D1217627

GUIDE TO THE EUROPEAN UNION

OTHER TITLES FROM THE ECONOMIST BOOKS

The Economist on America: 1843–1993
The Economist Guide to Economic Indicators
The Economist Numbers Guide
The Economist Style Guide

Pocket Finance
Pocket Manager
Pocket Marketing
Pocket MBA
Pocket Negotiator
Pocket Strategy

The Economist Pocket Asia
The Economist Pocket Europe
The Economist Pocket Latin America
The Economist Pocket USA
The Economist Pocket World in Figures

The
Economist

=== GUIDE TO ===

THE
EUROPEAN
UNION

Dick Leonard

The original and definitive guide

to all aspects of the EU

THE ECONOMIST IN ASSOCIATION WITH
HAMISH HAMILTON LTD

Published by the Penguin Group
Penguin Books Ltd, 27 Wrights Lane, London W8 5TZ, England
Penguin Books USA Inc., 375 Hudson Street, New York, New York 10014, USA
Penguin Books Australia Ltd, Ringwood, Victoria, Australia
Penguin Books Canada Ltd, 10 Alcorn Avenue, Toronto, Ontario, Canada M4V 3B2
Penguin Books (NZ) Ltd, 182–190 Wairau Road, Auckland 10, New Zealand

Penguin Books Ltd, Registered Offices: Harmondsworth, Middlesex, England

First published in 1988 as *Pocket Guide to the European Community*;
reprinted 1988; revised editions 1989, 1992
This edition published by Hamish Hamilton Ltd in association with
The Economist 1994

1 3 5 7 9 10 8 6 4 2

Copyright © The Economist Books Ltd, 1988, 1989, 1992, 1994
Text copyright © Dick Leonard 1988, 1989, 1992, 1994

All rights reserved. Without limiting the rights under copyright
reserved above, no part of this publication may be reproduced,
stored in or introduced into a retrieval system, or transmitted, in any
form or by any means (electronic, mechanical, photocopying,
recording or otherwise), without the prior written permission of
both the copyright owner and the above publisher of this book.

The greatest care has been taken in compiling this book. However,
no responsibility can be accepted by the publishers or compilers
for the accuracy of the information presented.

Where opinion is expressed, it is that of the author and does not
necessarily coincide with the editorial views of
The Economist Newspaper.

Printed in England by Clays Ltd, St Ives plc

A CIP catalogue record for this book is available
from the British Library

ISBN 0-241-00264-8

CONTENTS

List of tables

List of figures

Figure 1 **The European Union**

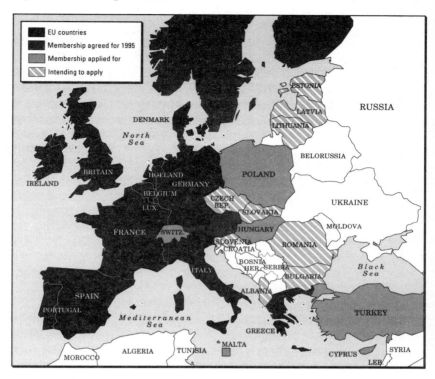

Membership		Applications for membership	
1958	Belgium	1987	Turkey
	France	1989	Austria
	Germany[1]	1990	Cyprus
	Italy		Malta
	Luxembourg	1992	Switzerland
	Netherlands	1994	Hungary
1973	Denmark		Poland
	Ireland		
	United Kingdom		
1981	Greece		
1986	Portugal		
	Spain		
1995	Austria		
	Finland[2]		
	Norway[2]		
	Sweden[2]		

1 East Germany joined as part of unified Germany in 1990.
2 Subject to national referendum.

INTRODUCTION

By the time that the European Union was formed in November 1993, the European Community, which it incorporated, had long established itself as a major force in the world, and its activities now impinge more and more on the lives of the citizens of its different member states. Yet the extent of public knowledge of the EU has tended to lag some way behind.

Many excellent books have been written about the EU. The majority of these have been addressed to specialists, or are concerned with one particular aspect of the Union's role. The purpose of this book is rather different. It is addressed specifically to lay people, and is intended to give a simplified account of the origin, history, institutions and functions of the Union in a form accessible to the intelligent reader with no previous knowledge of the EU.

The book is divided into five parts. Part I contains an account of the origins of the EC, followed by a historical account of its development up to and after the coming into force of the Treaty on European Union in November 1993. Part II describes in some detail the different institutions of the Community such as the European Commission, the Court of Justice, and so on. Part III deals with its competences, from agriculture to technological research. Part IV considers some specific problems, including enlargement and the continuing difficulties which the UK has experienced in adapting to EU membership, and concludes with an assessment of future prospects. Part V contains a series of appendixes which provide reference material on the Union and its institutions. Finally there are suggestions for further reading for those who wish to pursue the subject further.

The source of most of the figures and much of the factual information contained in this book is the European Commission and its publications, notably *European File*, *European Documentation* and *Basic Statistics of the Community*. Permission to reproduce this information is gratefully acknowledged.

I would like to dedicate this book to the memory of Dr Gertrud Heidelberger, my mother-in-law, an indomitable lady who represented all that is best in European culture.

Dick Leonard, Brussels, Summer 1994

NOTES

European Union or European Community?

In this book the terms European Union (EU) and European Community (EC) are often used interchangeably. Strictly speaking, the EC was incorporated into the EU in November 1993, when the Maastricht treaty came into force, but it continues to refer to the core of Union activities, for which the European Commission shares responsibility with the Council of Ministers, the European Parliament and the Court of Justice (see Part III). Other activities of the Union, notably foreign and security policy, and the co-ordination of immigration, police and judicial affairs, are organised on an intergovernmental basis.

Currency

All sums of money referred to in this book are denoted in ecus, the European currency unit, whose value is based on the weighted average of a "basket" of the currencies of the member states. On April 10 1994, the ecu was worth £0.77 and $1.13.

PART I

THE BACKGROUND

1

THE ORIGINS

Hitler was the catalyst

Adolf Hitler was the main catalyst of the European Community, although none of its leaders would readily admit him as a founding father. Like Charlemagne and Napoleon before him, Hitler brought together, by the sword, virtually the entire land area of the original EEC, destroying in the process the self-confidence of the nation states from which it sprang.

These were recreated in 1945, but no longer saw themselves as autonomous actors on the world stage. The governments of the three smallest – the Netherlands, Belgium and Luxembourg – decided in 1944, before the liberation of their territories had been completed, that their economic futures were inextricably intertwined. The Benelux Union came into force on January 1st 1948 as a customs union, with the intention of progressing to a full economic union at a later stage.

The Marshall Plan

The USA and the Soviet Union each gave the nations of Western Europe a strong shove in the direction of unity, one with apparently benign, the other with malign intentions. The Organisation for European Economic Co-operation (OEEC) was set up in 1947 in order to divide up among the member states the flow of US aid under the Marshall Plan. The aid programme was completed over three years, but the OEEC continued as a forum for promoting economic co-operation and freer trade among West European countries. It later widened its membership to include all the advanced industrial nations of the non-communist world, and changed its name in 1961 to the Organisation for Economic Co-operation and Development (OECD).

Fear of the USSR ...

If the USA, partly no doubt through self-interest, had contributed hope, the USSR contributed fear. Its brutal suppression of the countries of Eastern Europe, culminating in the communist takeover of Czechoslovakia in February 1948, forced several West European countries to come together for self-preservation. As early as March

17th 1948 the Treaty of Brussels was signed, providing for a 50-year agreement between the UK, France, Belgium, the Netherlands and Luxembourg known as the Western European Union (WEU). This provided "for collaboration in economic, social and cultural matters and for collective self-defence". In practice the WEU was largely superseded by the creation of NATO in 1949, although it remained in existence and its five original members were joined by West Germany and Italy in 1954.

... and Germany

Fear of the USSR in the post-war years was matched by fear of Germany, which had tried to overrun Western Europe in the second world war, and had also fought three ferocious wars with France over a period of 70 years. How to prevent a recurrence of these wars in the future occupied many minds in Western Europe, as elsewhere in the world, in the immediate post-war period. Two possible solutions presented themselves. The first was to ensure that Germany should not only remain divided (which the division of Europe between East and West seemed likely to secure, in any event), but that it should also be reduced to a permanent state of economic backwardness. Apart from intrinsic improbability, this solution had the serious disadvantage of conflicting with another West European priority: resisting the advance of Soviet communism. This pointed to the need not only for a German military contribution to western defence, but also for a strong economy which would help to satisfy the rapidly rising material expectations of West Europeans. It was this consideration which tipped the balance decisively towards the second proposed solution to "the German problem". This was that Germany (or West Germany at least) should be linked so organically with its neighbours, and that the link should appear so evidently in the self-interest of both Germans and all the other nationalities, that another war between the nations of Western Europe would become impossible.

Monnet's decisive role

The continental country most resistant to this concept was France, and it was fortunate that the most clearsighted and persuasive advocate of this approach was a Frenchman, Jean Monnet. If Hitler provided the impetus towards European unity, Monnet was indisputably its principal architect.

   He had a remarkable career, almost all of it devoted to international co-operation of a genuinely practical kind. Originally a salesman in the UK for his family firm of brandy distillers, he spent the first world war as a temporary civil servant co-ordinating the contributions of the French and UK economies to the joint war effort. Between the wars he acted as deputy secretary-general of the League of Nations, but in 1939 he was recalled to resume his role as an Anglo-French co-ordinator. It was his plan for a Franco-UK Union which Churchill put forward in 1940 in a vain attempt to forestall the French surrender to the Germans. Monnet spent the rest of the war years in London and Washington, once again co-ordinating the economic warfare of the allied nations.

He returned to France as a member of de Gaulle's government, and subsequently became head of the French planning organisation. In 1950 his moment of destiny came: it was his proposal that paved the way for the Franco-West German reconciliation which has been the essential condition for all subsequent progress towards European unity. The occasion was the Franco-West German dispute over the Saarland, which was largely fuelled by French fears that if its iron and coal industries were integrated with those of the rest of West Germany it would once again dominate the economy of Europe. France had tried unsuccessfully to annex the Saarland, which was overwhelmingly German in population, and, as in the post-1919 period, this attempt had poisoned relations between the two countries.

The Schuman plan

Monnet succeeded in capturing the ear of the French foreign minister, Robert Schuman, a man whose own personal history (as an Alsatian born in Luxembourg) had predisposed him to the advantages of European integration. Monnet's proposal, which was put forward by the French government as the Schuman Plan, was that the West German and the French coal and steel industries should be placed under a single High Authority which should supervise their development. "The solidarity between the two countries established by joint production will show that a war between France and Germany becomes not only unthinkable but materially impossible," Schuman said in launching his plan on May 9th 1950.

Other European countries were invited to join the plan, which was instantly accepted by Chancellor Konrad Adenauer on behalf of the West German government, which rightly saw it as the way to rejoin the European comity of nations on equal terms. Italy and the Benelux countries also quickly responded, and the Treaty of Paris (see page 29), signed on April 18th 1951, formally established the European Coal and Steel Community (ECSC), which came into being on August 10th 1952. Jean Monnet was its first president.

The UK stands aloof

One notable absentee was the UK, which had been invited to join but declined to do so, after having given the matter very little serious thought. The decision was taken by Clement Attlee's Labour government, but was confirmed by the Conservative government under Winston Churchill, which was elected in October 1951. The UK did not then regard itself primarily as being a European nation, and adopted a sniffily superior attitude to the new organisation, as was evidenced by the private remark of Churchill to his doctor in January 1952, "I love France and Belgium, but we must not allow ourselves to be pulled down to that level."[1]

The absence of the UK probably facilitated the construction of a community that was different in kind from the many other international organisations established during this period, such as the Council of Europe, the North Atlantic Treaty Organisation (NATO) or the General Agreement on Tariffs and Trade (GATT). Each of these bodies established a permanent secretariat; however, there was no question of it having any more than an administrative role. Decision-making was reserved for meetings of representatives of each of the member states. The ECSC was unique in being provided with a supra-national High Authority which was given wide powers to determine the direction of two key industries throughout the member states. There was provision for a Council of Ministers, a purely advisory Assembly (or indirectly elected Parliament) and a Court of Justice, but the High Authority was, and was intended to be, the main organ of decision-making.

The constitution of the ECSC, as spelled out in the Treaty of Paris, very closely reflected the views of Monnet, who wrote in his memoirs of the necessity of providing a firm institutional base to give effect to political intentions: "Nothing is possible without men: nothing is lasting without institutions."[1] He had intended that the ECSC would be paralleled by a common European defence force, which would supersede national armies and facilitate the rearming of West Germany without creating a specifically West German force. The same six governments – France, West Germany, Italy, Belgium, the Netherlands and Luxembourg – signed a treaty in May 1952 providing for the creation of a European Defence Community (EDC), for this purpose, but the French National Assembly in August 1954 finally declined to ratify the treaty.

Towards an economic community

The failure of the EDC had two significant consequences. West German rearmament proceeded on a national basis, and West Germany was admitted as a full member of NATO in October 1954. For his part, Monnet concluded that the path towards European unity lay through economic rather than military co-ordination. When his first term of office as president of the High Authority came to an end, in February 1955, he declined to accept a further term. Instead, he left to head a high-powered pressure group, the Action Committee for the United States of Europe (ACUSE), which included leading figures from the Socialist, Christian Democratic and Liberal parties of all the six member states.

ACUSE did not have to wait long for the first fruits of its activities. The foreign ministers of the Six met in Messina in June 1955 and appointed a committee under the chairmanship of the Belgian foreign minister, Paul-Henri Spaak, to investigate establishing a common market. This committee produced a report which was the basis of the Treaty of Rome, signed on March 25th 1957, establishing the European Economic Community (EEC). A separate treaty, signed in Rome on the same day, established the European Atomic Energy Community (Euratom). All six parliaments ratified the treaties, which came into effect on January 1st 1958, with the West German Walter Hallstein as first president of the EEC Commission.

The EEC's constitution largely paralleled that of the ECSC, but the supra-national element was significantly less. The EEC Commission, which was the counterpart of the High Authority, had substantially less power, and the Council of Ministers substantially more, than under the Treaty of Paris. In the early years of the EEC this difference was hardly apparent, as the confident and decisive figure of Hallstein dominated the development of the Community. But in 1965–66 his authority was successfully challenged by France's President Charles de Gaulle (see page 10), and he subsequently resigned. None of his successors has wielded as much power as he had done, and since his departure the supremacy of the Council of Ministers (the representatives of the different member states) over the supra-national commission has been evident.

Amalgamation

The three communities – the ECSC, Euratom and the EEC – were formally amalgamated on July 1st 1967. They became jointly known as the European Community (EC), or sometimes the European Communities, although the abbreviation EEC remained in common use to denote the combined organisation.

---

1 Alfred Grosser, *The Western Alliance: European-American Relations since 1945*, London, Macmillan, 1980, pages 121 and 102.

2

EVOLUTION

The EEC might have broken up during its first year of operation. On June 1st 1958, five months after its foundation, General Charles de Gaulle became prime minister (and subsequently president) of France. His followers had bitterly opposed its creation; however, de Gaulle saw it as a useful means of extending French influence, and during his early years in power he encouraged its development.

Three months after coming to power he had a momentous meeting with the West German chancellor, Konrad Adenauer, which, in the words of the French historian, Alfred Grosser, turned out to be a case of "love at first sight".[1] Grosser quotes de Gaulle as writing in his memoirs: "From then until mid-1962, Konrad Adenauer and I were to write to each other on some 40 occasions. We saw each other 15 times ... we spent more than 100 hours in conversation." From this mutual attraction sprang an enduring alliance which has proved to be the mainspring of the Community ever since. It was formalised in the Franco-West German Treaty of January 22nd 1963, which provided for the co-ordination of the two countries' policies in foreign affairs, defence, information and cultural affairs.

This co-ordination has been spasmodic, but whenever France and West Germany have acted together within the Community their influence has been enormous and they have generally been able to achieve their objectives. Where they have not done so, the Community has tended to drift and has found it difficult or impossible to agree on a course of action. For many years West Germany, while the stronger of the two powers economically, was content to play the subordinate role. When West German leaders' views differed from those of France, they were often willing to defer to their partners, or at least refrain from carrying their opposition to extremes.

An encouraging start

With the background of the Franco-West German entente, the benefit of strong economic growth in all six member states and the enthusiastic encouragement of the USA, the Community got off to a tremendous start in the first years after 1958. Intra-Community trade leapt ahead, increasing by 28.4% annually during the first ten years of the EEC, while the average increase of imports from third countries was 10%.

The timetable for removing all internal tariffs and quota restrictions was originally intended to be completed in successive stages by December 31st 1969. It was, however, twice accelerated, and the process was completed 18 months ahead of schedule, on July 1st 1968. Simultaneously with the removal of internal tariffs, a common external tariff was erected, based on an average of the duties previously levied by the member states, with some downward adjustment. This, too, was completed 18 months early, and the Community collaborated with the USA in the Kennedy round of the GATT, which resulted in a further 35% cut, on average, in its external tariff.

The other economic objective spelled out in considerable detail in the Rome treaty was the development of a common agricultural policy (CAP), based, however, on protectionism rather than free trade. In fact the two major prongs of the EEC were widely regarded as offering quid pro quos to West Germany and France. Free trade for industry accorded with the interests of West German manufacturers, and a guaranteed market for agricultural produce with those of French farmers. Despite the provisions in the Rome treaty, the CAP proved much more difficult to launch than the customs union, but in January 1962, after what a commission publication describes as "lengthy and often bitter negotiations and the longest negotiating marathon in the Community's history",[2] the Council of Ministers adopted the basic regulations for a common market in agriculture.

Foreign policy gap

The economic progress made by the Six (as the founder members of the Community were known) soon showed up a glaring omission in the Rome treaty, in that no mention was made of political co-operation. At a summit meeting in February 1961, the heads of government of the Community agreed that a political union should be set up between the Six. A committee chaired by the French politician, Christian Fouchet, produced two successive plans to bring this into effect. But neither the Fouchet Plan nor the Second Fouchet Plan was approved, due to a basic difference between the larger and smaller member states. The larger states, particularly Gaullist France, thought that they should effectively direct the foreign policy of the Six. The smaller Benelux countries, on the other hand, fearing the prospect of domination, wanted a more equal say. In the end nothing came of the proposal, except that the heads of government agreed to hold regular meetings for general political consultation. Despite this decision, no further summit was held until six years later, and it was only after December 1974, when the European Council (see page 46) was formalised, that the heads of government began to meet regularly on a three times a year basis (reduced to twice a year in 1986).

Other European countries began to take note of the economic success of the Community. Greece and Turkey both applied to become associated states during 1959, while the UK government, whose earlier attempt to negotiate a wider free trade area within the OECD had ended in failure, became alarmed at the prospect of being left out in the cold. It took the initiative in organising the European Free Trade Association (EFTA), which linked it much more loosely with six of the smaller West European states. Together with Austria, Denmark, Norway, Portugal, Sweden and Switzerland,[3] it signed the Stockholm Convention, establishing EFTA, on January 4th 1960.

The UK knocks at the door

Yet no sooner had this Convention been signed than the UK government, led by Harold Macmillan, reappraised its position once again and decided that EFTA was much too small a grouping to meet its trading interests (it had a combined population of no more than 90m compared with 170m in the Six). In July 1961 the UK applied for full membership of the EEC, followed shortly afterwards by Ireland, Denmark and Norway.

The application was welcomed by five of the Six, but it soon transpired that President de Gaulle was lukewarm if not actually hostile to the entry of an "Anglo-Saxon" nation. Detailed accession negotiations began in November 1961, but soon became bogged down as the UK negotiators strove, perhaps ill-advisedly, to achieve a mass of detailed concessions on agriculture, Commonwealth trade and future relations with the other EFTA countries. Meanwhile de Gaulle bided his time, but in January 1963, following Macmillan's Nassau agreement with President Kennedy on the supply of Polaris missiles which confirmed the French president's view that the UK's links with the USA took priority over any European commitment, he promptly vetoed the UK application at a press conference in Paris. The other three applicant countries accordingly withdrew their own applications.

The other five members states were aghast at the French action, but were unwilling to bring matters to a head. The EEC without the UK was a misfortune, in their view; without France it would be an impossibility. So they reluctantly acquiesced in de Gaulle's action, and only one week later the Franco-West German Treaty was signed. Three years later a UK Labour government, under Harold Wilson, made a renewed attempt to secure entry, but once again de Gaulle applied a veto, and once again his EEC partners submitted to his will.

Hallstein versus de Gaulle

At the head of the European Commission during the first nine years was Professor Walter Hallstein, formerly a close aide and confidant of Adenauer, whose name was previously associated with the so-called Hallstein doctrine, under which West Germany refused to have diplomatic relations with any government which recognised the East German regime. Hallstein had been the leader of the West German delegation to the Schuman Plan conference in 1950, and he enjoyed a large fund of French as well as West German goodwill at the outset of his presidency which greatly helped him to keep up the momentum. After several years, however, the gap between his own beliefs in a supra-national Europe and the more nationalistic approach of President de Gaulle became more and more apparent, and it was probably only a matter of time before a clash would occur.

The occasion might have been a difference over foreign policy or the rejection of UK membership. In the event, it was the decision-making process within the Council of Ministers which led to the break. During the early years of the Community most decisions within the council needed to be taken, under the terms of the Rome treaty, by unanimity. From 1966 onwards, when the transitional period came to an end, a wide range of decisions should have been reached by qualified majority voting (see pages 43–44). President de Gaulle was not willing to contemplate the possibility of France being outvoted on major issues and when, in June 1965, France found itself in a minority of one against commission proposals on the financing of the CAP, the provision of its own financial resources and extending the budgetary powers of the European Parliament, he refused to allow decisions to be taken. For the next six months France boycotted all meetings of the Council of Ministers, and its "empty chair" policy was only abandoned in January 1966, when the so-called Luxembourg compromise (see page 43) was reached. This effectively gave all member states a right of veto when their "very important interests" were concerned. Not long afterwards Hallstein, who rightly concluded that the Luxembourg compromise had severely undermined the role of the commission as the principal initiator of policy, submitted his resignation.

The transformation of farming

One of the most profound changes within the Community during the 1960s and 1970s was the transformation of its agriculture. Not only did productivity and production shoot up, making the Community more than self-sufficient in most temperate products, but the number of people working on the land fell sharply, from 15.2m in 1960 to 5.8m in 1984 in the original six member states. The process would have gone even further if the Mansholt Plan, named after Dr Sicco Mansholt, the agricultural commissioner and later president of the commission, had been adopted. This plan, put forward in 1968, would have provided generous financial inducements for increasing the size of holdings, mechanising farming operations and taking some 5m ha of poorer land out of cultivation. A much watered down programme was eventually approved by the Council of Ministers in 1972, but unfortunately it did nothing to cure the emerging problem of structural surpluses nor to lighten the burden on the Community's funds of production guarantees.

Another significant development was the conclusion, in 1963, of the Yaoundé Convention, signed in the capital of Cameroon with 18 African states which were former dependent territories of EEC member states. The convention provided for the duty-free access of all their exports, except for certain products covered by the common agricultural policy, and for financial aid to be provided through the European Development Fund and the European Investment Bank. The first Yaoundé Convention was replaced in 1969 by Yaoundé II, and subsequently by four successive conventions bringing in many of the developing countries of the Commonwealth, signed at Lomé (Togo) in 1975, 1979, 1984 and 1989 (see Chapter 34). Lomé IV, signed by 69 African, Caribbean and Pacific states (the ACP states), continues the programme until 2000.

An EC summit conference at The Hague, in December 1969, marked an important step forward. The conference finally approved the proposals for financing the common agricultural policy, the creation of the Community's own financial resources (see pages 74–75) and the extension of the European Parliament's budgetary powers, which had earlier been blocked by France. It agreed that the Community should proceed to the establishment of an economic and monetary union to be completed by 1980 (which proved to be a wildly over-optimistic target date), and it commissioned a report on ways of improving foreign policy co-ordination between member states. This report, which was written by the Belgian diplomat, Etienne Davignon (later an influential commissioner), was approved ten months later. Since then the foreign ministers of the member states have met "in political co-operation" at frequent intervals, as have senior officials of the different foreign ministries, the idea being to discuss and if possible harmonise foreign policy opinions and activities (see Chapter 35).

Enter Denmark, Ireland and the UK

President de Gaulle's resignation in 1969, followed by his death the following year, removed the main obstacle to UK accession. His successor, Georges Pompidou, was less inflexible and the new West German chancellor, Willy Brandt, strongly urged him to agree to an enlargement of the Community. The Danish, Irish, Norwegian and UK governments all renewed their applications and, after much hard bargaining, treaties of accession were signed in Brussels on January 22nd 1972. Norway narrowly rejected the treaty terms (by 53% to 47%) in a referendum in September 1972, but the other three countries formally became members on January 1st 1973.

Denmark and Ireland also held referenda on EC accession, which produced majorities in favour of, respectively, 83% and 63%. The UK did not initially do so, although the issue of accession was highly divisive. The prime minister, Edward Heath, pursued the objective of UK membership with great determination, and succeeded in rallying a large majority of the Conservative Party behind him. The Labour Party, however, was badly split on the issue, with the majority coming down decisively against. A defiant minority of 69 Labour members of Parliament, led by Roy Jenkins, insisted on voting against a three-line whip, in favour of the terms which Heath had negotiated, in a House of Commons vote in October 1971. The Labour Party subsequently resolved to hold a retrospective referendum on continued UK membership if it won the next general election.

The government of Harold Wilson, which came to power in 1974, first as a minority government, later with a tiny majority, fulfilled this undertaking in June 1975 after having "renegotiated" the terms of entry. The main change secured was the institution of a "corrective mechanism" which was intended to prevent excessive UK contributions to the EC budget. The mechanism was later to prove inoperative, but the referendum produced a decisive vote (67%) in favour of continued UK membership, and it seemed as though the controversy was at an end.

Denmark and the UK left EFTA on their accession to the EC, but were not required to sever their trading links, as the remaining EFTA members negotiated industrial free trade agreements with the Community and formed a sort of "outer ring", sharing in the benefits of tariff-free trade, except for agricultural produce, without having to accept any of the obligations of EC membership.

Problems of enlargement

The 1973 enlargement, which increased the Community's membership from six states to nine, and its population from 191m to 255m, was expected to give it a fresh wind and enable it to develop further and faster during the 1970s. These hopes were largely unfulfilled. In part, this was due to the fact that the enlarged EC lacked an agreed programme for its medium-term development, which the Rome treaty, with its precise timetable for progressing to a customs union and its outline of the basic constituents of a common agricultural policy, had provided in the first years of the Community. Moreover, the nine members formed a less cohesive grouping than the original six, and the persistence of hostility to the EC among large sections of the population in the UK and Denmark made it difficult for these two countries to accommodate themselves to the essential process of compromise and "give and take" that the smooth operation of the Community required.

The biggest blow to the Community's development, however, was undoubtedly the prolonged economic recession which followed the Yom Kippur war of 1973, and the consequent quadrupling of petroleum prices. All the member states suffered from mounting inflation and unemployment, and most of them saw their balance of payments slide into severe deficit. Moreover, efforts to co-ordinate energy policies of the member states proved elusive, as did attempts to find a common economic strategy to enable the Community to hoist itself out of the recession. The member governments all felt constrained, to varying degrees, to implement austerity policies in their own countries, and it became increasingly difficult to persuade them to release resources for the introduction of new common policies under the aegis of the Community.

Yet at the Paris EC summit in December 1974 agreement was reached on the establishment of the European Regional Development Fund (ERDF, see pages 137–140), whose purpose was to help close the gap between the most disadvantaged and the more favoured regions within the Community. Although the ERDF provided assistance to all the member states, its main beneficiaries during its first ten years of operations were the UK, Ireland and Italy.

The European Council

The same summit conference took three other important decisions.

It resolved that henceforth the heads of government should consult among themselves much more frequently, and instituted the European Council (see Chapter 6), which should meet three times a year and consider important foreign policy questions as well as the affairs of the Community. It decided that the European Parliament should be elected by direct universal suffrage from 1978 onwards (later postponed until 1979). And it appointed Leo Tindemans, the then Belgian prime minister, to compile a report on European union by the end of 1975.

Tindemans duly reported one year later, proposing a series of measures, including a common foreign policy, an economic and monetary union, European social and regional policies, joint industrial policies as regards growth industries, policies affecting EC citizens and a substantial reinforcement of Community institutions. The report was discussed on several occasions by the European Council but no action was taken on it, an outcome which reflected the general lowering of the horizons of West European leaders so far as European union was concerned.

The appointment of Roy Jenkins as president of the commission, for four years from January 1977, was seen as a most encouraging development. A senior political figure, who had been deputy leader of the Labour Party as well as chancellor of the exchequer and home secretary, he had (together with Edward Heath) been the most energetic and consistent campaigner for UK adhesion to the EC. His admirers from many member states hoped that his arrival in Brussels would give the Community the added momentum which the enlargement four years earlier had failed to provide.

Jenkins proved a resourceful and diligent president but, partly due to lack of support from the UK government, first under James Callaghan and then under Margaret Thatcher, his presidency did not quite match up to expectations. He did, however, have two undoubted achievements to his credit. He established the right of the president of the European Commission to attend the annual Western economic summits as the representative of the Community, despite stubborn resistance from President Valéry Giscard d'Estaing and only lukewarm support from Callaghan. And he was one of the architects of the European Monetary System (EMS, see pages 103–105), which came into effect in March 1979.

The European Monetary System

The European Monetary System (EMS) has compensated, to some extent, for the failure of the earlier aspiration to achieve a full economic and monetary union by 1980. Based on a European currency unit (the ecu), the EMS comprises an exchange and intervention mechanism, credit facilities and a vehicle to ease the path of the less prosperous Community countries. Proposed by Jenkins in a speech in Florence, it was taken up by the West German chancellor, Helmut Schmidt, who, in conjunction with Giscard d'Estaing, was able to secure its acceptance by the European Council during three successive meetings in 1978. Despite the UK refusal to join its exchange rate mechanism during its first eleven years, it was credited with having done a great deal to dampen down currency fluctuations and to encourage co-operation in financial policies between member states.

International trading relations developed continuously through the 1970s. The centrepiece was the Tokyo round of GATT negotiations between the European Community and 99 other participants. Given the background of world recession and rising unemployment (which had already reached 10m in the Community as a whole, and was subsequently to rise to 16m), the results of the round were remarkable, leading as they did to further cuts in customs duties, averaging about one-third, which came into effect from 1980.

The Community greatly extended its network of bilateral trade and aid agreements with developing countries. Agreements with the Maghreb countries (Tunisia, Algeria and Morocco), signed in 1976, were followed by others with the Mashreq countries (Egypt, Syria, Jordan and Lebanon) in 1977. An agreement had been reached with Israel in 1975, and one with Yugoslavia was concluded in 1980, which enabled the Community to implement a global Mediterranean policy. In Asia more limited agreements were made with Sri Lanka (1975), Bangladesh and Pakistan (1976), and India (1981), while a co-operation agreement was reached with the five ASEAN countries in 1981.

In Latin America agreements with Uruguay (1973), Mexico (1975) and Brazil (1980) were followed by a co-operation agreement with the five-nation Andean Pact in 1983. The third Lomé Convention, concluded in December 1984, covered trade with 66 African, Caribbean and Pacific countries, and provided aid worth 8,500m ecus for the period 1985–90 (see pages 206–207).

Attempts to secure a framework for the expansion of trade with communist countries made little progress. Talks with Comecon, the Soviet-dominated organisation for economic co-operation, continued from 1977 to 1980 but no agreement was reached, and the dialogue was only resumed in 1986, following Gorbachev's rise to power. Trade agreements were, however, concluded with China and Romania, and sectoral agreements with some other communist states (see pages 83–84).

Greece enters the Community

Meanwhile further enlargements of the EC appeared on the agenda when three countries which had recently emerged from dictatorial or military rule applied to become full members. Greece tabled its application in 1975, and Portugal and Spain in 1977. The negotiations with Greece proceeded relatively smoothly, partly because the Greek government took the view that it had to secure entry at all costs and therefore did not haggle much over the terms, taking the view that its bargaining power would be greatly increased once it was inside the Community. It duly became a member on January 1st 1981.

The negotiations with Spain and Portugal were much more difficult, and not only because these two countries adopted a more stringent negotiating stance than Greece. There was far more opposition from within the Community itself, particularly in France, to their accession, largely because farmers in southern France, and also in Italy and Greece, feared competition from their Spanish rivals. There was a lively apprehension that France would again veto a membership application, and although this did not happen, President Giscard d'Estaing, in 1980, deliberately set out to slow down the negotiations.

Although Giscard d'Estaing played a negative role in this context, his overall influence on the Community was a positive one. Throughout his seven years as president he worked in close partnership with the West German chancellor, Helmut Schmidt, with whom he shared a very considerable commonality of views, despite their different political backgrounds. Able to converse freely to each other in English, they sat side by side at meetings of the European Council, and were often able to steer it in the direction in which they both wanted to go. In so far as anybody provided leadership to the Community during those seven years it was Schmidt and Giscard.

In 1981–82 both lost power and their successors, who were François Mitterrand and Helmut Kohl, signally failed to reproduce the Schmidt–Giscard relationship. Accordingly a vacuum appeared at the apex of the Community, and for several years it drifted helplessly, seemingly unable to tackle the mounting problems that it faced. A contributory factor was that Jenkins's term as president of the commission ended at about the same time, and his successor, the Luxembourger, Gaston Thorn, carried insufficient weight to be able to fill the gap.

A maze of problems

As the 1980s began, the Community was faced by a series of distinct problems which became increasingly entwined as the years went by; no solution was found until 1984. The issues were as follows.

- The prospect of disproportionately high UK payments to the budget.
- The threatened exhaustion of budget resources, allied to the need to curb the amount spent on the CAP.
- The need to reform the Community's institutions in order to speed up decision-making and to make them more accountable.
- The need to respond to the technological challenge of the USA and Japan if Europe was not to become an industrial back-water.
- The need to remove internal barriers within the Community.
- The enlargement negotiations with Spain and Portugal.

The UK budget problem for several years proved the most intractable, partly because of the personalities involved, including Margaret Thatcher, whose combativeness was an unwelcome revelation to her fellow heads of government. The fact that the UK was liable to pay an unacceptably high net contribution, once its transitional stage had come to an end, came to light during the closing months of James Callaghan's Labour government in 1979. The basic reason for this was that despite indications given during the negotiations and renegotiations for membership, agriculture continued to take the lion's share of the Community's budget. As a large importer of food, the UK was paying a disproportionately high amount in import levies, but as a relatively small food producer it was getting much less than its proportionate share back in payments under the CAP.

When Mrs Thatcher became prime minister in 1979 she took an extremely robust line in defence of UK interests, and managed to obtain from the other member states in May 1980 a temporary agreement limiting UK contributions for 2–3 years while a longer-term solution was sought. An unfortunate by-product of Mrs Thatcher's hard-hitting campaign was to rekindle anti-EC feeling within the Labour Party, whose annual conference in 1980 passed a resolution calling for UK withdrawal. Under the leadership of Michael Foot, this then became part of Labour's manifesto for the 1983 general election.

The search for a long-term solution went on until 1984, practically monopolising the agenda of several meetings of the European

Council before a settlement was reached, which, in the opinion of many, could have been obtained a great deal earlier if cooler counsels had prevailed.

Budgetary crisis

The UK budget dispute inevitably got bound up with the looming crisis in the general budgetary affairs of the Community, in that its "own resources" were proving inadequate to meet the many demands on its budget. The proceeds of customs duties and agricultural levies were declining each year, and the day was fast approaching when the EC's only other resource – a maximum take equal to a 1% rate of VAT throughout the Community – would be exhausted. The member states were divided between those that were prepared to raise the VAT limit and those (including especially the UK) that were more interested in budget-cutting, particularly in the large part of the budget (around 70%) devoted to agriculture.

Those that wished to expand the budget pointed to the desirability, which the commission was repeatedly asserting, of a major expansion of Community expenditure on technological research, in order to enable European firms to obtain a share in world markets that would otherwise be monopolised by US and Japanese suppliers of "third industrial revolution" products. In parallel with this was a growing realisation that, in order to compete at all, Western Europe must turn itself into the "common market" it was supposed to be, and rid itself of the innumerable barriers to free trade which still existed a quarter of a century after the Community had been established.

Progress towards removing these barriers in the internal market was being thwarted by the failure of the Council of Ministers to agree on a vast number of proposals for liberalisation which had been tabled over the years by the commission. The backlog, largely resulting from the council's unwillingness to apply the majority voting rules of the Rome treaty, acted as a spur to proposals to speed up and democratise the decision-making process which emanated, in particular, from the European Parliament. Finally, frustration was growing dangerously in both Spain and Portugal at the slowness of their entry negotiations, and there was a widespread feeling within the Community itself that these two newly democratic countries were not receiving the encouragement that they deserved.

Mitterrand's initiative

Like his predecessors, as president of France François Mitterrand eventually made his own considerable mark on the history of the EC. After all the above-mentioned problems had been incessantly

argued for several years, to no measurable effect, he apparently
determined that solutions to several of them should be reached during the course of the French presidency of the Council of Ministers,
in the first half of 1984. In order to achieve this he had to rise above
narrow French interests, so far as Spanish entry and the size of any
budget rebate for the UK was concerned. This he succeeded in
doing, and at the Fontainebleau summit, in June 1984, agreement
was reached on the UK budget issue, on increasing the Community's own resources, on restraining agricultural spending and on
clearing the way for the admission of Spain and Portugal.

The settlement for the UK was based on a yearly rebate of 66% of
the difference between its VAT contribution and its share of EC
expenditure. In exchange for this, Mrs Thatcher agreed that the
general limit of VAT contributions should be raised from 1% to 1.4%.
It was also agreed that in future agricultural spending would rise in
each year by a smaller proportion than the overall rise in expenditure, which should have meant that the percentage of the budget
devoted to the CAP would decline year by year.

The 1992 programme

A year later, at the Milan summit, progress was made on two other
issues: a seven-year timetable was agreed for removing 300 barriers
to the internal market (see Chapter 15); and it was agreed to hold
an inter-governmental conference to discuss amendments to the
Rome treaty and other ways of speeding up and democratising the
decision-making process. This led to the Single European Act,
adopted in Luxembourg in December 1985 and implemented, after
ratification by all 12 national parliaments (which involved referenda in Denmark and Ireland), in July 1987 (see page 44).

The programme for the completion of the EC's internal market
became known either as the 1992 programme or, in some member
states, the 1993 programme. The ambiguity arose from the target
date of December 31st 1992 by which time all 300 measures were
intended to be implemented. The original idea came from Jacques
Delors, but credit for the detailed planning and the enthusiastic
way in which the programme was launched should go to the then
UK commissioner for internal market affairs, Lord Cockfield.
Despite initial scepticism, it soon became clear that the programme
would be substantially completed within the timetable laid down
and that it would bring considerable economic benefits to all the
member states. Beyond that, it gave a new sense of purpose to the
Community and helped to create the atmosphere in which further
initiatives to broaden and deepen the EC appeared both practical

and desirable. By the end of December 1992 almost 95% of the programme had in fact been legislated.

Meanwhile agreement was reached on launching several EC research programmes (see pages 128–132), as well as the Eureka programme which also involved several non-EC European countries, although the budgets agreed for them were substantially less than the commission would have liked. It seemed that the EC had woken from its slumbers, and at last was tackling the most urgent problems on its agenda. Unfortunately, however, new obstacles arose to imperil some of the agreements reached. The Spanish and Portuguese entry negotiations were successfully terminated, but at the last moment their ratification was put in doubt by a stratagem of the Greek government. It refused to endorse the entry terms unless Greece received more economic aid from the Community. Greece was eventually bought off by the institution of the Integrated Mediterranean Programmes (see pages 140–141), which provided for 6,600m ecus to be spent over seven years. Most of this sum has been applied to the modernisation of the Greek economy, but Italy and southern France have also been beneficiaries.

Enter Spain and Portugal, and a new budget crisis

No sooner had Spain and Portugal taken their places in the Community in January 1986 than the budgetary measures agreed at Fontainebleau began to come unstuck. In the face of falling world prices, and the steep decline in the value of the dollar in 1986 and 1987, the cost to the EC of export refunds for its food exports rose dramatically. It became politically impossible to adhere to the guidelines for agricultural expenditure, and within a year of the VAT limit being raised from 1% to 1.4% the available funds for the Community budget were once again exhausted. By the beginning of 1987 it was clear that the Community would face a budget deficit for the year of 5 billion–6 billion ecus, with agricultural expenditure greatly exceeding the planned appropriations, and with no prospect in sight of reconciling the EC's political and financial objectives within the existing budgetary framework. Under the leadership of Jacques Delors the commission then produced a programme which became known as the "Delors package", designed to put the funds of the Community on a more assured basis, while reinforcing control over farm spending and releasing resources for priority objectives including, especially, research and the expansion of the so-called structural funds (the regional and social funds and the guidance section of the EAGGF[4]), which the commission argued should be doubled, in real terms, by 1992.

A new beginning

It took three meetings of the European Council to reach agreement on the Delors package, partly because of the reluctance of Margaret Thatcher to accept proposals for controlling future expenditure which she regarded as less than watertight, and partly because of her determination that any new basis for budgetary contributions should include arrangements for abating the UK share which would be at least as generous, and as secure, as those agreed at Fontainebleau in 1984. Finally, however, at an emergency summit meeting in Brussels in February 1988, she agreed with the other 11 national leaders on proposals largely based on those put forward by Delors one year earlier.

The Brussels agreement meant that the Community could make a new start. A new budget limit was set at 1.2% of the total GNP of the Community, equivalent to 1.9–2.0% of VAT contributions as calculated on the previous basis. This enabled a budget of 43.8 billion ecus to be agreed for 1988, compared with actual expenditure of 37 billion ecus the previous year. By 1991 the budget had increased to 55.6 billion ecus. Under the agreement reached, a fourth resource based directly on the national share of GNP was added to the three main existing sources of revenue. The Fontainebleau agreement, under which 66% of the UK's net contribution is refunded, was written into the new dispensation.

The other main features of the agreement were that the structural funds were to be doubled, in real terms, by 1993, with more focus on economically backward areas, while much stricter control was to be applied to agricultural spending. In future this was not to grow by more than 74% of the annual growth rate of GNP, and so-called "stabilisers" would be applied progressively to reduce the level of subsidy for products in excess supply. Moreover, "set-aside" payments would be made to encourage farmers to take less fertile land out of production.

EMU back on the agenda

With this settlement under their belts, the EC leaders felt free to seek to revive the dormant project for economic and monetary union. At the Hannover summit of June 1988, which reappointed Jacques Delors for a further two years from January 1989, a committee was set up under his chairmanship with a mandate to study and report on means of preparing for monetary union. The summit noted that progress made towards achieving the 1992 programme for completing the internal market was now "irreversible" and that the Single European Act had succeeded in its objective of speeding up decision-making. At the subsequent Rhodes summit, in December 1988, it was noted that almost half the legislation involved in the 1992 programme had been adopted by the Council of Ministers, and the meeting reasserted the importance of the social aspects of the single market. The commission drew up proposals for a Community charter of fundamental social rights, which it hoped to have approved at the Madrid summit in June 1989. In the meantime, however, the Community had been treated to yet another example of UK reluctance to commit itself to progress towards closer European integration. The new crisis, if crisis it was, was due to Mrs Thatcher's strident attack on the European Commission during a highly publicised speech to the College of Europe at Bruges in September 1988, accusing it of accumulating power for its own sake and of trying to create an "identikit European personality".

Mrs Thatcher's speech (which was widely characterised as "Gaullist") was followed by a deliberate policy of nit-picking over commission proposals, which was ill-received not only in other member states but in the UK as well, particularly when it was perceived as directly contrary to specific UK interests. One such case was the rejection, on legalistic grounds, of the Lingua programme of support for foreign language teaching, of which the UK was likely to be the principal beneficiary. Mrs Thatcher's campaign, which clearly embarrassed several of her own ministers, reached its climax in the third election to the European Parliament in June 1989 when, on her initiative, the Conservative Party's appeal was couched in narrow nationalistic terms.

The very poor showing of the Conservatives in that election, and the strong support received both by the Labour Party and the Greens, seems to have had a chastening effect on the UK prime minister. This certainly appeared to be the case at the Madrid summit, which followed one week later. The main item on the agenda was the report of the Delors Committee on monetary union. This committee, composed mainly of the 12 central bankers of the member states, had proposed a three-stage process, leading to full currency union and a European system of central banks. It was agreed that the first stage, which involved all 12 member states adhering to the exchange rate mechanism of the EMS, should begin on July 1st 1990 while preparations should be made for an inter-government conference which would prepare the two subsequent stages and agree necessary amendments to the Rome treaty. While predicting that the UK would vote against the holding of such a conference, but would nevertheless go along with it, Mrs Thatcher acquiesced in these decisions and confirmed that the UK would join the exchange rate mechanism once certain conditions had been met. She declined, however, to endorse the Social Charter approved by the other 11 leaders, which was signed by them later in the year.

Downfall of communism

Meanwhile momentous changes were occurring in Eastern Europe which were to have a profound effect on the European Community. By the summer of 1989 both Poland and Hungary were well on the way to a peaceful transition from communism to democracy, and in the following months hardline communist rule crumbled in East Germany, Czechoslovakia, Bulgaria and, after violent resistance, in Romania. The newly liberated states instinctively looked to the Community as a source of economic assistance, but also as a potential guarantor of their democratic development.

The Community responded with emergency aid and loans to Poland and Hungary, and at the Western economic summit in July 1989, the European Commission was asked to co-ordinate a much wider Western aid operation involving 24 donor nations (the members of the OECD). This programme was later opened up to include Czechoslovakia, Bulgaria, Romania and Yugoslavia, and all of these countries signed trade and co-operation agreements with the EC, as did the Soviet Union itself in December 1989.

A similar agreement was negotiated with the communist government of East Germany, but before it came into effect Germany was united on October 3rd 1990. Six months before, the EC heads of government, at an emergency summit in Dublin, agreed that, subject to transitional arrangements, the territory of the former German Democratic Republic should be integrated into the Community without any revision of the treaties, as soon as unification was legally established. So East Germany joined the EC, as part of the Federal Republic, without any of the long-drawn-out negotiations which had preceded earlier enlargements of the Community.

Central and Eastern Europe

No such quick transition awaited the other countries of central and Eastern Europe, although all their leaders, including those of Yugoslavia and later still, in early 1991, of Albania, declared that their long-term objectives would be membership of the Community. Instead, ten-year association agreements, involving trade concessions, financial assistance and co-operation over a wide range of activities, were signed with Poland, Hungary and Czechoslovakia in December 1991. These agreements specifically acknowledged that the countries involved would eventually be eligible for full membership. Negotiations for similar agreements followed soon after with Romania, Bulgaria, Albania and the three Baltic states of Estonia, Latvia and Lithuania, whose independence was recognised in September 1991. By early 1994 so-called Europe Agreements had been signed with each of these countries, as well as the Czech Republic and Slovakia, to replace the earlier agreement reached with Czechoslovakia. Ukraine signed a partnership agreement with the EU in March 1994, by which time negotiations were well advanced for comparable agreements with Russia and the former Soviet republics of Belarus, Kazakhstan and Kyrgystan. Unlike those with Eastern European countries, these agreements do not hold out the prospect of eventual membership. By contrast, this was implied in a Trade and Economic Co-operation Agreement signed with Slovenia in April 1993. Comparable agreements will almost certainly be offered to the other former Yugoslav republics as soon as a secure peace is established.

The EC was, in fact, deeply involved almost from the outset in trying to achieve a peaceful settlement to the warfare which broke out following the declaration of independence by Slovenia and Croatia in June 1991. The European Council, meeting in Luxembourg on June 28th–29th, immediately dispatched a team of foreign ministers to try to arrange a ceasefire, and subsequently a peace conference opened in The Hague, under EC auspices, in September 1991 under the chairmanship of Lord Carrington, the former UK foreign secretary. Teams of EC monitors were sent to Yugoslavia to see that the ceasefire was respected. It held in Slovenia but not in Croatia, where over a dozen further ceasefires broke down, a third of the country was overrun by Serbian forces and the federal Yugoslav army, and great death and destruction was caused before, after diplomatic intervention by the UN, a peace of exhaustion set in, reinforced by the arrival of a large UN peace-keeping force in March 1992. This was the first time that the EC had attempted to play an international mediating role beyond its own boundaries. Later in 1992 a similar scenario was played out in Bosnia-Hercegovina, although the EC role was more marginal and the UN intervened, if ineffectively, at an earlier stage.

The EC also became heavily involved in Western efforts to provide material assistance to the former Soviet Union. Already in June 1990 the EC heads of government had asked the commission to consult with the Soviet government and to prepare proposals for short-term credits and longer-term support for structural reform. In December 1990 aid programmes of 750m ecus for food and 400m ecus for technical assistance during 1991 were approved, although the latter programme was temporarily suspended as a protest against Soviet repression in the Baltic states.

After the unsuccessful coup in August 1991 a more extensive aid programme was initiated which, following the dissolution of the Soviet Union in December 1991, was widened to include assistance not only to Russia but to all the other former Soviet republics. Six of these claim to be European states: Armenia, Azerbaijan, Belarus, Georgia, Moldova and Ukraine. Several have already indicated an interest in eventual membership of the EU, but none is likely to be a viable candidate until well into the next century, although the other states of central and Eastern Europe might conceivably qualify by the end of the present decade.

Meanwhile the EC had taken the initiative in setting up the European Bank for Reconstruction and Development (EBRD), with an initial capital of $10 billion subscribed by 40 countries. Its purpose is to help the former communist countries to develop into free-market economies (see pages 67–68).

Inter-governmental conferences

The rapid completion of German unification proved possible only because other states were convinced of West Germany's peaceful intentions and the solidity of its democratic institutions. Nevertheless, Chancellor Helmut Kohl, who took the lead in pushing the process through, was convinced that only if a unified Germany was firmly entrenched in a more democratised European Community would it be acceptable to its neighbours. Accordingly, on the eve of the Dublin EC summit of April 1990, in conjunction with France, the German government launched an initiative to ensure that new and decisive steps should be taken towards closer European unity. The following June a further summit meeting in Dublin agreed to establish a second inter-governmental conference (IGC), to run parallel with that on economic and monetary union (EMU), to recommend changes which would lead to "political union" within the Community. It was agreed that both the conferences would be convened in December 1990, with a view to completing their work in time for the member states to ratify their proposals by the end of 1992.

Although all the member states agreed to the establishment of the two IGCs, it was evident that the UK government, still led by Margaret Thatcher, was the least enthusiastic and was unlikely to accept the far-reaching proposals for change which other member states, with France and Germany in the lead, were putting forward with increasing urgency. Although Mrs Thatcher finally agreed in early October 1990 to let the pound enter the exchange rate mechanism of the EMS, 11 and a half years after it was first established, her hostility towards EMU remained unabated. Three weeks later, at a summit meeting in Rome, she was outvoted by 11 to 1 on the starting date for the second stage of EMU. Her intemperate reaction to this rebuff triggered the challenge which led to her replacement as prime minister by John Major at the end of November.

Major lost no time in mending fences with his fellow EC leaders at the second Rome summit, which followed on December 14th–15th 1990. It was then that the two IGCs, which were manned respectively by the finance and foreign ministers of the 12 member states, were formally convened. As their work proceeded over the following months it became evident that there was no longer a serious risk of the UK being totally isolated in both conferences. It seemed more likely that compromises would be reached, involving rather slower progress towards EMU than had originally been proposed, while the changes effected by political union would be less radical than France and Germany had been seeking.

Maastricht treaty

So it proved when the European Council met at Maastricht in December 1991 to consider a draft treaty based on the work of the two IGCs. After two days of hard bargaining the Treaty on European Union was approved, but only after John Major had insisted on two opt-out clauses so far as the UK was concerned. The practical effect of these opt-outs may not be great, but they symbolised once again that the UK, or at least the UK government, still did not feel thoroughly at ease within the European family.

The Maastricht treaty is described in some detail in Appendix 8, and is discussed in Chapters 17, 22 and 35. It undoubtedly represents the most important development in the EC's history since the signing of the Treaty of Rome. Not only does it set out a detailed timetable for achieving economic and monetary union, at the latest by 1999, and provide for the development of common foreign and defence policies, but it also introduces a new concept of EC institutions. A protocol signed by 11 member states, from which the UK excluded itself, opens the way to the implementation of Social Charter legislation in those 11 countries. Finally, the treaty commits the EU to establish a further inter-governmental conference in 1996 to review the working of the Maastricht changes and to set the ground rules for the Union well into the 21st century.

Question marks began to appear against the Maastricht treaty in June 1992, when a referendum in Denmark narrowly went against ratification (50% to 49.3%). Although a further referendum in Ireland, later the same month, produced a strong majority in favour, the alarming prospect arose that French voters would turn the project down in a closely contested ballot in September 1992. Although closer European integration was widely supported in France, there was a serious risk that voters would take the opportunity to administer a rebuff to the unpopular Socialist government which had, quite unnecessarily, called the referendum. In the event a narrow majority (51.05% to 48.95%) approved the treaty.

There were also serious difficulties in securing ratification in the UK, where the prime minister, John Major, had great trouble in overcoming opposition within his own Conservative Party. As he was unwilling to renounce the opt-out that he had secured on the Social Charter, he was unable to count on consistent support from the opposition Labour and Liberal Democratic parties to get the treaty through the prolonged procedures required for ratification by the House of Commons. After considerable delays, which tried the patience of the UK's European partners, the ratification bill was finally approved by the House of Commons on May 20th 1993, and by the House of Lords on July 20th, enabling the UK instrument of ratification to be deposited in early August.

Nine months earlier, at the Edinburgh summit in December 1992, concessions had been made to the Danish government enabling Denmark to opt out of a single European currency, on a similar basis to that agreed for the UK, and a number of other – largely cosmetic – interpretations of the treaty were agreed in order to encourage Danish voters to reconsider their earlier rejection. Consequently, in a further referendum in May 1993, the Danes approved the treaty by 56.7% to 43.3%.

There was yet another delay when German opponents of the treaty sought a ruling declaring it incompatible with the German constitution, despite its having been adopted by an enormous majority in the German Parliament. This attempt was overruled by the German Constitutional Court on October 12th 1993, and the German instrument of ratification was deposited on the same day. This removed the last obstacle, and the treaty finally came into force on November 1st 1993, ten months later than planned. Since then the European Community has been generally known as the European Union (EU).

The difficulties over securing ratification in Denmark, France, Germany and the UK were widely seen as a demonstration that EC political leaders had moved too far ahead of public opinion in their own countries in deciding to push ahead towards closer European integration. The former UK prime minister, Margaret Thatcher, characterised it as a "treaty too far". There was some force in this criticism, and it is true that public knowledge of the provisions of the Maastricht treaty was not extensive, but it is more likely that the undoubted tailing off of enthusiasm for the EU was due to three other factors. These were the economic recession, which struck virtually all European countries, though with varying force, between 1990 and 1994; turmoil in the currency markets which led to UK and Italian withdrawal from the exchange rate mechanism in September 1992, and the abandonment of the narrow bands within the ERM ten months later; and dismay at the apparent failure of EU efforts to bring peace to former Yugoslavia.

New enlargement

In January 1995 four of the EFTA countries – Austria, Finland, Sweden and Norway – should become full members of the EU. This will be the culmination of a process which began with the launching of the 1992 programme in 1985. All seven EFTA countries, anxious not to be excluded from the development of a single market of more than 370m people, sought means by which they could share in the expected benefits. On the initiative of Jacques Delors, the EC offered to negotiate to set up a European Economic Area (EEA), which would permit the EFTA states to join in the 1992 programme at the price of accepting many of the obligations of the EC member states.

The EEA treaty was signed in 1992, but was rejected in a referendum in Switzerland. When it finally came into force in January 1994 it included only Iceland, in addition to Austria, Finland, Sweden and Norway, which were already well advanced in negotiations for full membership of the EU. The door was left open for Liechtenstein to join at a later date, when it had revised its economic relationship with Switzerland. Switzerland had also applied for full membership, but its application was held in abeyance following the referendum decision on the EEA. The four other applicant states completed their negotiations in March 1994 and providing their membership terms are approved in referendums to be held in all four countries between June and December 1994 they will take their places in a Union of 16 nations in January 1995.

1 Alfred Grosser, *op. cit.*, page 189.
2 Steps to European Unity, *European Documentation*, 1985.
3 The UK, Denmark and Portugal subsequently left EFTA on joining the EC, but Finland, Iceland and Liechtenstein became EFTA members.
4 The European Agricultural Guidance and Guarantee Fund.

3

TREATIES

The Treaty of Rome

The bible of the European Community, which provides the ultimate authority for the greater part of its decisions and responsibilities, is the Treaty of Rome, signed on March 25th 1957 by representatives of Belgium, France, West Germany, Italy, Luxembourg and the Netherlands. It was actually only one of two treaties signed in Rome by the same signatories on the same day; the other established Euratom, the European Atomic Energy Community. Six years earlier on April 18th 1951 the six countries had signed the Treaty of Paris, setting up the European Coal and Steel Community (ECSC).

The Treaty of Rome is a bulky document comprising 248 articles and an additional 160 pages of annexes, protocols and conventions. The first four articles, quoted here in their entirety, define the purposes of the European Economic Community, and the principal institutions to be created to ensure their achievement.

Article 1   By this Treaty, the HIGH CONTRACTING PARTIES establish among themselves a EUROPEAN ECONOMIC COMMUNITY.

Article 2   The Community shall have as its task, by establishing a common market and progressively approximating the economic policies of Member States, to promote throughout the Community a harmonious development of economic activities, a continuous and balanced expansion, an increase in stability, an accelerated raising of the standard of living and closer relations between the States belonging to it.

Article 3   For the purposes set out in Article 2, the activities of the Community shall include, as provided in this Treaty and in accordance with the timetable set out therein:

(a) the elimination, as between Member States, of customs duties and of quantitative restrictions on the import and export of goods, and of all other measures having equivalent effect;

(b) the establishment of a common customs tariff and of a common commercial policy towards third countries;

(c) the abolition, as between Member States, of obstacles to freedom of movement for persons, services and capital;

(d) the adoption of a common policy in the sphere of agriculture;

(e) the adoption of a common policy in the sphere of transport;

(f) the institution of a system ensuring that competition in the common market is not distorted;

(g) the application of procedures by which the economic policies of Member States can be co-ordinated and disequilibria in their balances of payments remedied;

(h) the approximation of the laws of Member States to the extent required for the proper functioning of the common market;

(i) the creation of a European Social Fund in order to improve employment opportunities for workers and to contribute to the raising of their standard of living;

(j) the establishment of a European Investment Bank to facilitate the economic expansion of the Community by opening up fresh resources;

(k) the association of the overseas countries and territories in order to increase trade and to promote jointly economic and social development.

Article 4

1. The tasks entrusted to the Community shall be carried out by the following institutions:

- an ASSEMBLY
- a COUNCIL
- a COMMISSION
- a COURT OF JUSTICE

Each institution shall act within the limits of the powers conferred upon it by this Treaty.

2. The Council and the Commission shall be assisted by an Economic and Social Committee acting in an advisory capacity.

Articles 5–248   These articles deal with the following areas.

- 5–8: the setting up of the Community during a transitional period of 12 years.

- 9–11: free movement of goods.
- 12–29: the establishment of a Customs Union.
- 30–37: the elimination of quantitative restrictions.
- 38–47: provisions for agriculture.
- 48–73: the free movement of persons, services and capital.
- 74–84: the requirements for a common transport policy.
- 85–102: competition policy, taxation and the approximation of laws.
- 103–116: economic and trade policy.
- 117–128: social policy.
- 129–130: the establishment of a European Investment Bank.
- 131–136: the association of overseas countries and territories.
- 137–198: the composition and powers of the various Community institutions.
- 199–209: financial provisions.
- 210–248: the legal personality of the Community, the admission of additional members, the setting up of the institutions and various miscellaneous points. Article 240 states that "The Treaty is concluded for an unlimited period". The treaty came into effect on January 1st 1958.

Other treaties

A number of other treaties, protocols and conventions have been signed by the member states over the years, which supplement the original provisions of the Treaty of Rome. The most important of these are as follows.

1   The treaty amalgamating the three European Communities (ECSC, EEC and Euratom), signed in Brussels on April 8th 1965, usually known as the EC treaty.
2   The treaty concerning the admission of Denmark, Ireland, Norway and the UK, signed in Brussels on January 22nd 1972. (Norway subsequently declined to ratify this treaty after a referendum.)
3   Equivalent accession treaties with Greece, signed in 1980, with Spain and Portugal, signed in 1985, and with Austria, Finland, Sweden and Norway, signed in 1994.
4   The Single European Act, signed in 1986 which, among other provisions, amended several articles of the Treaty of Rome regarding voting procedures in the Council of Ministers, while somewhat enlarging the legislative powers of the European Parliament. The main objective was to facilitate the adoption of the programme of nearly 300 measures to complete the Community's internal market (see pages Chapter 15). These were the first substantial amend-

ments to the Treaty of Rome in its first 30 years in operation.

5   The Treaty on European Union, otherwise known as the Maastricht treaty, agreed in December 1991 and signed in February 1992. This was a much more thorough-going revision of the Rome treaty, comprising two major sets of provisions: those aiming at the establishment of an economic and monetary union (EMU), at the latest by January 1st 1999; and those defined as steps towards the achievement of a political union, involving common foreign and defence policies. Other provisions extended or defined more precisely the Community's competences in other policy areas and amended the powers of various EC institutions. This treaty is summarised in Appendix 8.

PART II

THE INSTITUTIONS

Under the Treaty of Rome, four main institutions have been established to give effect to the provisions of the treaty. The following is a simple definition of their functions.

- The European Commission initiates policies and implements those already decided upon.
- The Council of Ministers decides, or legislates, on the basis of proposals brought forward by the commission.
- The European Parliament has a largely advisory role.
- The European Court of Justice interprets the Community's decisions and the provisions of the treaty in the event of dispute.

The Community institutions continue their function under the Treaty on European Union (the Maastricht treaty). In addition, powers have been acquired by the European Union that are not subject to the institutions of the EC, but are dealt with on an inter-governmental basis. These include a common foreign and security policy (see pages 215–216) and co-operation over judicial, police and immigration issues. Strictly speaking the EU is now a hybrid organisation consisting of the EC, with its carefully defined division of powers between its constituent institutions, and an additional inter-governmental component. Part II of this book describes in some detail the principal EC institutions.

4

THE COMMISSION

The European Commission is the executive organ of the Community. It is often seen as the embodiment of the European idea as its members, while appointed by national governments, are under no obligation to them, and their total loyalty is pledged to the interests of the Community as a whole. Each commissioner, on assuming office, makes the following solemn declaration.

> I solemnly undertake:
> To perform my duties in complete independence, in the general interest of the Communities;
> In carrying out my duties, neither to seek nor to take instructions from any Government or body;
> To refrain from any action incompatible with my duties.
> I formally note the undertaking of each Member State to respect this principle and not to seek to influence Members of the Commission in the performance of their task.
> I further undertake to respect, both during and after my term of office, the obligations arising therefrom, and in particular the duty to behave with integrity and discretion as regards the acceptance, after I have ceased to hold office, of certain appointments or benefits.

To the extent that the reality falls short of these aspirations, the commissioners will be failing in their allotted role, and the purposes of the Community will be imperfectly realised.

The commissioners

The commission currently consists of 17 members, two each from the five larger states (France, Germany, Italy, Spain and the UK) and one each from the seven smaller members (Belgium, Denmark, Greece, Ireland, Luxembourg, the Netherlands and Portugal). They were appointed for a four-year term by the Council of Ministers, on the nomination of their own national governments. The term of office is renewable, and at the end of each four-year period typically about half of the commissioners have been reappointed, the remainder being replaced by new nominees. Most of the commissioners are politicians, usually from the governing party (or parties) in the member states, but the UK practice has invariably been for one of its nominees to come from the main opposition party, even though the choice is made by the prime minister of the day. A minority of commissioners have been senior administrators, trade union leaders or businessmen.

The presidency

The president of the commission has hitherto been appointed for a two-year term, although in practice this has normally extended to four years, virtually automatically. Each four-year commission term is referred to colloquially under the name of its president; for example, the Jenkins commission, the Thorn commission, the Delors commission. Under the Maastricht treaty the arrangements for appointing the commission have been changed. From January 1st 1995 the term of office of both the commission and the president will be five years. In future the governments of the member states will be required to consult the European Parliament before nominating the president of the commission. They must also consult the president-elect before nominating the other commissioners. The president and other members of the commission will then be subject to approval, as a body, by a vote of the European Parliament. Only if this vote is positive will the president and the commission be formally appointed by the governments of the member states.

The Maastricht treaty also changes the provisions regarding vice-presidents of the commission. Hitherto six commissioners have been designated by the Council of Ministers as vice-presidents, a distinction which has had little practical significance, except that they have drawn somewhat larger salaries than their colleagues. In future, according to the treaty, the commission itself "may appoint a vice-president or two vice-presidents from among its members". The commissioner (or commissioners) thus chosen will presumably be seen much more clearly as deputising for the president when occasion demands. Under the enlargement treaties negotiated with Austria, Finland, Sweden and Norway, each country will have a member of the commission, whose size will increase to 21 in January 1995 if all four of these countries ratify their adhesion to the EU.

The president of the commission is often misleadingly compared with a prime minister of a member state in relation to his or her cabinet. In fact the president's dominance over his colleagues is normally much less. He neither selects nor dismisses them, and does not determine what portfolios they should hold. His influence on this point is considerable, as he makes a proposal for the distribution of responsibilities at the outset of each term of office, but the actual decision is taken by the commissioners themselves, if necessary by majority vote.

Responsibilities of commissioners

Commissioners are each allocated an area of responsibility under the treaty, and parts of the administrative machine will report directly to them (see Appendix 3 for the current distribution of responsibilities). They also have the assistance of a small cabinet of half a dozen personal appointees who not only act as advisers but also customarily intervene on the commissioners' behalf at all levels of the commission's bureaucracy.

Decision-making in the Community

There are five ways in which the institutions of the Community are able to change or influence the law in the member states. The Council of Ministers and/or the commission is able to issue:

- regulations
- directives
- decisions
- recommendations
- opinions.

Legislation, as normally understood, is undertaken through regulations and directives. Both are initiated by the commission and adopted by the Council of Ministers, in most cases after having received an opinion from the European Parliament and, when appropriate, the Economic and Social Committee. Regulations are of general applicability: they are binding in their entirety and directly applicable in all member states. Directives are binding on the member states to which they are addressed as regards the result to be achieved, but leave the form and methods of achieving it to the discretion of the national authorities (most often this is achieved by passing national legislation, based on the directive).

Decisions by the council or the commission, derived from the authority bestowed by the Rome treaty or through regulations or directives already approved, may be addressed to a government, an enterprise or an individual. They are binding in their entirety on those to whom they are addressed. Recommendations and opinions are not binding. (See also Figure 2.)

A sixth way in which national laws are affected is by case law

Figure 2 **The Community's decision-making process**

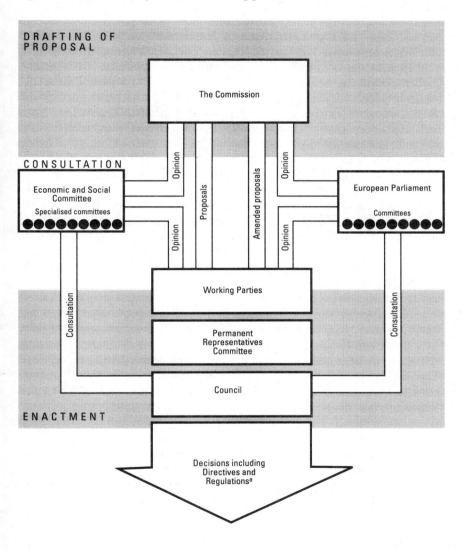

a Subject, in certain cases, to the co-operation and co-decision procedures of the European Parliament

Source: European Commission

resulting from decisions taken by the Court of Justice, whose role is to interpret the Rome treaties affecting the European Community, and to adjudicate in disputes between the other institutions or between any of them and one or more member states (see Chapter 9).

Responsibilities of the commission

The responsibilities of the commission are listed in Article 155 of the Rome treaty. They have been summarised as being those of initiative, implementation and supervision.

Initiative. The treaty gives a general responsibility to the commission to ensure that its provisions are carried out, but it also gives it the specific right to put proposals before the Council of Ministers, which in most circumstances is unable to make decisions in the absence of such a proposal.

Implementation. The commission is entrusted with the implementation of the decisions taken by the council. In respect of the coal and steel industries, the commission itself has a wide range of decision-making powers, inherited from the former High Authority of the ECSC, which it may exercise without reference to the Council of Ministers. It also has substantial autonomous powers relating to competition policy and the running of the common agricultural policy. The commission administers the various funds established by the Community (the Agricultural Guidance and Guarantee Fund (EAGGF), Social Fund, Regional Fund, Cohesion Fund, and so on). It prepares a draft budget which must be approved by the council and the European Parliament. It also negotiates international agreements on behalf of the Community, though these can only be concluded by the council.

Supervision. The commission supervises the implementation of Community law by the member states. Whenever it concludes that a member state has infringed its treaty obligations it is required to deliver an "opinion" to this effect, and may afterwards bring an action in the Court of Justice against the state concerned.

Location

The commission is based in Brussels, and normally occupies the Berlaymont building, a purpose-built glass-fronted building constructed in 1969. In early 1992 the Berlaymont was closed down, and will be comprehensively reconstructed over a period of 5–6 years, due to the risk of infection from the large amounts of asbestos contained in the original structure. In the meantime the commission and its immediate staff are housed in the nearby Breydel building, while the remainder of the personnel are housed in a score of other locations.

Staff

The commission employs about 15,000 people, one-third of whom are concerned with interpreting or translating between the nine official languages of the Community (English, French, German, Italian, Dutch, Danish, Greek, Spanish and Portuguese). A further 1,350 commission employees are engaged in scientific research work at Ispra in Italy, Culham in the UK, Geel in Belgium and various other centres.

The staff, part of which is based in Luxembourg, is organised in 23 directorates-general (from External Relations to Financial Control) and 12 special services (Secretariat-General, Legal Services, Statistical Office, and so on).

Working practices

The commission meets as a body every Wednesday morning, and if there is a heavy agenda the meeting may be resumed after lunch. Additional meetings are frequently scheduled, occasionally in more relaxed surroundings, to discuss particular topics or long-term perspectives. Decisions within the commission are normally adopted on the basis of a simple majority vote, and subsequently the principle of collective responsibility applies.

While all official documents are translated and meetings involving national officials are simultaneously interpreted into all nine languages, most day-to-day business within the commission is conducted in French or English.

5

THE COUNCIL OF MINISTERS

If the commission is the institution representing the general European interest, the Council of Ministers is certainly that in which the particular interests of each member state are brought to bear. It is unquestionably the most powerful of the Community's organs and, in the words of the Directorate-General for Research of the European Parliament, "It has now evolved into the actual centre of political control in the European Community".[1]

Structure

The council consists of representatives from each of the member states, and its meetings are also attended by at least one commissioner as well as by officials of its own secretariat. The membership, however, is constantly changing. If agriculture is on the agenda agricultural ministers will attend; industry ministers will come for industrial matters; and finance ministers will attend when the budget is being discussed.

The foreign ministers' meeting, held at least once a month except in August, is known as the General Affairs Council. As well as discussing foreign policy matters, foreign ministers are supposed to exercise general co-ordination over the work of the other ministerial councils and to tackle particularly complicated and/or urgent matters which do not readily fall within the scope of their more specialist colleagues. It is also their task to prepare the now twice-yearly meetings of the heads of government, known as the European Council (see Chapter 6).

The presidency

The council has a rotating chairmanship or presidency, with ministers from each member state taking turns for a six-month period in the chair. The foreign minister of the state concerned assumes the title of president of the Council of Ministers, and the foreign ministry of his or her country undertakes, with the help of the council secretariat, the organisation of the council's business during the six months. A period will thus be characterised as that of the French presidency, the Dutch presidency, and so on, according to which nationality is in the chair.

It is accepted that it is part of the presidency's duty to oil the wheels of the Community and to strive to get agreement on as many issues as possible. The presidency is therefore expected to exert itself to produce compromise proposals whenever there is a deadlock and to cajole its own national representatives as well as those of other member states to modify their demands.

During the course of each presidency there will be a summit meeting (or European Council) of heads of government in the country concerned, while most of the specialist councils will hold informal meetings, usually in a secluded country house, for an exchange of views on long-term issues, uncomplicated by the mass of more ephemeral items which normally clutter their agenda. Such informal gatherings are known in Eurocircles as Gymnich-type meetings, after Schloss Gymnich in western Germany where the first of them was held.

Permanent Representatives

Few items reach the agenda of council meetings without having been previously discussed, usually exhaustively, at a lower level. Each member state maintains a large delegation in Brussels, known as its Permanent Representation. These are staffed not only by diplomats but by officials from each of the domestic ministries which is liable to be affected by decisions taken by the EC. They are backed up by further officials in their home capitals who are deputed to liaise with them.

Coreper. The heads of delegations, the Permanent Representatives, who have the rank of senior ambassadors, meet at least once a week in the Committee of Permanent Representatives, known by its French language initials as Coreper. Coreper will work methodically through all the issues which are awaiting ministerial decision. If, on the basis of instructions which they have received from their national governments, the Permanent Representatives find themselves in complete agreement on a draft proposal it is normally placed on the council agenda as an "A" point. This would then, except in the unusual event of a government having a last minute change of mind, be adopted without discussion at a subsequent council meeting. More often the Permanent Representatives find that their viewpoints are still fairly wide apart, and the proposals are referred to expert groups, at a lower level, for more detailed discussion. In most cases it is only when no more than one or two governments are in disagreement with the rest that an issue is passed on to the Council of Ministers in the hope of getting a decision.

Other working groups.   Even though the Permanent Representatives are highly versatile, they cannot possibly maintain a uniform level of expertise on all the highly detailed topics which may appear on their agenda. A substantial range of subjects is entrusted to their deputies who have a parallel weekly meeting, known as Coreper II, while agricultural issues are by tradition invariably dealt with by the Special Committee for Agriculture (SCA), consisting of senior officials of national ministries or of the agricultural councillors at the Permanent Representations. A large number of working groups staffed by less senior officials meet regularly to haggle over the details of virtually every proposal for Community legislation.

Legislative role

Unlike in a nation state, where the parliament is responsible for enacting legislation, the legislative role in the EC is performed by the Council of Ministers. Community legislation, known as directives or regulations (see pages 36–37), can only be initiated by the commission. The opinion of the European Parliament and frequently of the Economic and Social Committee must in most cases be sought, but the proposals are adopted (or not, as the case may be) by the council. Again, contrary to the practice of national parliaments, the legislative function takes place behind closed doors, although hardly in secret as the large Brussels press corps is normally extensively briefed after each meeting of the council by spokesmen for each of the national governments concerned.

Meetings

In its various forms, the council meets around 80–90 times during the course of a year, usually for one day, sometimes for two and occasionally for longer. Often two or three different meetings are taking place simultaneously, with, for example, foreign ministers in one conference chamber, transport ministers in another and finance ministers in a third.

Making decisions

When a proposal actually reaches a council meeting, except as an "A" point, it is by no means assured of being adopted. The Treaty of Rome lays down precise rules on decision-making within the council, but these have not been applied in the manner originally intended. Under Article 148 of the treaty, decisions may be taken:

- by a simple majority;
- by a qualified majority (now 54 votes out of 76);
- unanimously.

Simple majority decisions are restricted to minor matters, often of a purely procedural nature. Under the Rome treaty it was envisaged that most decisions would be reached by a qualified majority, leaving the unanimity rule for a limited number of issues of major importance. During a transitional period, which was intended to end in 1965, unanimity was prescribed for a much wider range of issues, but at the very moment that the Community was scheduled to change over to qualified majority voting a major crisis broke out between the French Gaullist government and the other five original members of the EEC (see page 10).

The Luxembourg compromise

As a result of this crisis the five members reluctantly acquiesced in the so-called "Luxembourg compromise" in order to ensure continued French membership of the Community. The operative sentence of this was:

> Where, in the case of decisions which may be taken by a majority vote on a proposal from the Commission, very important interests of one or more partners are at stake, the Members of the Council will endeavour, within a reasonable time, to reach solutions which can be adopted by all the Members of the Council while respecting their mutual interests and those of the Community, in accordance with Article 2 of the Treaty.

If subsequent practice had accorded with the actual wording of the "compromise", which referred specifically to "very important interests", it might not have affected the decision-making process very often. In practice, however, the council showed extreme reluctance to bring any issue at all to a vote, and the unanimity rule was effectively extended to a vast range of decisions which could not conceivably be regarded as affecting the "very important interests" of member states. Accordingly the Luxembourg compromise has seldom been formally invoked. One occasion was in May 1982 when the British government attempted to block a farm price settlement for purely tactical reasons related to a quite different issue (the British budget dispute). The other members refused to accept the validity of the British claim and proceeded to approve each of the 20-odd draft regulations involved in the settlement by qualified majority voting.

Amendments under the Single European Act

Since then there has been a growing feeling, shared by the French government, that qualified majority voting should be used more often. While the Luxembourg compromise, which had no legal force, still stands, the Single European Act, which came into force in July 1987, amended the Treaty of Rome to reduce the number of issues on which unanimity was required. In particular, qualified majority voting was authorised for most of the 300 or so measures which had to be adopted if the 1992 programme to complete the EC's internal market was to be ratified. The Maastricht treaty, which came into force in January 1993, also extended the range of issues to which qualified majority voting would apply, including transport and the environment. Consequently in the areas concerned it is no longer possible for proposals to be held up for years because one or two member states object to them.

Decisions are taken

In view of the above it is hard to see how any decisions are made at all, given the difficulty of persuading 12 separate nation states to sink their differences. In fact many decisions are taken on a "log-rolling" basis, governments giving way on particular points on which they are not convinced in exchange for concessions on often quite unrelated issues.

Allocation of votes

Under the system of qualified majority voting the member states are allocated votes very roughly in proportion to their size. Germany, France, Italy and the UK have ten votes each, Spain eight votes, Belgium, Greece, the Netherlands and Portugal five votes each, Denmark and Ireland three votes each and Luxembourg two votes. As 54 votes (out of 76) are needed for a proposal to be adopted, it follows that a "blocking minority" must muster 23 votes. Thus three large states acting together, or two large states plus one small one (except for Luxembourg), can block a proposal but it would require at least five of the smaller states (with five votes each or fewer) to do so. This arithmetic will change in January 1995 if four new members join the European Union. Austria and Sweden will have four votes each, and Finland and Norway three, increasing the total number of votes to 90. It will then be necessary to win 64 votes for a decision to be taken, raising the blocking minority to 27. In the face of objections from the British and Spanish governments, which wanted to make it more difficult for majority decisions to be taken, it was agreed by the Council of Ministers in

March 1994 that if between 23 and 26 votes were cast against a proposal a decision should be delayed "for a reasonable period of time" while a compromise was sought.

Other council responsibilities

As well as adopting EC legislation, the council has joint responsibility with the European Parliament (whose role, however, is a subordinate one) to adopt the Community budget. It also has the power of appointment to the other institutions, such as the Economic and Social Committee and the Court of Auditors. The multifarious nature of its activities has been well summarised by a former British Permanent Representative, Sir Michael Butler, who wrote:

> In one sense, Coreper and the council together are a forum for a permanent negotiation between member governments on a wide range of issues simultaneously. In another, they are the legislature of the Community. In a third, they are the senior board of directors taking many of the day-to-day decisions on its policies.[2]

Location

The council and its secretariat are based in the Charlemagne building in Brussels, next door to the commission's headquarters in the Berlaymont. A much larger building, just across the road, was due to come into use late in 1994. During three months of the year (April, June and October), however, its meetings are held in Luxembourg, a legacy from the merger of the three Communities which took place in 1965, the former ECSC having been based in Luxembourg.

1 Fact Sheet 1/B/2, European Parliament, Directorate-General for Research, 1987.
2 Michael Butler, *Europe: More than a Continent*, Heinemann, London, 1986, page 30.

6

THE EUROPEAN COUNCIL

The Treaty of Rome makes no provision for meetings of the heads of government of the member states, and during the first ten years of the EEC they met on only three occasions. Yet it gradually became clear that a more regular exchange of views was necessary to give a sense of strategic direction to the Community and to resolve problems to which the Council of Ministers and the European Commission had not been able to find solutions through the EC's normal processes.

Inauguration

In December 1974 it was formally decided at a summit meeting in Paris that the heads of government should meet three times each year under the title of the European Council.[1]

Starting in Dublin in March 1975, the European Council duly met on this basis until December 1985, when it was agreed that only two meetings a year would henceforward be held. During 1990, however, two additional "emergency" summits were held, making four meetings in all during the course of the year. A further emergency summit was held in April 1991 in Luxembourg. It seems probable that, in future, 3–4 meetings of the European Council will be held each year. These meetings take place in the member state currently holding the presidency of the Council of Ministers, and its prime minister (or, in the case of France, its president) takes the chair and is responsible for the organisation of the meetings.

Status

The Single European Act, adopted in December 1985, gave legal recognition to the European Council without, however, defining its powers.

In fact it has had the same status as an ordinary meeting of the Council of Ministers, although it has usually avoided giving formal effect to the decisions it has taken, leaving it to a subsequent meeting of foreign ministers to adopt them on a "rubber stamp" basis. Indeed, a major purpose of the European Council is that its deliberations are informal. They take place without the presence of national officials, the heads of government sitting round the table being accompanied only by their foreign ministers, while the president of the commission is supported only by one vice-president. The more sensitive discussions normally take place in the intervals between the actual sessions (which are spread over two days), particularly during and after dinner on the evening of the first day when most if not all of the heads of government speak in English and simultaneous interpretation is dispensed with.

Its increasing influence ...

The European Council has, to a large extent, replaced the commission as the motor of the Community, and this was especially notable during the period 1974–81, when President Valéry Giscard d'Estaing and Chancellor Helmut Schmidt co-operated closely to play a leadership role. Their joint departure within a few months heralded the beginning of a period of 2–3 years in which few significant decisions were taken by the European Council. The deadlock was broken at Fontainebleau in June 1984 when, largely due to the initiative of President François Mitterrand, a solution was finally found to the British budget problem (see pages 17–18) which had plagued the Community for several years, and the way was cleared for the admission to membership of Spain and Portugal.

Since then the green light for other major new Community initiatives – such as the launching of the 1992 programme, the acceptance of a united Germany within the EC, the convening of inter-governmental conferences on economic and monetary union and on political union, and the offer of economic aid to the former Soviet Republics – has been given at meetings of the European Council. It was also the European Council which agreed the Single European Act at Luxembourg in December 1985, and the Treaty on European Union at Maastricht in December 1991.

Such major and difficult issues can only be resolved at the summit, as only the heads of government have the authority and the political clout not only to impose unwelcome decisions but also to reconcile them with political forces and pressure groups back in their home countries.

... holds up decision-making on minor issues

On the debit side, however, is the undoubted fact that the existence of regular summit meetings actually retards decision-making on many less far-reaching issues which would otherwise be resolved at a lower level. Time and again the heads of government have been called upon to discuss technical matters on which their subordinates have failed to agree because they were unwilling to take the responsibility. The European Council ought not to have to act as a final court of appeal, except on issues of the first importance, but it seems condemned to do so.

---

1 Formally "the heads of state and government". In fact the only head of state who attends is the president of France, the other countries being represented by their prime ministers.

7

THE EUROPEAN PARLIAMENT

The European Parliament is intended to bring a measure of democratic control and accountability to the other institutions of the EC. Its powers, however, are severely restricted; it is not the legislative authority of the Community, and its status compares very badly with that of all of the national parliaments in the different member states. The European Parliament is the successor to the Assembly of the ECSC, which was established in Strasbourg as a purely advisory body in September 1952. It had 78 members, all of them members of national parliaments who had been deputed to attend the Assembly as an ancillary duty to their main functions. The Assembly was expanded to 142 members in 1958, when its competences were extended to the EEC and Euratom, which merged with the ECSC seven years later. Its membership was increased to 198 in 1973, with the accession of Denmark, Ireland and the UK, and its powers (particularly in the budgetary field) were modestly increased under treaties signed in Luxembourg in April 1970 and in Brussels in July 1975.

Direct elections instituted in 1979
Much more significant was the institution of direct elections to the Parliament in June 1979 when 410 members were elected, during a four-day period from nine member states, to a greatly enlarged Parliament. In the second direct elections in June 1984, 434 members (or Euro-MPs) were elected from ten member states, comprising 81 each from France, West Germany, Italy and the UK, 25 from the Netherlands, 24 from Belgium and Greece, 16 from Denmark, 15 from Ireland and 6 from Luxembourg. They were later joined by 60 Spanish and 24 Portuguese members, making a total of 518. Yet this much larger Parliament of 518 full-time members directly elected by over 100m voters was given no greater formal power than had been enjoyed by the previous appointed Assembly of part-timers. The predictable result was constant conflict between the parliamentarians and the Council of Ministers, and a high degree of frustration among Euro-MPs.

Euro-MPs

Euro-MPs are elected for fixed five-year terms, and the next election is due in June 1999. Under Article 138 of the Rome treaty there should be a common electoral system in all member states, and the Parliament itself proposed such a system in 1982 and again in 1993. However, the Council of Ministers was unable to agree to this, largely because of the reluctance of the UK government to abandon its first-past-the-post system in favour of proportional representation (PR). Thus the first four direct elections have been held with different systems operating in all the member states, although all except the UK have used variations of PR.

Salaries.   Euro-MPs are paid the same salary as MPs in their own countries which means that there is a wide variation, with the Portuguese being paid the least and the French and West Germans the most. In addition there are generous travel, attendance, research and secretarial allowances which are paid on the same basis to all members.

Political groups.   Euro-MPs do not sit in national delegations but in cross-national political groups. At the end of the 1989–94 Parliament there were eight of these, with 23 members choosing to remain non-affiliated. The membership was made up as follows.

Party of European Socialists	198
European People's Party (Christian Democrats)	162
Liberal, Democratic and Reformist Group	44
Greens	28
European Democratic Alliance	20
Rainbow Group	16
Technical Group of the European Right	14
Left Unity Group	13
Non-affiliated	23

The Party of European Socialists comprised Labour, Socialist or Social Democratic parties in all 12 member states, including the former Italian Communist Party, renamed the Party of Democratic Socialism, which had wound up its own separate group in January 1993. The Left Unity Group consisted mostly of French Communists. British Conservative MEPs, who previously had joined with Danish Conservatives in a separate group known as the European Democratic Group, became members of the European People's Party in 1992, although the Conservative Party itself declined to affiliate to the European Federation of Christian Democratic parties. The European Democratic Alliance was made up of French Gaullists and Irish Fianna Fáil members, while the Rainbow Group consisted mostly of regionalist and nationalist parties. There was a very small left-wing majority in the Parliament, but the centre-left predominated as the Socialists and the Christian Democrats, who together made up more than two-thirds of the membership, reached an agreement to co-operate on a wide range of issues. Voting in the European Parliament is less disciplined than in most national parliaments and ad hoc coalitions are often formed on individual issues which cross normal ideological and national barriers. There is, accordingly, often some uncertainty about how the Parliament may vote.

Elections to the European Parliament

Since 1979 the European Parliament has been elected simultaneously in all the member states. The term of office is five years, with no provision for early dissolution. There should be a common electoral system but, as mentioned above, agreement on this has not yet been reached. Consequently each member state has used its own system which, in most cases, resembles that used for the election of its own national Parliament.

There have been four direct elections as follows.

- The 1979 election was held in nine member states on June 7th–10th 1979. Greece, which joined the Community on January 1st 1981, subsequently elected 24 members on October 18th 1981.
- The 1981 election was held in ten member states, on June 14th–17th 1984. Spain and Portugal, both of which joined the EC on January 1st 1986, subsequently elected 60 and 24 members respectively, on June 10th and July 19th 1987.
- The third election, when all the states polled simultaneously, was held on June 15th–18th 1989.
- The fourth election, for an enlarged house comprising 567 members, took place on June 9th–12th 1994.

Further members will be elected separately during 1995 to represent Austria, Finland, Sweden and Norway, assuming that these four countries have joined the Union by that date. The next full election will be in June 1999. The electoral systems used in 1994, and the number of members for each country, are shown in Table 1.

Table 1   European Parliament election, 1994

Country	Seats	Voting method
Belgium	25	PR, regional lists
Denmark	16	PR, national lists
France	87	PR, national lists
Germany	99	PR, regional lists
Greece	25	PR, national lists
Ireland	15	PR, single transferable vote
Italy	87	PR, regional lists
Luxembourg	6	PR, national lists
Netherlands	31	PR, national lists
Spain	64	PR, regional lists
Portugal	25	PR, national lists
UK	87	plurality
of which:		
Northern Ireland	3	PR, single transferable vote

Powers of the European Parliament

The European Parliament has supervisory powers over the commission and the council, the right of participation in the legislative process and budgetary powers.

Supervisory powers. These are defined by the Treaty of Rome as including the right to put questions, written or oral, to the commission, to discuss its Annual General Report, to discharge the annual budget and to adopt a motion of censure which would lead to the resignation of the commission as a body. Thus in 1993 some 3,588 written and 850 oral questions were put to the commission, and a further 523 written and 475 oral questions to the Council of Ministers. These were answered by ministers from the country currently holding the presidency, who attend each plenary session of the Parliament for this purpose. Since December 1981 the practice has grown up that the prime minister of this country makes a personal report to the Parliament after each meeting of the European Council. The Parliament is able to exercise more intensive supervision over the commission than the treaty envisages, as members and senior officials of the commission attend meetings of its committees and the commission submits its annual programme of work in advance to the Parliament, as well as its annual report, which can only be used as the basis for retrospective checks.

Yet the power of the Parliament to dismiss the commission has, so far at least, remained largely a theoretical threat. The motion of censure may be carried only by a two-thirds majority of the votes cast, representing a majority of the Euro-MPs. It is not possible to censure a particular commissioner, which might well prove a more effective sanction. In practice Euro-MPs have regarded the power as analogous to possession of a nuclear weapon, the consequences of actually using it being regarded as too horrible to contemplate. Moreover, the Parliament has seldom been at loggerheads with the commission as a whole; its arguments have mainly been with the Council of Ministers against which it has no such sanction.

Legislative role. The legislative role of the Parliament is essentially an advisory one. The treaties designate a large number of areas in which the Council of Ministers cannot enact legislation without first consulting the European Parliament. In practice, in addition to this mandatory consultation the Parliament is normally invited to submit an opinion on any other draft directives or regulations tabled by the commission. Amendments proposed by the Parliament may be incorporated by the commission when it presents a revised draft to the council, and it has undertaken to explain to the Parliament the reasons why an amendment has not been adopted.

The legislative role of the Parliament has been significantly strengthened by the Single European Act, which came into effect in July 1987, and by the Maastricht treaty, which took effect in November 1993. This provides for processes of consultation and co-decision by the Parliament which strengthen its ability to amend legislation and, through a "negative assent" procedure, gives it the right to veto certain legislation by a vote of a majority of its members. The Maastricht treaty gives the Parliament a new right of initiative, whereby it may by a majority vote require the commission to propose action in any area. The treaty also gives the right to any EC citizen to petition the Parliament if the matter is of direct and individual concern, and it authorises the Parliament to appoint an ombudsman to receive complaints about deficiencies in the administration of EC institutions. The Parliament may, at the request of a quarter of its members, set up a temporary committee to examine allegations of infringement or bad administration of Community law, unless the matter is *sub judice*. Despite these changes the Parliament still falls far short of being an equal partner of the Council of Ministers in the legislative process.

Budgetary powers. The budgetary powers of the Parliament are more substantial. It is officially designated as jointly forming the budgetary authority with the Council of Ministers, and no budget may be adopted without its agreement. Even so its influence, though considerable, is clearly less than that of the council, as a brief description of the process will make clear.

There are five stages in the budgetary process.

1 The tabling of the preliminary draft budget, which is the responsibility of the commission. This is laid before the Council of Ministers by September 1st of the previous year.

2 The council amends the preliminary draft, invariably reducing the expenditure proposed, and establishes the draft budget, which is submitted to the Parliament by October 5th.

3 The Parliament has 45 days to state its position; it may propose modifications to the compulsory part of the budget and amendments to the non-compulsory part. The compulsory part (currently 66% of the whole) consists of expenditure on policies directly arising out of the treaties, mainly agriculture. The non-compulsory part covers other policies adopted by the EC, and this expenditure the Parliament is free to amend, although it may not increase it beyond a so-called "maximum rate" set by the council each year.

4 The council takes a final decision on the Parliament's proposed modifications to the compulsory expenditure, which it may reject. If the modifications involve no increase in expenditure they require only a qualified majority for acceptance by the council; if any increase is involved a positive majority is required to reject them. The council may also reject the Parliament's amendments on the non-compulsory side. In that case a compromise has to be reached between the two institutions by means of a "conciliation procedure".

5 The Parliament may amend these modifications and it then adopts the budget. It may decline to do so by a two-thirds majority of the votes cast, representing a majority of all members.

The Parliament has refused to adopt the budget on three occasions, which resulted in the Community entering a new calendar year without a budget being approved. When this happens, total expenditure is restricted during each month to one-twelfth of the total budgeted for the previous year. On each of these occasions the Parliament subsequently adopted a revised draft which differed only marginally from the budget it had originally rejected. On the whole it has enjoyed more success when it has used the established conciliation procedures and has played off one member state against another in the Council of Ministers than when it has gone for outright rejection. Every year, however, there is a struggle of wills between the council and Parliament, with the latter invariably wanting a larger budget and one less heavily committed to agriculture. Euro-MPs are intensely dissatisfied with their inability to amend compulsory expenditure and with the council's power to determine the "maximum rate".

Location
The member states have not yet fulfilled their obligation under the treaties to establish a single seat for the Parliament, and its effectiveness is undermined by the geographical fragmentation of its work. The monthly plenary sessions are held in Strasbourg, with additional meetings in Brussels, most committees meet in Brussels and the bulk of the secretariat is based in Luxembourg. This, plus the fact that it needs to conduct its business in nine different languages with simultaneous interpretation, and the requirement that all documents shall be translated into each of the nine languages, greatly increases the cost of running the institution, which in 1991 amounted to some 508m ecus ($590m or £355m).

Most Euro-MPs would undoubtedly prefer that the Parliament's activities should be concentrated in Brussels, but the Luxembourg and French governments are vehemently opposed to this and they have prevented a decision on a permanent seat from being taken. Under the treaties this would need to be unanimous. The European Parliament itself, however, can largely control its own provisional arrangements, and it has shown itself pusillanimous in not deciding to hold its plenary sessions in Brussels. It seems that many Euro-MPs prefer to complain rather than to risk upsetting their own governments by taking decisive action.

Sessions
The Parliament normally meets in plenary session for one week in each calendar month except August, with additional part sessions in March and October to consider its opinions on agricultural prices and the annual budget. Much of its work, however, takes place in committees or subcommittees, of which there are currently 45. These usually meet during two other weeks each month, leaving at least one week free for party or constituency activities.

8

THE ECONOMIC AND SOCIAL COMMITTEE

A purely advisory body, the Economic and Social Committee (ESC) must nevertheless be consulted by the European Commission and the Council of Ministers over a wide range of issues. The Treaty of Rome specifies a number of areas where consultation is mandatory before directives and regulations may be approved, but the council and the commission customarily consult with the ESC over many other issues. In general terms, there is in practice little hindrance to the ESC offering opinions on any subject on which its members may wish to pronounce.

Membership

The membership of the ESC is made up of interest groups throughout the Community, and it provides a useful sounding board for their representatives whenever legislation which concerns them is envisaged. The members are divided into three groups:

- Group I representing employers;
- Group II representing workers;
- Group III representing various interests such as consumers, farmers, the self-employed, academics, and so on.

Members are appointed by the Council of Ministers on the nomination of their governments, which normally consult with the interest groups most concerned (particularly the trade unions and employers' organisations) before choosing their nominees.

The current membership is 189, consisting of 24 each from France, Germany, Italy and the UK, 21 from Spain, 12 each from Belgium, Greece, the Netherlands and Portugal, 9 each from Denmark and Ireland and 6 from Luxembourg. The members are appointed for a renewable term of four years; the current term of office ends in September 1994. The ESC elects its own chairman, who serves for two years, and it is customary to rotate the chairmanship between the three groups. ESC members are part-timers, who are allowed time off from their normal jobs.

Location and working practices

The headquarters of the ESC is in Brussels and it meets there every month. Its detailed work is, however, undertaken in specialist sections (currently nine in number) which draft opinions for approval by the ESC meeting in plenary session. The sections are as follows.

- Agriculture
- Transport and Communications
- Energy and Nuclear Questions
- Economic and Financial Questions
- Industry, Commerce, Crafts and Services
- Social Questions
- External Relations
- Regional Development
- Protection of the Environment, Public Health and Consumer Affairs

On issues such as workers' rights to be consulted or to participate in management, the ESC normally splits on left-right lines, with the members of Groups I and II on opposing sides. In these circumstances the members of Group III are left with the casting votes, and more often than not they have tended to come down predominantly on the trade union rather than the employers' side. On most questions considered by the ESC, however, divisions occur within each group rather than between them. The influence of the ESC, which by 1992 had given over 2,000 opinions, is in any event seldom significant on controversial political matters. Where it can, and does, influence the content of Community legislation is on more technical issues, where the expertise of its members is often brought to bear.

Committee of the Regions

A similar body, known as the Committee of the Regions, was appointed under the Maastricht treaty provisions, and met for the first time in March 1994. This committee is asked to give its opinion on proposed EC legislation likely to have a particular impact on the various regions of the member states. Like the ESC, with which it shares premises and secretariat, it has 189 members appointed for a four-year renewable term. The national membership quotas are the same as for the ESC.

9

THE COURT OF JUSTICE

The task of ensuring that the law is applied throughout the Community in accordance with the provisions of the treaties is devolved upon the European Court of Justice,[1] based in Luxembourg.

Composition

The court currently comprises 13 judges (one from each member state and one other) and six advocates-general.

The judges are chosen by the Council of Ministers, on the nomination of member states, "from persons whose independence is beyond doubt and who possess the qualifications required for appointment to the highest judicial offices in their respective countries or who are juriconsultants of recognised competence" (Article 167 of the Treaty of Rome). They are appointed for a renewable term of six years, half the court being renewed every three years. The advocates-general are appointed on the same basis.

The judges select one of their number to be president of the court for a renewable term of three years. For more important cases, and invariably in cases brought by a member state or a Community institution, the court sits as a single body. Other cases are assigned to chambers set up within the court: there are currently four chambers composed of three judges and two chambers composed of six judges. At any stage a chamber may refer a case to the full court if it considers that it raises points of law requiring definitive rulings.

Jurisdiction

In general six types of cases come before the court or its chambers.

- Disputes between member states.
- Disputes between the EC and member states.
- Disputes between the institutions.
- Disputes between individuals, or corporate bodies, and the Community (including staff cases).
- Opinions on international agreements.
- Preliminary rulings on cases referred by national courts.

The last type of case is of crucial importance for ensuring that Community law is uniformly applied throughout the EC. It illustrates an essential difference between the Court of Justice and the US Supreme Court, with which it is often compared. Both courts are supreme in the sense that there is no appeal against their decisions. But the US court is at the apex of a structure of federal, state and district courts, all of whose rulings may be appealed upwards to it. The Court of Justice is, by contrast, the only EC court within the Community, and has no hierarchical relationship to the lower courts, all of which form part of one of 12 different legal systems. When a case comes before a national court involving Community law, which takes precedence over national laws, if there is any question as to the effect of the Community law with regard to that case it should be referred to the Court of Justice for a preliminary ruling, which the judges in the national court must then apply in giving their own judgments. In the application and interpretation of purely national laws, which of course make up the great bulk of cases in other courts, the Court of Justice has no jurisdiction whatever.

Court procedure

Proceedings before the court may be initiated by a member state, a Community institution (most often the commission) or by a corporate body or individual (providing he or she has a direct personal interest in the subject of the case). The court procedure involves two separate stages, one written and one oral.

In the first stage, on receipt of a written application from a plaintiff, the court establishes that it falls within its jurisdiction and that it has been lodged within the time limitations determined by the treaties. The application is then served on the opposing party, which normally has one month in which to lodge a statement of defence. The applicant has a further month to table a reply, and the defendant one more month for a rejoinder.

Each case is supervised by a judge-rapporteur, who is appointed by the president. On receipt of all the documents the judge-rapporteur presents a preliminary report to the court, which decides whether a preparatory enquiry (involving the appearance of the parties, requests for further documents, oral testimony, and so on) is necessary, and whether the case shall appear before the full court or be assigned to one of the chambers. The president then sets the date for the public hearing, at which the two sides appear before the judges, present their arguments and call evidence if they so wish. The judges and the advocate-general (whose role is somewhat similar to that of the public prosecutor in French courts) put to the parties any questions they think fit. Some weeks later the advocate-general gives his opinion, at a further hearing, analysing the facts and the legal aspects in detail and proposing a solution to the dispute.

The advocate-general's opinion often gives a clear indication of which way the judgment will go, but this is not invariably the case. The judges consider their ruling in private, on the basis of a draft prepared by the judge-rapporteur. If, during their deliberations, they require additional information they may reopen the procedure and ask the parties for further explanation, oral or written, or order further enquiries.

The judgments of the court are reached by majority vote; where the court is equally divided the vote of the most junior judge is disregarded, although in most cases it is arranged that an uneven number of judges will be sitting (the quorum for the full court is seven). The judgment is given at a public hearing, which, on average, occurs some 18 months after the receipt of an application.

Case load

The case load of the court has built up steadily since its foundation in 1953. Altogether some 8,293 cases had been brought before the Court by December 31st 1993. Table 2 gives a detailed breakdown of all the cases heard in the six years up until that date. Given the importance and complexity of the common agricultural policy, it is not surprising that agriculture leads the number of direct actions brought before the court. The largest number of cases referred for preliminary rulings also concerns agriculture, with a substantial number concerning the free movement of goods and social security and free movement for workers.

Much the largest number of cases concern complaints brought by employees of the different EC institutions on such matters as recruitment, salaries, promotion, disciplinary procedures, and so on, which under national administrations would go to employment tribunals. It is an anomaly that the Court of Justice, whose primary function should be to rule on significant issues of Community law, should have its timetable clogged up with a mass of petty cases, most of which could be adequately dealt with at a far lower level.

Court of First Instance

The Single European Act (see page 44), which took effect in July 1987, provided for the establishment of a Court of First Instance, which would hear certain classes of cases brought by individuals,

Table 2   **Court of Justice: cases 1988–93 analysed by subject matter (as at December 31st, 1993)**

	Direct actions	Preliminary rulings
Accession	2	2
Agriculture	575	217
Approximation of laws	57	11
Brussels Convention	–	33
Commercial Policy	35	21
Company Law	25	21
Competition	74	64
Economic Policy	1	–
Energy Policy	1	–
Environmental and Consumer Affairs	70	11
European Investment Bank	1	–
External Relations	22	15
Free movement of goods	66	202
Free movement of persons	52	173
Law governing the Institutions	22	6
Principles of the Treaty	7	7
Regional Policy	1	–
Rules of Procedure	2	–
Social Policy	47	97
State Aid	53	3
Taxation	39	96
Transport	24	20
Total EEC Treaty	**1,176**	**999**
Financial Provisions	–	2
Law governing the Institutions	3	–
State Aid	2	–
Iron and Steel	9	2
Total ECSC Treaty	**14**	**4**
Procurement	2	–
Protection of the Population	4	–
Safety Control	1	–
Law governing the Institutions	1	–
Total EAEC Treaty	**8**	**–**
Financial and Budgetary Provisions	11	–
Law governing the Institutions	1	–
Privileges and Immunities	–	3
Staff Regulations	4	3
Total EC	**21**	**6**
Total	1,219	1,009

including actions brought by officials of the Community. This court, which consists of 12 judges, began work in September 1989. The removal of staff cases from the work of the main court should shorten the delay in arriving at judgments in other cases.

Who brings the cases

Cases involving member states are often initiated by the commission, normally alleging failure to carry out their obligations under the treaties. Occasionally one member state is brought to court by another. As Table 3 shows, Italy has figured most frequently in cases both as a complainant and, more notably, as a defendant. The Italian Parliament is notoriously slow in passing laws, and a large number of these actions have been for failure to apply directives, adopted by the Council of Ministers, within the appointed time. The commission easily heads the lists both of complainants and defendants. It is its responsibility to take action, against individuals and companies as well as member states, to ensure that the treaties are being applied, for example in competition cases. On the other hand it is the commission which is the defendant in virtually all actions alleging loss or damage caused by the carrying out of EC policies.

Occasionally cases have involved one institution lodging a complaint against another. The Council of Ministers has more than once initiated action against the Parliament for allegedly exceeding its budgetary powers, while the Parliament took the council to court for failure to implement a common transport policy within the period foreseen by the Rome treaty.

Beneficial effect of judgments

The judgments of the court have helped to consolidate the Community, ensuring that its citizens as well as national governments are both protected by, and subject to, the provisions of Community law. It has been effective in many of its judgments in preventing governments from backsliding from the obligations which they (or their predecessors) assumed in signing the treaties. And, although it has few sanctions against member states – being unable, for example, to send erring ministers to prison – its judgments have nearly always been complied with, although on occasion after some delay, and sometimes following a further ruling by the court. The Maastricht treaty has given the court the power to impose fines on member states failing to comply with its judgments within a time-limit set by the commission.

One particular judgment has provided a useful stimulus to the removal of non-tariff barriers to intra-Community trade. In 1979

Table 3 **Complainants and defendants, 1954–93**

Direct actions brought by:		Direct actions brought against:	
Belgium	12	Belgium	149
Denmark	5	Denmark	20
Germany	40	Germany	75
Greece	19	Greece	87
France	41	France	123
Ireland	11	Ireland	46
Italy	50	Italy	286
Luxembourg	7	Luxembourg	57
Netherlands	31	Netherlands	47
Portugal	5	Portugal	6
Spain	35	Spain	22
UK	20	UK	35
Total brought by member states	276	Total brought against member states	953
Commission	980	Commission	1,469
Council	4	Council	240
European Parliament	16	Commission and Council	446
Individuals or firms	1,870	European Parliament	28
		Other institutions	4
		Individuals or firms	6
Total	3,146	Total	3,146

Source: Court of Justice.

and 1980 the court ruled in the "Cassis de Dijon" case that where a product (in this case a category of alcoholic drink, but it has subsequently been applied to particular foodstuffs) is legally retailed in one member state, its sale cannot be prohibited in another member state except on the grounds of risk to public health.

1 Not to be confused with the European Court of Human Rights, based in Strasbourg, which was set up by the Council of Europe, under the European Convention of Human Rights, signed in 1950. All the member states of the EC recognise the jurisdiction of this court in human rights cases.

10

THE COURT OF AUDITORS

The least known of the EC's institutions is the Court of Auditors, based in Luxembourg. It was established only in 1977, when it replaced an earlier Audit Board which had less sweeping authority.

Membership
There are 12 members, one from each member state, who are chosen from persons who belong or have belonged to external audit departments in their own countries, or who are otherwise specially qualified. They are appointed for a renewable six-year term by the Council of Ministers, and appoint their own chairman from among their number for a renewable term of three years.

Responsibilities
The court's task is to examine all accounts of revenue and expenditure of Community institutions, and of any other bodies set up by the EC, to ensure that all revenue has been received and all expenditure incurred in a legal manner. It also has the responsibility of ensuring that the financial management has been sound. Its function is similar to that of bodies like the Comptroller and Auditor General's department in the UK.

An influential role
The court produces an annual report, as well as periodic specific reports undertaken at the request of any of the Community's other institutions or on its own initiative. It has frequently thrown up evidence of wasteful expenditure, especially on support to agriculture, and occasionally of financial misconduct. Its role is highly influential, and its reports have led to a considerable tightening up of EC procedures.

11

THE EUROPEAN INVESTMENT BANK

The European Investment Bank (EIB) is both a Community institution and a bank. Established in 1958, under Article 130 of the Rome treaty, it is the EC's bank for financing capital investment promoting the balanced development of the Community. It raises the bulk of its financial resources on capital markets (where it has a AAA rating), and on-lends the proceeds, on a non-profit making basis, for capital investment meeting priority EC objectives. The major part of its lending activity is focused on the Community's less prosperous regions. It also contributes towards deploying EC development aid programmes, notably under the co-operation or association agreements which the Community has concluded with 12 countries in the Mediterranean region and with 69 African, Caribbean and Pacific countries under the fourth Lomé Convention (see Chapter 34).

Members and financial resources
The members of the EIB are the 12 member states of the EC. They have collectively subscribed the bank's capital of 57.6 billion ecus (of which 4.32 billion ecus is paid up). Up to the end of 1992 the bank had raised some 126 billion ecus in loans. During 1992 it borrowed 13 billion ecus and lent 17 billion ecus.

Activities in the EC
Loans went to each of the member states. Italy and the UK have long been the major recipients, but both Spain and Portugal (which already benefited from EIB loans before their accession to the Community) are rapidly increasing their drawings from the bank.

EIB loans within the Community during 1990 were principally for regional development, energy, industry, advanced technology, the modernisation and conversion of enterprises, transport, telecommunications and other infrastructure development, and environmental protection.

Location and structure
The EIB is based in Luxembourg. Its Board of Governors consists of the finance ministers of the member states, who meet once a year.

Figure 3 **Finance provided by the European Investment Bank, 1973–92[a]**
(m ecus at current prices)

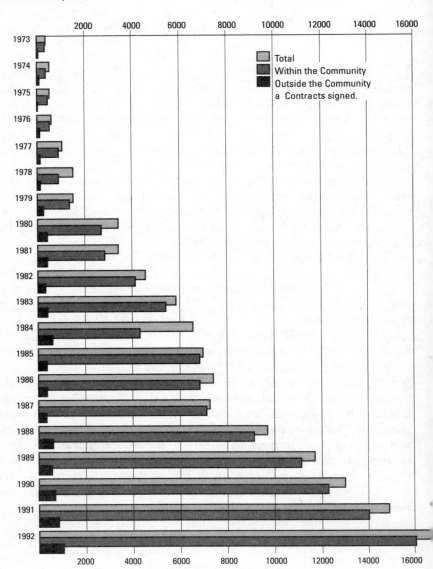

Total
Within the Community
Outside the Community
a Contracts signed.

Table 4 **Geographical breakdown of loans granted, 1991–92**

	1991 m ecus	%	% of total	1992 m ecus	%	% of total
Within EC						
Belgium	115.6	0.8		396.6	2.5	
Denmark	538.6	3.7		690.8	4.3	
Germany	1,300.1	9.0		1,663.9	10.3	
Greece	366.9	2.5		377.5	2.3	
France	1,924.4	13.3		1,895.1	11.7	
Ireland	236.9	1.6		303.5	1.9	
Italy	4,000.7	27.7		3,796.9	23.5	
Luxembourg	28.6	0.2		42.8	0.3	
Netherlands	175.4	1.2		154.4	1.0	
Portugal	1,002.1	6.9		1,230.4	7.6	
Spain	2,342.5	16.2		3,020.6	18.7	
UK	2,090.5	14.5		2,407.2	14.9	
Other	300.4	2.1		159.7	1.0	
Total within EC	14,422.8	100.0	94	16,139.7	100.0	94.8
Outside EC						
ACP states	389.5	42.5		252.0	28.2	
Mediterranean countries	241.5	26.4		320.8	35.9	
Eastern Europe	285.0	31.1		320.0	35.8	
Total outside EC	916.0	100.0	6	892.8	100.0	5.2
Total loans	15,338.8			17,032.5		

Source: European Investment Bank.

It also has a part-time Board of Directors (21 members nominated by the member states and one member nominated by the European Commission), and a full-time Management Committee of the bank's president and six vice-presidents. They are appointed by the Board of Governors, on the nomination of the Board of Directors, for a renewable six-year term.

European Bank for Reconstruction and Development

Since 1990 the EIB has been lending money to countries in Eastern Europe to help towards their transition to market economies. It also contributed to the establishment in April 1991 of the European Bank for Reconstruction and Development (EBRD), with headquarters in London, whose specific function it is to lend money for this purpose. Although 40 countries participated in its establishment, more than half of the EBRD's capital of $10 billion was contributed by the European Community and its member states. The EIB's share in the new bank's capital is 3%.

12

THE BUREAUCRACY:
FACTS, FIGURES AND COSTS

Number of employees

Despite frequent suggestions that the EC has a vast bureaucracy, the Community's payroll is modest compared with that of the national civil services of the member states. The European Commission has fewer than 16,000 employees excluding 1,350 working in scientific research institutes, while the remaining institutions together employ about half that number. The total number of employees at the end of 1993 is shown in Table 5.

Table 5   **EU employees, end-1993**

	Permanent	Temporary
Commission	14,403	743
Research institutions	1,159	191
Council of Ministers	2,170	–
Parliament	3,243	547
Court of Justice	691	81
Court of Auditors	335	67
ESC	510	–
Total	22,511	1,629

Recruitment

Recruitment to the commission's staff, apart from a limited number of senior posts to which national governments make nominations, are filled by open competition, the competitions being advertised periodically in the *Official Journal* of the Community, and in leading newspapers in the member states. Normally there is an upper age limit for new recruits, which effectively means that most Eurocrats join early in their careers, in their 20s or early 30s. Appointments are made without regard to race, creed or sex and, in principle, no posts are reserved for nationals of any specific state. In practice there are unofficial national quotas designed to ensure that each member state gets a reasonable share of posts at each level of the administration. Otherwise the general qualifications are as set

out in Article 28 of the Community's Staff Regulations.
An official may be appointed only on condition that:

(a) he is a national of one of the Member States of the Communities,
unless an exception is authorised by the appointing authority, and
enjoys his full rights as a citizen;
(b) he has fulfilled any obligations imposed on him by the laws
concerning military service;
(c) he produces the appropriate character references as to his
suitability for the performance of his duties;
(d) he has ... passed a competition based on either qualifications or
tests, or both qualifications and tests;
(e) he is physically fit to perform his duties; and
(f) he produces evidence of a thorough knowledge of one of the
languages of the Communities and of a satisfactory knowledge of
another language of the Communities to the extent necessary for the
performance of his duties.

Candidates for posts as interpreters or translators must have a
good knowledge of two Community languages other than their own.

Training
In addition to its permanent staff, the commission makes provision
for the in-service training of about 200 stagiaires each year. The
training lasts for 3–5 months, and the posts are open, also on a competition basis, primarily to recently graduated students. There is no
guarantee of future employment, but the "stages" provide excellent
experience for those interested in future careers at a European
level, either with the Community or otherwise.

Salaries
The remuneration of members of the commission is linked to the
maximum of the A1 scale. The president of the commission receives
138% of this (£168,775), vice-presidents 125% (£152,875) and commissioners 112.5% (£137,590). In each case they also qualify for the
various allowances paid to employees, notably the expatriation
allowance, which adds 14% to the above figures for all except the
Belgian commissioner.

EU employees pay income tax to the Community (currently at a
standard rate of 25%) rather than to the country in which they are
employed, and the rates of pay are set rather higher than for
national civil servants in order to compensate for living and working in a different country. In addition to basic salaries, there are

family allowances and expatriation allowances, and a number of other "perks", such as free education for children at one of the European schools maintained by the commission. The salary scales are published from time to time in the *Official Journal*, where they are expressed monthly in Belgian francs. The approximate annual equivalents in pounds, as of 1994, are shown in Table 6.

Table 6 **Basic salaries in each category and in the Language Service, 1994 (£)**

Category A

A1	Director-general	96,630–122,300
A2	Director	85,750–110,240
A3	Head of Division	71,015–101,010
A4	Principal Administrator	59,660–83,070
A5		49,190–69,585
A6	Administrator	42,510–58,745
A7		36,590–45,695
A8	Assistant Administrator	22,360–33,665

Category B

B1	Principal Administrative Assistant / Senior Administrative Assistant	42,510–58,745
B2	Senior Technical Assistant	36,830–48,915
B3	Senior Secretarial Assistant / Administrative Assistant	30,895–40,945
B4	Technical Assistant	26,720–35,435
B5	Secretarial Assistant	23,885–26,910

Category C

C1	Executive Secretary / Principal Secretary / Principal Clerical Officer	27,255–34,945
C2	Secretary/Shorthand-typist	23,705–30,755
C3	Clerical Officer	22,115–28,150
C4	Typist	19,980–25,645
C5	Clerical Assistant	18,425–20,690

Category D

D1	Head of Unit	20,820–27,195
D2	Skilled Employee	18,985–24,645
D3	Skilled Worker / Unskilled Employee	17,670–22,965
D4	Unskilled Worker	16,660–18,710

Language Service

LA3	Head of a Translation or Interpretation Division	71,015–101,010
LA4	Head of Translation or Interpretation Group	59,660–83,070
LA5	Reviser, principal translator, principal interpreter	49,190–69,585
LA6	Translator	42,510–58,745
LA7	Interpreter	36,590–45,695
LA8	{ Assistant translator { Assistant interpreter	22,360–33,665

PART III

THE COMPETENCES

The European Union is still a long way from becoming the political union to which its founders aspired, and which has several times been reaffirmed, most recently at Maastricht in December 1991, by the EC's heads of government as their eventual aim. It is far from being a European government, and its progress has been markedly lopsided. The removal of customs duties between member states and the development of a common agricultural policy long remained the most concrete achievements of the Community, but there are many other areas of economic activity where it has a competence, which is often shared, to a varying extent, with that of the member states. The Maastricht treaty enshrined the principle of "subsidiarity" by asserting that decisions should be "taken as closely as possible to the citizens", but nevertheless extended the competences of the EC institutions in several directions. Part III surveys the principal fields of action of the Community without, however, purporting to provide a comprehensive account of all of its activities.

13

FINANCING THE UNION

The EU's budget is modest compared with that of the member states, no more than around 2% of the sum of the national budgets. In 1994, according to the European Commission, each EU citizen paid an average of 200 ecus to the Union, and perhaps 50 times that amount to their own country. Despite this disparity, the EU's budget has been a source of periodic dispute between the member states and between them, the commission and the Parliament.

Revenue

Sources

The EC's sources of revenue have changed over the years. The ECSC, which has its own operational budget (393m ecus in 1994), has always been financed by a levy on the production of coal and steel firms. The general Community budget was originally financed by a system of national contributions based mainly on the GDP of the member states. In 1970 it was decided progressively to replace these contributions by the Community's "own resources". These consist of sources of revenue which, while collected in the main in the member states, belong to the Community as a right. At present they consist of four separate elements.

1 Customs duties, levied on products imported from outside the Community.
2 Agricultural levies, charged on imports of various foodstuffs to bring the price up to Community level plus levies on products in surplus supply.
3 A proportion of value-added tax. By far the largest element, this was originally set at a maximum of 1% of the final selling price of a common base of goods and services (this was necessary, as both the rates and the incidence of VAT vary widely from one country to another). The limit was raised to 1.4% in 1986, but will gradually drop from 1.4% back to 1.0% between 1995 and 1999.
4 Contributions from member states. Based on the member state's share of the total GNP of the Community, the size of this contribu-

tion is to be limited to that which would bring the total revenue of the EC to a maximum of 1.2% of the Community's GNP in 1993 and 1994, gradually rising to a maximum of 1.27% in 1999.

Budgetary reform

The fourth resource was added in 1989, following the agreement on budgetary reform reached at the Brussels summit of February 1988. For the first time for several years the Community was thus able to have a budget based on an amount of available own resources sufficient to finance all its political, economic and social operations. For several years previously a growing shortfall had had to be met by non-refundable advances from the member states. Table 7 shows the estimated revenue for 1993 and 1994.

The previous methods of financing the budget had become increasingly unsatisfactory, and the 1986 and 1987 budgets were only balanced by various forms of creative accountancy. The yield from customs duties had slowly declined as the Community's external tariffs were adjusted downwards, and agricultural levies fell as the EC became self-sufficient in an increasing number of products. This put pressure on the VAT contributions which were already up to the maximum level of 1.4% of the value of purchases in the Community within a year of the ceiling being raised from 1%. The addition of the fourth resource enabled the long-term planning of budgetary commitments until 1992, later extended to 1999.

Table 7 **Budget revenue, 1993–94 (m ecus)**

	1993[a]	1994[b]
Agricultural levies	1,032.1	1,023.4
Sugar & isoglucose levies	1,115.3	1,242.2
Customs duties	12,259.6	14,021.5
Own resources collection costs	-1,440.7	-1,628.7
VAT own resources	35,560.0	35,850.5
GNP-based own resources	16,555.7	18,988.8
Balance of VAT and GNP-based own resources from previous year	-1,129.6	[c]
Budget balance from previous year	1,004.0	[c]
Other revenue	500.0	515.8
Total	65,456.4	70,013.5
% GNP		
Maximum own resources which may be assigned	1.20	1.20
Own resources actually assigned to the budget	1.11	1.19

Source: European Commission. [a]Outturn. [b]Estimate. [c]Token entry.

Expenditure

Figure 4 (page 77) shows the expenditure provided for in the EU's general budget of 1994, and compares it with 1973, the first year in which the UK was a member. The principal elements in the budget are described below.

Agriculture and fisheries. 49.6% of expenditure in 1994, a sharp reduction on previous years. The main reason why agriculture absorbs such a high proportion of the budget is that it is the one area of major expenditure where a substantial amount of publicly financed support passes through the EU's budget. It threatens to crowd out programmes in other areas, for example, technological research, where the Union ought to be making a far larger contribution. Efforts have been made in recent years to curtail agricultural spending, and at least to ensure that it rises at a slower rate than EC expenditure as a whole (see pages 125–127).

Regional policy. Some 12.2% of expenditure in 1994. In 1973 there was no regional spending in the budget. The European Regional Development Fund was established in 1975, following the accession in 1973 of the UK, Denmark and Ireland. It helps to finance development programmes, infrastructural investment and industrial and service projects in poorer regions and areas particularly hit by the recession. The fund normally operates on the basis of matching contributions from the member state concerned. Under the Maastricht treaty, a new Cohesion Fund (2.5% of expenditure in 1994) was established to provide assistance for infrastructure investment in the four poorest member states: Greece, Portugal, Spain and Ireland.

Social policy. Approximately 8.8% of expenditure in 1994, a small percentage increase over 1973 despite the massive increase in unemployment in the intervening years. Most of this expenditure is through the European Social Fund, which co-finances training and retraining schemes and aid for recruitment. In 1988 it was agreed that total expenditure on the "structural funds", that is the regional fund, the social fund and the agricultural guidance fund, would double by 1993. By 1994 they amounted together with the Cohesion Fund to 31.6% of the total budget.

Energy, research, industry, transport and the environment. These accounted for only 4.3% of Union spending in 1994, which is evidently only a tiny fraction of the amount spent by member states in these fields. The largest proportion went on research, which was widely seen as being a totally inadequate response to the research efforts of the USA and Japan. Attempts by the commission to persuade the member states sharply to increase the appropriations for research have so far met with only partial success.

Development co-operation. 5.5% of expenditure in 1994, mainly on food aid and assistance to East European countries, the former Soviet Union and Mediterranean, Asian and Latin American countries. Additionally, the Lomé Convention provides for financial and technical aid to 69 African, Caribbean and Pacific countries, which is in practice financed separately from the EU budget through national contributions and loans from the European Investment Bank (see Chapter 34).

Appropriations and expenditure

The procedure for approving the annual budget is described on pages 53–55. Total estimated expenditure for 1994 was 70,013m

Figure 4 **The Community budget, 1973[a] and 1994[b]**

(general budget, current prices, % share of totals)

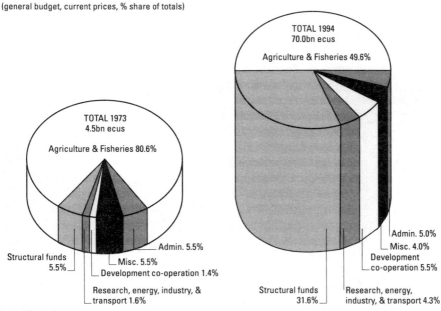

TOTAL 1994
70.0bn ecus

Agriculture & Fisheries 49.6%

TOTAL 1973
4.5bn ecus

Agriculture & Fisheries 80.6%

Admin. 5.5%
Misc. 5.5%
Development co-operation 1.4%
Research, energy, industry, & transport 1.6%
Structural funds 5.5%

Admin. 5.0%
Misc. 4.0%
Development co-operation 5.5%
Research, energy, industry, & transport 4.3%
Structural funds 31.6%

a Actual expenditure.
b Budget estimates.
c Including regional and social and, for 1994, the Cohesion Fund.

Source: European Commission

ecus. (The actual appropriations were for 73,444m ecus, but each year the actual expenditure tends to fall short because not all the commitments are taken up.) The main appropriations for 1994 are shown in Table 8.

Table 8   **General EU budget, 1994 appropriations**

Sector	m ecus
Common agricultural policy	36,465
Structural operations (incl. Cohesion Fund)	23,176
Internal policies (other than structural operations)	4,360
External action	4,296
Administrative expenditure	3,617
Reserves	1,530
Total	73,444
Payment appropriations required as % of GNP	1.19
Own resources ceiling as % of GNP	1.20

Source: European Commission.

Table 9   **Financial perspective, 1987–99 (bn ecus, 1992 prices)**

Commitment appropriations	1987	1992	1999
Common agricultural policy	32.7	35.3	38.4
Structural operations (incl. Cohesion Fund)	9.1	18.6	30.0
Internal policies (other than structural operations)	1.9	4.0	5.1
External action	1.4	3.6	5.6
Administrative expenditure	5.9	4.0	3.9
Reserves	–	1.0	1.1
Total	51.0	66.5	84.1
Payment appropriations required	49.4	63.2	80.1
as % of GNP	1.05	1.15	1.26
Own resources ceiling as % of GNP	–[a]	1.20	1.27

Note: Average annual GNP growth: 1987–92 (actual) 3.1%; 1992–97 (projected) 2.5%.

[a]Except VAT 1.4%.

Source: EC Commission.

Expenditure proposals for 1993–99

In February 1992 the commission published its proposals for expenditure over the five-year period 1993–97, the so-called Delors II package. Largely to meet the commitments agreed at the Maastricht summit some weeks earlier, the commission proposed that the budget should increase by rather less than one-third, from 66.5 billion ecus in 1992 to 87.5 billion ecus in 1997. In order to permit this, the limit on EU "own resources" should be raised from 1.2% to 1.37% of GNP. The member states were unwilling to see EU expenditure rise by so great an amount. Instead, they agreed at the Edinburgh summit in December 1992 a less ambitious increase to be spread over seven years from 1993 to 1999. Under this agreement appropriations (at 1992 prices) may rise to 80.1 billion ecus by 1999 and the limit on own resources will increase to 1.27% of GNP. Table 9 shows the estimated financial commitments for 1999, compared with 1992 and 1987, in terms of 1992 prices. The table also gives the estimated expenditure, which is normally somewhat lower than the commitments undertaken.

14

TRADE

Removal of tariff barriers

The Treaty of Rome provided for the removal of all tariff barriers inside the Community within 12 years, and in fact the original six member states completed the process 18 months early, in 1968. Later entrants proceeded in stages: the UK, Ireland and Denmark by 1977; and Greece by 1986. Spain and Portugal, which joined the Community in 1986, removed all their tariffs against other EC members by the end of 1992. As internal tariffs were removed, a common external tariff was introduced against the goods of other countries. Originally set at an average of around 10%, this has gradually been reduced, following successive rounds of negotiations in the General Agreement on Tariffs and Trade (GATT), and the weighted average of EU customs duties now stands at just under 5%, a little lower than in the USA but higher than in Japan. Under the GATT Uruguay round agreement reached in December 1993, this weighted average will fall to around 3%.

Member states represented by EU

The treaty stipulated that the EC should represent its members in matters of external trade, and the member states formally transferred some of their sovereign powers to the Community. As a result some 157 countries established diplomatic relations with the EC. Most of these have embassies or missions in Brussels which often double up with embassies accredited to Belgium, although the EU role is in most cases by far the more important. The EU, normally represented by the commission, speaks for the member states in the GATT and the North Atlantic Fisheries Organisation.

The EC signed agreements with over 120 countries as well as some 30 multilateral agreements. Most of them concerned EC trade, and their effect was profoundly to modify its pattern. The trading arrangements fall into four main categories: EFTA; other developed countries; state trading countries; developing countries.

EFTA

EU's largest trading partner

Since 1973 the EC has formed an industrial free-trade area with the seven countries of the European Free Trade Association (EFTA): Austria, Finland, Iceland, Liechtenstein, Norway, Sweden and Switzerland. Customs duties and restrictions on trade in manufactured goods were abolished, and some reciprocal concessions were made for agricultural produce. This has effectively extended the size of the common market for manufactures to 370m people. EFTA is the EU's largest trading partner.

European Economic Area

Following the launch of the EC's single market programme, the EFTA countries expressed a desire for closer association with the Community. Negotiations began in December 1989 to establish a European Economic Area (EEA) in which the EFTA states would assume many of the obligations and disciplines of EC membership, including the acceptance of the free movement of capital, persons and services, in return for sharing in most of the expected benefits of the single market programme. The negotiations ended in autumn 1991 and the EEA should have started on January 1st 1993. However, the agreement was turned down in a referendum in Switzerland in December 1992, and following further negotiations with the remaining countries it only came into effect in January 1994, with Switzerland left out and Liechtenstein's membership deferred to a later date. It seems likely, however, that it will act as no more than a staging post on the way to full EU membership. Austria, Finland, Norway and Sweden are expected to become members of the EU in January 1995, while a Swiss application remains in abeyance (see also pages 223–224).

Other developed countries

North America

Trade relations with the USA are largely governed by agreements in the GATT. Both sides profess free-trade principles, but each often accuses the other of protectionist tendencies and/or of giving unfair advantages to its own exporters through state subsidies. Disputes concerning agriculture and steel, in particular, became increasingly frequent during the 1980s, leading on occasion to the introduction of counter-measures which were usually withdrawn when the other side belatedly offered concessions. A full-scale trade war, which would be as deeply damaging to both sides as to world trade as a whole, has several times seemed a distinct possibility, but so far at least cooler counsels have prevailed when tension has mounted.

Canada is in a similar position to the USA, although in 1976 a framework agreement was concluded which established mechanisms for commercial and economic co-operation. In November 1990 a transatlantic declaration was signed between the EC, the USA and Canada, providing for closer co-operation in areas of common interest and a more permanent dialogue to resolve or contain the trade disputes which would inevitably continue to occur.

Japan

The EU's trading relations with Japan have been difficult, largely due to the substantial trade deficit. Japan imports less than half as much from the Union than it exports to it. This imbalance is particularly painful because Japanese exports are focused on a relatively small number of sectors – cars, electronics, audio-visual equipment, computers and telecommunications – where European firms have been struggling to maintain or achieve a viable share in the world market. Although Japanese tariffs are, on average, lower than the EU's, the Union has repeatedly called for the removal of non-tariff barriers and for more decisive action by the Japanese authorities to open up their domestic market to foreign imports.

Meanwhile, Japanese exports to Europe have been curbed by a variety of measures, some taken by individual member states rather than by the EU itself, such as "voluntary" limitation agreements on the number of Japanese cars that may be imported in any one year. The commission has increasingly resorted to anti-dumping measures to restrict the importation of goods such as photocopiers, computer printers and electronic typewriters; and imports of colour TV sets, numerically controlled machine tools, CD players, video recorders and microwave ovens have been formally or informally restricted in recent years.

High-level meetings with Japanese ministers and officials take place regularly, as well as quadrilateral meetings that include the USA and Canada. The pressure applied at these meetings resulted in Japanese initiatives to encourage importers and to ease or remove impediments in their domestic markets. The Japanese trade surplus with the EC more than halved in the five years to 1990, but it rose steeply again during 1991 and succeeding years. The EC pressed for further market-opening measures to be taken by Japan, which blamed lack of enterprise by EC exporters for their failure to increase their penetration of the market. In July 1991 the

EC and Japan signed a joint declaration providing for close economic and political co-operation in the future. A Trade Assessment Mechanism (TAM) was established in 1993 to find out why EU businesses which perform well internationally fare less well in Japan, and to propose action to remove internal obstacles to trade. Meanwhile negotiations were proceeding to phase out EC restrictions on Japanese car exports, which were not, however, expected to gain completely free access to the EU market before January 1st 2000.

Australasia

Australia and New Zealand have no trade agreements with the EU. They are, however, important trading partners, supplying food and raw materials and taking mainly manufactured goods from the Union. Australian and New Zealand food exports to the UK were adversely affected when the UK joined the EC. New Zealand was partially compensated by the award of temporary export quotas for cheese and butter. The cheese quota expired after five years, but the arrangements for importing a limited amount of butter have been extended, despite the EU's own excess production.

Former communist countries

Trade with the countries of central and Eastern Europe before the collapse of communist rule in 1988–90 was hampered by the lack of normal trading relations and by the inherent inefficiencies of command economies. A mutual recognition agreement was reached in June 1988 with Comecon, the economic organisation linking most of the communist countries, which was wound up in 1991. This opened the way to the establishment of diplomatic relations between the EC and individual East European countries as well as Cuba. Trade and co-operation agreements were subsequently signed with Poland, Hungary, Czechoslovakia, Bulgaria, Romania and the Soviet Union. At the same time considerable economic and technical aid was made available to the first three countries (see page 208), and humanitarian aid was given to Bulgaria, Romania and the Soviet Union.

Association agreements

Negotiations began in 1990–91 with a view to concluding far-reaching association agreements (known as Europe Agreements) with the new democracies of central and Eastern Europe, which would provide tariff-free access for most of their manufacturing goods while maintaining restrictions on their free export of textiles and agricultural products. The first three agreements were con-

cluded with Czechoslovakia, Hungary and Poland in December
1991. The agreement with Czechoslovakia was later replaced by
separate agreements with the Czech Republic and Slovakia, and
others were signed with Bulgaria and Romania. Less comprehensive agreements were subsequently concluded with Albania, Slovenia, the three Baltic states and Ukraine, and negotiations were well
advanced with Russia by the end of 1993. A trade agreement with
former Yugoslavia, concluded in 1970, is no longer in operation. The
Union has a large deficit with the former Comecon countries,
largely because of Soviet energy sales to Western Europe, and has
been anxious to build up its export of manufactured goods.
Progress, however, has been slow. It has been further impeded by
the quasi-collapse of the Soviet economy.

Developing countries

The Mediterranean

The Community concluded association or co-operation agreements
with 12 Mediterranean countries (excluding Albania and Libya).
These give duty-free access to all, or most, of their industrial products, specific concessions for some of their agricultural produce and
a certain amount of financial aid in the form of grants and loans. A
similar agreement came into force in January 1990 with the countries belonging to the Gulf Co-operation Council.

Three countries have association agreements. In 1987 Turkey
applied for full membership (see page 221), while Cyprus concluded
a customs union which will include agricultural produce and will be
completed in stages up to 1997. The third association country,
Malta, and Cyprus applied for full membership in 1991.

The ACP

In Africa, the Caribbean and the Pacific, 69 states are members of
the Lomé Convention (see Appendix 7), which frees the signatories
from all customs duties on 99.5% of their exports to the Union, with
no reciprocal concessions required on their part.

Asia

Countries such as India, Bangladesh, Pakistan and Sri Lanka benefit from the EC's generalised system of preferences, which gives
developing countries duty-free access for finished and semi-finished
goods. The EC also has separate economic and development agreements with India and Pakistan, and a co-operation agreement with
the Association of South-East Asian Nations (ASEAN): Brunei,

Indonesia, Malaysia, the Philippines, Singapore and Thailand.

Latin America

There are economic and trade co-operation agreements with most of the principal countries, including the five members of the Andean Pact and the six countries of the Central American isthmus. All the Latin American countries benefit from generalised preferences.

Trade policy

Industrial products

The external trading policy of the EC is based on free trade, or the aspiration to achieve it, so far as industrial products are concerned, although this attitude has been greatly modified in relation to Japan. Notable exceptions are shipbuilding, steel (see Chapter 24) and textiles. Textile imports into the EC have been regulated by the Multi-Fibre Arrangement (MFA). The MFA was a deal between the USA, the EC and low-cost suppliers conceived in 1973, to open up markets to developing country suppliers while the ailing textile industries of the industrialised world were slowly run down. It soon became apparent, however, that it was being used as a protectionist device to keep imports from developing countries at modest levels. Under the Uruguay round agreement the MFA will be gradually dismantled over a period of ten years and the EU market will be progressively opened up to textile imports.

Agriculture

Agricultural trade is governed by protectionism. Apart from special arrangements to buy quotas of sugar from India and the ACP countries at guaranteed prices, virtually no temperate agricultural products are imported into the EU since the agricultural levies (see Chapter 19) effectively make them uncompetitive. This will be less true in the future as a result of the Uruguay round (see page 127). The EU remains, however, the world's largest food importer. It still has a substantial deficit in its agricultural trade because of its purchases of tropical products and animal feed.

EU the world's leading trader

The result of these arrangements is that the EU is the world's leading trader. The EC was responsible in 1989 for 15.6% of world trade (average of exports and imports), compared with 13.8% for the USA and 8.1% for Japan. In relation to the total economic activity within its area, the EU is much more dependent on trade than either of its main rivals. In Belgium and Luxembourg imports and exports make up some 60% of GDP, and Spain (14%) is the only member state where they amount, on average, to less than 20% of GDP.

The Union needs to trade to this extent because of its paucity of energy and raw materials. Nearly 45% of its energy needs are met by imports, as well as three-quarters of other vital raw materials. In order to pay for these it needs to export mainly finished products to the rest of the world. Although internal trade between member states has expanded enormously since the establishment of the Community in 1958, its share of world trade has somewhat declined in the face of much stronger competition from Japan and from newly industrialised countries such as South Korea, Brazil and Singapore. The EC's share in a much larger volume fell from 22% in 1958 to 15.6% in 1989.

Table 10 **EC trade[a], 1991**

Country	Imports m ecus	% of GDP	'000 ecu/ head	Exports m ecus	% of GDP	'000 ecu/ head	Balance[b] m ecus
EC 12[c]	1,199,380	23.6	3.5	1,116,050	22.0	3.2	– 83,230
EC 12[d]	493,808	9.7	1.4	423,467	8.3	1.2	– 70,341
Belgium & Luxembourg	102,321	64.3	10.2	95,013	59.7	9.5	– 7,308
Denmark	26,674	25.3	5.2	29,298	27.8	5.7	+2,624
France	200,118	20.6	3.5	184,746	19.0	3.2	–15,372
Germany	314,735	24.7	3.9	323,947	25.4	4.0	+9,212
Greece	17,411	30.5	1.7	7,015	12.3	0.7	– 10,396
Ireland	16,833	48.0	4.8	19,534	55.7	5.5	+2,701
Italy	147,197	15.8	2.5	136,755	14.7	2.4	– 10,442
Netherlands	110,899	47.2	7.3	108,212	46.0	7.2	–2,687
Portugal	21,089	38.0	2.1	13,158	23.7	1.3	– 7,931
Spain	72,666	17.0	1.9	51,351	12.0	1.3	– 21,315
UK	169,437	20.8	2.9	147,123	18.0	2.6	– 22,314
Canada	95,387	20.1	3.5	102,631	21.6	3.8	+7,244
Japan	191,046	7.0	15.4	253,822	9.3	20.5	+62,776
USA	393,914	8.7	1.6	340,435	7.5	1.3	– 53,479

[a]Trade with the rest of the world, including intra-EC trade.

[b]+ = export surplus; – = import surplus.

[c]Internal and external.

[d]External.

Source: Eurostat.

Table 11 **Total exports by partner countries, 1991 (%)**

Exporting country	Total exports	Destination EC 12	USA	Japan	Rest of world	of which: ACP
EC 12	100	61.6	6.4	2.0	30.0	1.4
Belgium/Lux'bourg	100	75.2	3.8	1.2	19.9	1.1
Denmark	100	54.1	4.8	3.6	37.5	1.1
France	100	63.6	6.0	2.0	28.4	2.6
Germany	100	53.8	6.3	2.5	37.4	0.8
Greece	100	63.5	5.7	1.0	29.8	1.4
Ireland	100	74.4	8.7	2.3	14.7	0.8
Italy	100	59.0	6.9	2.2	32.0	1.1
Netherlands	100	76.2	3.8	0.9	19.0	1.2
Portugal	100	75.1	3.8	0.9	20.3	4.4
Spain	100	66.4	4.6	0.8	28.2	1.3
UK	100	56.3	11.0	2.2	30.5	2.0
Canada	100	8.1	74.2	4.8	12.9	0.4
Japan	100	18.8	29.3	–	51.9	1.2
USA	100	24.4	–	11.4	64.1	1.9

Source: Eurostat.

Table 12 **Total imports by partner countries, 1991 (%)**

Importing country	Total imports	Origin EC 12	USA	Japan	Rest of world	of which: ACP
EC 12	100	58.6	7.7	4.3	29.4	1.6
Belgium/Lux'bourg	100	70.6	5.9	3.7	19.7	2.0
Denmark	100	54.2	5.8	3.1	36.9	0.3
France	100	64.2	8.3	2.9	24.6	2.1
Germany	100	54.5	6.1	5.3	34.1	1.0
Greece	100	60.2	4.3	6.6	28.8	1.2
Ireland	100	69.1	15.1	3.8	12.0	0.9
Italy	100	57.7	5.6	2.4	34.2	1.3
Netherlands	100	59.0	8.1	5.4	27.5	1.8
Portugal	100	71.9	3.4	2.9	21.8	3.0
Spain	100	59.8	7.9	4.4	27.9	2.9
UK	100	50.2	12.5	5.7	31.6	1.5
Canada	100	10.9	62.9	7.5	18.8	0.8
Japan	100	13.4	22.7	–	63.8	0.8
USA	100	17.4	–	18.5	64.1	2.9

Source: Eurostat.

Figure 5 **Where the EC traded, 1992**

($bn, current prices)

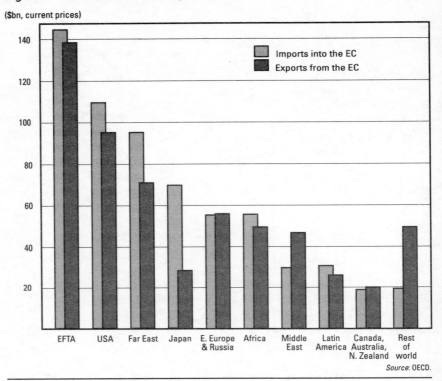

Source: OECD.

Figure 6 **Shares of world exports, 1990**

($mn)

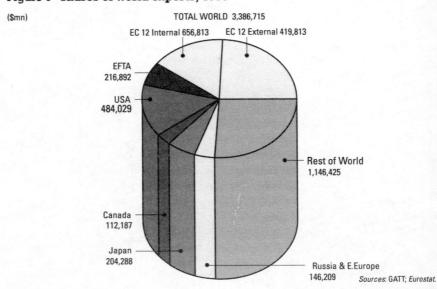

Sources: GATT; Eurostat.

Figure 7 **Trade as a percentage of GDP, 1991**

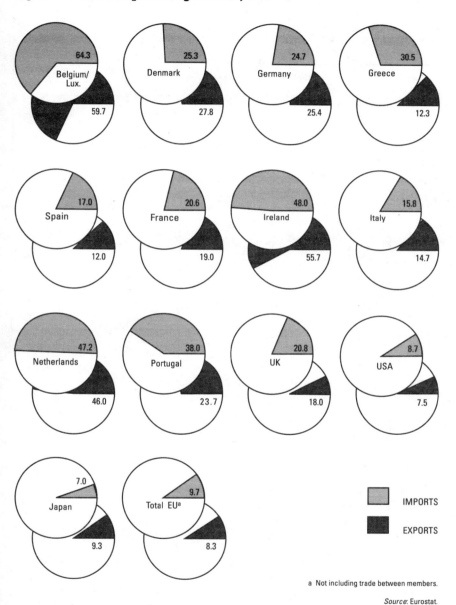

a Not including trade between members.

Source: Eurostat.

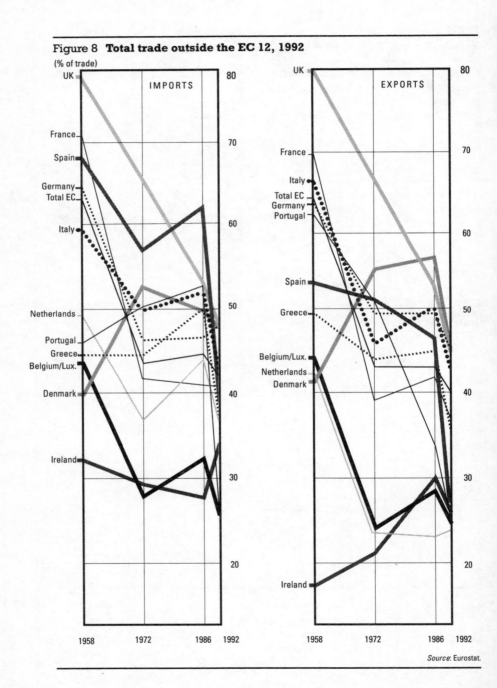

Figure 8 **Total trade outside the EC 12, 1992**

(% of trade)

IMPORTS

EXPORTS

Source: Eurostat.

Figure 9 **EC external trade, 1962 and 1990**

(%share of total value)

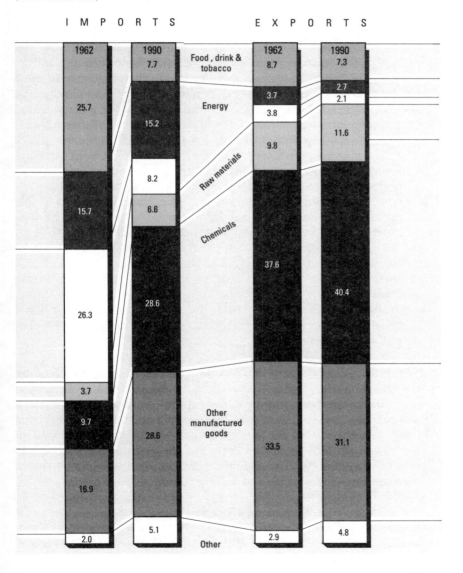

I M P O R T S   E X P O R T S

1962	1990		1962	1990
25.7	7.7	Food, drink & tobacco	8.7	7.3
	15.2	Energy	3.7	2.7
15.7	8.2		3.8	2.1
	6.6	Raw materials	9.8	11.6
26.3	28.6	Chemicals	37.6	40.4
3.7				
9.7	28.6	Other manufactured goods	33.5	31.1
16.9	5.1			
2.0		Other	2.9	4.8

Source: European Commission.

15

THE SINGLE MARKET

"Common market" proved to be elusive

In the early 1980s concern was expressed with growing urgency that 15 years or so after the six founding members of the EC had abolished all quota restrictions and duties on their internal trade, the Community was still far from being the "common market" which it was usually called.

- Frontier formalities delayed and added to the cost of transporting goods from one member state to another.
- It was still impossible for many EC citizens to pursue their professional duties in another member state, despite the provisions of the Rome treaty concerning free movement.
- Service industries such as insurance were prevented from operating on a Community-wide basis.
- Differential indirect tax rates distorted intra-Community trade.
- Public procurement contracts in each member state were effectively reserved for national suppliers rather than being put out to open tender.

An influential report to the European Parliament by two leading economists, one French and the other British,[1] estimated that such restrictions cost every worker in the Community the equivalent of a week's wages every year. It was evident that the Community was largely failing to reap the benefits which a unified market of 321m people (following Spanish and Portuguese accession in 1986) should provide in relation to the smaller population base of both of its main industrial rivals, the USA and Japan.

The European Council takes action

The problem was discussed at successive meetings of the European Council between 1982 and 1985. At several of these the heads of government pledged themselves to the completion of the internal market as a high priority, but this had little noticeable effect. An enormous backlog of draft directives and regulations, tabled by the

European Commission, had built up in the Council of Ministers, which was often prevented from taking a decision through the resistance or hesitancy of only one member state.

Finally, in 1985, more decisive action was taken at two consecutive European Council meetings (at Brussels in March and at Milan in June). In Brussels it was decided to instruct the commission to draw up a detailed programme with a specific timetable for completing the single market by 1992. In Milan it was resolved to summon an inter-governmental conference which would consider, among other matters, the desirability of amending the Rome treaty to enable qualified majority voting to be applied to most of the internal market issues which had previously required unanimity. This eventually led to the Single European Act, which came into force on July 1st 1987 (see page 44).

White paper on single market drawn up

The call from the Brussels summit was soon answered by the commission, which produced a white paper drawn up by Lord Cockfield, the commissioner responsible for the internal market, in time for it to be approved at Milan. This document listed some 300 actions which would need to be taken if the single market was to be achieved. These were divided into three categories:

- the removal of physical barriers;
- the removal of technical barriers;
- the removal of fiscal barriers.

Physical barriers. The white paper set as its target the total abolition, not simply the alleviation, of frontier controls by 1992. Measures which would relax and simplify existing controls – beginning with the introduction in 1988 of the so-called Single Administrative Document (SAD) which replaced up to 70 forms previously required by truck drivers crossing internal EC frontiers – were set out, paving the way for the complete removal at the end of the period of all restrictions on goods and individual travellers.

Technical barriers. The second part of the white paper was intended to remove the barriers created by different national regulations and standards. The commission proposed that its laborious programme to harmonise national standards for thousands of different manufacturing processes should be replaced by a system of mutual recognition of national standards, pending the adoption of European standards. The EC should instead confine itself to laying down minimum health and safety requirements which would be obligatory in all member states. Other proposals included:

- the liberalisation of public procurement;
- the establishment of a common market for services such as transport, banking, insurance and information marketing;
- the free movement of capital throughout the Community;
- the removal of legal restraints on the formation of EC-wide companies; and
- the adoption of a Community trademark system.

Fiscal barriers.　The third part of the white paper was mainly concerned with the approximation of VAT and excise-duty rates throughout the Community. The commission did not consider that total harmonisation was necessary for the completion of the internal market. It would be content to see rates varying by +/–2.5% of whatever target rate or norm was chosen.

Target dates set in timetable for completion

The timetable for completing the internal market set target dates for each of the 300 proposals, both for the commission to table draft directives or regulations and for their adoption by the Council of Ministers. Despite the enthusiasm of the heads of government, there was a great deal of scepticism as to whether the programme would be carried out. Yet it soon gathered momentum, due partly to the dedication which Jacques Delors and Lord Cockfield brought to the task of following up the white paper proposals. The 1992 target aroused intense interest, both within the member states and in other countries, whose governments and traders feared the consequences of a more integrated European market from which they might be excluded. Lord Cockfield was not reappointed in January 1989 to serve in the second Delors Commission, but by then his programme was progressing without interruption, helped by the new voting procedures under the Single European Act which speeded up progress in the Council of Ministers. The 300 measures were later consolidated into 282 proposed directives or regulations. By the target date of December 31st 1992 no fewer than 258 of these (over 90%) had been adopted by the Council of Ministers, and 79% were already being implemented by the member states. In some cases, notably concerning the harmonisation of indirect taxes (see Chapter 18), there had been a certain watering down of the original proposal, but it was undeniable that the great bulk of the programme was legislated as planned.

The Schengen Agreement

The biggest failure was that, though all customs controls on goods were abolished at internal EU frontiers on January 1st 1993, systematic passport checks continued to be made at many frontier crossings, particularly at seaports and airports. Already several years earlier some governments, notably that of the UK, had argued that to abolish border checks would cause problems relating to the control of terrorism, illegal immigrants and drug-trafficking, and the containment of animal-borne diseases. It was in order to bypass this opposition that, in June 1990, five member states decided to go ahead on their own with an agreement to do away with all their internal EC frontiers, while strengthening controls at external borders. Thus the Schengen Agreement, named after the Luxembourg village where it was signed, was concluded by Belgium, France, Germany, Luxembourg and the Netherlands. Two important areas covered by the agreement are as follows.

External borders. The objective is to harmonise visa requirements and to issue visas which would be valid for all the Schengen countries. It is envisaged that a common list will be drawn up of about 100 countries whose citizens would require entry visas. A joint list of suspect individuals would also be compiled, and a watch kept out for them at external frontiers. Political asylum procedures would also be aligned.

Judicial matters. Provision is made for close co-operation in cases involving irregularities in taxation, excise duties and customs payments, while sentences delivered in courts in one member state may be served in the country where the offender resides. Police forces will co-operate more closely, and will have the right of hot pursuit over borders, although France will not allow actual arrests to be made on its territory by foreign police forces. The Schengen Information Service, to be established in Strasbourg, will collate files on people and goods sought by the police in each member state. Safeguards were agreed concerning the confidentiality of these files. The Schengen countries will harmonise their laws on the ownership and use of weapons and will co-operate closely to combat drug-trafficking.

The agreement was due to come into force early in 1992, but there were repeated delays and it will probably only take effect towards the end of 1994. In the meantime Italy, Portugal, Spain and Greece had already adhered to the agreement by mid-1992, leaving only three member states outside. These countries – Denmark, Ireland and the UK – which are all on the geographical periphery of the Community are, for differing reasons, unlikely to sign the agreement in the foreseeable future. At least nine countries, however, should meet the white paper objective of abolishing internal border controls on individuals only two years late.

Cecchini report

The 1992 programme was launched in the belief that it would bring substantial economic benefits to the nations and people of the Community. In an attempt to quantify the benefits the commission appointed an expert committee presided over by Paolo Cecchini, a recently retired senior EC official. Its report, published in 1988 and based on a survey of 11,000 industrialists and econometric modelling, estimated that over 5–6 years the cumulative impact of the measures would add 4.5% to the GDP of the member states, reduce price levels by around 6%, create an extra 2m jobs and "put Europe on an upward trajectory of economic growth lasting into the next century".

1 Albert, M. and Ball, R.J., *Towards European Economic Recovery in the 1980s*, Report to the European Parliament, 1983.

16

COMPETITION POLICY

There was little point in creating a customs union, the EC's founding fathers thought, if free competition between firms from different member states could be thwarted by cartels and restrictive agreements. Thus Articles 85 and 86 were inserted into the Treaty of Rome. The first outlaws deals between companies to fix prices, share out markets, limit production, technical development and investment, and other restrictive practices. The second bans "abuses of dominant position" by firms or groups of firms. Furthermore, Articles 92–94 forbid government subsidies that distort or threaten to distort competition.

The commission has wide powers
The power to prevent such abuses is in the hands of the commission, which can act without reference to the Council of Ministers, though its decisions may be, and often are, challenged before the Court of Justice by the companies concerned. The commission acts either on its own initiative or following complaints by member states, companies or individuals. Several hundred cases are dealt with each year involving firms with household names as well as more obscure ones – some in both categories having their headquarters outside the EU – and covering a range of industries and products.

In many instances cases are resolved by voluntary policy changes by the countries or companies concerned. A famous example was when IBM was accused, in 1980, of abusing a dominant position in the computer market by withholding information on new products and "bundling" its products (that is, selling several of them together in a package, so that customers must either take all of them or none). After spending a small fortune in lawyers' fees, IBM eventually backed down in 1984 and came to a voluntary agreement with the commission to modify its trading practices. In other cases the commission finds in favour of the accused or it finds the case proved, and orders policy changes or imposes fines, sometimes running to millions of ecus (there is no limit to such fines, although they may not amount to more than 10% of the actual sales affected by the abuse with which a company is charged).

The commission has wide powers of investigation. Its staff can visit companies without warning to demand access to documents and to take away photocopies as evidence. It then holds hearings with the companies concerned to discuss the case before giving its verdict. Convicted firms may appeal to the Court of Justice against both the conviction and the size of the fine, which has sometimes been reduced on appeal. The court has built up a large body of case law. EC competition law takes precedence over national law and is directly applicable in member states. Businesses and individuals believing themselves to be victims of infringements of EC competition rules can bring direct actions before national courts.

Any agreements that may fall foul of the Rome treaty provisions must be notified in advance to the commission. Companies may apply for a "negative clearance", which means that free competition is not threatened, or for an "exemption", which spares a restrictive agreement from the overall ban if substantial public benefits (as defined in the treaty) can be demonstrated. The commission is empowered to declare illegal and order the termination of an agreement or other unacceptable practices at any time.

The commission has banned are the following types of agreement.

- **Market-sharing agreements.** For example, the quinine cartel (1969), which led the commission to impose its first fines; the sugar producers' cartel (1973); and the zinc and flat glass manufacturers' cartels (1984), which were fined a total of 4m ecus.
- **Price-fixing agreements.** For example, the dye-stuffs cartel (1969), which controlled 80% of the European market. It was the first case in which firms with head offices outside the Community were fined by the commission.
- **Exclusive purchase agreements.** These have been banned for a wide variety of products ranging from gramophone records to heating equipment.
- **Agreements on industrial and commercial property rights.** The exclusive use of patents, trademarks or works of art is not necessarily exempt from competition rules. In a 1982 case, involving maize seed, the Court of Justice ruled against the total territorial protection granted by a patent licensing contract.
- **Exclusive or selective distribution agreements.** For example, those, such as in the motor car trade, which seek to restrict parallel imports. Among companies which have been heavily fined, or otherwise penalised, for applying such agreements have been Ford, AEG-Telefunken and the Moët-Hennessy group.

Enforcement has become more rigorous

The commission was somewhat lax in applying the competition policy until 1977, since when there has been a substantial increase in its activity. This is largely because the individual commissioners holding the competition portfolio since that year have been far keener on exercising their powers than their predecessors. The commission has, however, continued to use its power to give industrial exemptions or en bloc waivers, where it judged that the threat to competition was small or non-existent and was outweighed by the likely public benefits. It has been particularly concerned not to hamper co-operation between small and medium-sized enterprises, and it has identified a number of types of agreement which it feels should escape the general ban. These are as follows.

- Exclusive representation contracts given to trade representatives.
- Small-scale agreements, based on turnover (not more than 50m ecus) and market share (not more than 5%).
- Subcontracting agreements.
- Information exchanges between companies, joint studies and joint use of plant.

The commission also takes account of the economic climate facing companies seeking individual exemptions. If there is a long-term downturn in demand for a product, it has been known to authorise firms to co-ordinate a run-down in overcapacity. This occurred, for example, in the synthetic fibre sector in 1984.

Jurisdiction over mergers ...

Until 1990 the commission had no specific power to prevent mergers, though it intervened on several occasions, using the general authority given to it under Articles 85 and 86 of the Rome treaty, when it believed that they posed a threat to effective competition in the Community. As long ago as 1973 it sought agreement on a regulation which would give it powers to vet cross-border mergers in advance, while leaving member states to police mergers within their own territories. The proposal was revived in 1987, and following detailed negotiations with the member states finally came into effect on September 21st 1990. It gave the commission jurisdiction over larger-scale company mergers and takeovers affecting more than one member state and exceeding certain thresholds. The main thresholds concerned were:

- 5 billion ecus for the worldwide turnover of the companies concerned; and
- 250m ecus for the individual turnover within the EC of at least
two of the companies concerned, while no more than two-
thirds of this turnover should be concentrated within a single
member state.

Projected mergers which meet these criteria must be reported in
advance to the commission, which will decide within one month
whether there is a possibility that they would breach the competition rules of the EC. If no such possibility is discerned, the merger
may go ahead; otherwise an investigation will be launched which
must be completed within a further four months.

When worldwide turnover is less than 2 billion ecus the commission has no jurisdiction. It falls to a national anti-trust body, such
as the Monopolies and Mergers Commission in the UK. Within the
2 billion–5 billion ecus bracket the national authorities will be
responsible, unless they ask the European Commission to carry out
an investigation on their behalf. The commission regarded the
thresholds as being too low, and gave notice that it would propose
before 1993 that the main threshold should be lowered from 5 billion ecus to 2 billion ecus.

In the event, the commission reported in July 1993 on the working of the merger control regulation and recommended that the
thresholds should be reviewed by 1996. In the first two and a half
years of operation it had received 164 formal notifications of proposed mergers, of which 17 cases fell outside the scope of the regulation. Of the other 147 cases, 131 (nearly 90%) were cleared within
the initial one-month deadline, and enquiries were opened concerning the remaining 16. Of these, seven were later approved condi-
tionally, two without condition and five were withdrawn. In only
one case, the proposed acquisition in 1991 of the Canadian aircraft
manufacturer De Havilland by a Franco-Italian consortium,
Aérospatiale-Alenia, was the merger prohibited. Neither the Rome
nor the Paris treaty makes any distinction between private and
publicly owned firms, so that neither nationalisation nor privatisa-
tion proposals, in themselves, would conflict with them. State-
owned concerns, however, must respect the EC's competition law in
the same way as any privately owned company. In 1980 a directive
was adopted providing for financial "transparency" in dealings
between member states and state-owned enterprises.

... and government subsidies

Government subsidies to either publicly owned or private firms are normally banned if they distort or threaten to distort competition. Some types of aid are exempt from control, including: special help at times of natural disasters; aid to depressed regions; and aid to promote new economic activities.

Member states are supposed to notify the commission of all aid planned, and it decides whether the aid can be exempted from the treaty rules. It has the power to order the repayment of unauthorised aid and may impose fines on member states that break the rules. Two examples occurred during 1988, when the competition commissioner, Sir Leon Brittan, required both the French and the British governments to secure repayment of illegal state aids that they had provided. The French government reluctantly agreed to reclaim FFr6 billion (about £600m) paid to Renault, which had then failed to fulfil the conditions the commission had attached to the project. The British government was also forced to seek repayment of the secret "sweeteners", worth £44m, that it had paid to British Aerospace as an inducement to buy the Rover car company.[1]

During the 1970s and early 1980s the commission approved guidelines for state aid to industries that were especially hard hit by the recession. It insisted that such aid must be exceptional, limited in duration and geared directly to the objective of restoring long-term viability by reducing capacity in struggling sectors. In four industries most severely affected – shipbuilding, textiles, synthetic fibres and steel (see Chapter 24) – special provisions were made. Most aid awards are made under schemes that were approved many years ago, so in 1990 the commission embarked upon a review of all systems of aid existing in the member states. This review, which is being carried out under Article 93 (1) of the Rome treaty, should enable changes in the economic and industrial situation due to the completion of the internal market to be taken into account. In principle, the commission believes that all categories of state aid should be kept to a minimum, and as it seeks to enforce the rules more rigorously they are increasingly coming into conflict with national governments under political pressure to maintain employment opportunities for their own citizens.

1 In February 1992 the Court of Justice ruled that the commission had not followed the correct procedure in requiring the repayment of the £44m. The commissioner for competition, Sir Leon Brittan, commented: "It is clear that the judgment relates wholly to procedural matters and does not touch the merits of the actual decision. I shall therefore be recommending the commission to reopen the case by commencing formal proceedings."

17

ECONOMIC AND FINANCIAL POLICY

Lack of co-ordination in economic policy...

Although Article 103 of the Rome treaty requires member states to determine their economic policies in consultation with each other, as yet little co-ordination has been achieved. In so far as most governments followed rather similar policies in the 1970s and 1980s, it was because they were reacting to worldwide economic pressures rather than a result of joint planning of their overall strategies. Thus, despite regular discussions between ministers, there was no common European policy on pooling energy supplies, containing inflation or reducing unemployment. The annual economic reports produced by the commission gave advice to national governments, but were by no means binding upon them.

Broad discussions do take place between the heads of government at meetings of the European Council, when "the economic and social situation in the world and in the Community" is invariably an item on the agenda. More detailed exchanges take place between economic and finance ministers, who meet approximately every two months in Ecofin[1] councils, and sometimes more frequently in the Monetary and Economic Policy committees. The governors of the central banks of the member states also meet regularly in their own consultative committee. National leaders are thus well informed about each other's views and policies, and no doubt take them into account to some extent, but each government remains firmly in charge of its own economic policy.

...means EU element is ancillary

Nor is the EU's budget sufficiently large to have a significant macroeconomic effect on the West European economy in a manner comparable with the way in which national budgets point their economies in an expansionist or deflationary direction. In so far as there is an EU element in the economic policy of member states, it is undoubtedly an ancillary one, and seems likely to remain so for the foreseeable future.

Loans made by EC institutions

There are two areas, however, where the EC undoubtedly plays a significant part. One is in raising loans on behalf of member states, the other in regulating fluctuations in exchange rates. During 1993, for example, EC institutions made well over 20 billion ecus available, principally through the following channels.

- The European Investment Bank (see Chapter 11) lent some 17.7 billion ecus within the Union. Three-quarters went towards developing the economy of the less prosperous regions. Other projects which received EIB assistance included energy saving, the modernisation and redevelopment of industry, new technologies and environmental protection.
- The European Coal and Steel Community lent approximately 918 million ecus, mainly for productive investment in the coal and steel industries. In addition, it financed projects which aim to improve the marketing and transport of coal and steel, and schemes to bring new industries to coal and steel areas. It also financed the building or modernisation of workers' homes.
- Euratom, which has a loan facility of 4 billion ecus mainly for investments in the nuclear energy and nuclear fuels sectors, made no new loans during 1993 because of the unfavourable situation in the industry.
- The Edinburgh Growth Initiative, agreed at the December 1992 Edinburgh summit, under which a new temporary lending facility of 5 billion ecus was established within the EIB, while a European Investment Fund was created with a capital of 2 billion ecus, which it was hoped would cover guarantees between 10 billion and 16 billion ecus. The EIF will target its activities on large infrastructure projects associated with trans-European networks (TENs) and on small and medium-sized enterprises (SMEs).

There is also a facility available for short-term loans to member states in temporary balance of payments difficulties. In 1993 8 billion ecus was lent, all to Italy.

The European Monetary System

The European Monetary System (EMS) was devised primarily as a means of stabilising currency fluctuations within the EC, following the breakdown in the early 1970s of the fixed-rate exchange system established by the 1944 Bretton Woods agreement. The first attempt, in 1972, to regulate European currencies within the so-called "snake", with permitted fluctuations of +/-2.25%, was largely unsuccessful. Only West Germany, Denmark and the Benelux countries were able to remain within these limits. The EMS, which was originally proposed by Roy Jenkins in October 1977, was a more ambitious project, in which the exchange rate mechanism (ERM) was bolstered by various financial solidarity mechanisms and a common currency unit (the ecu).

Under the ERM each participating currency has a central rate against the ecu. Only eight currencies[2] participated initially, the UK "temporarily" staying out when the system was inaugurated in March 1979. The three later entrants to the EC – Greece, Spain and Portugal – felt that they were not yet ready to join. Spain eventually joined in June 1989 and the UK followed suit in October 1990, an earlier decision having consistently been blocked by Mrs Thatcher, who only agreed to the move a month or so before she left office. Portugal joined in April 1992, leaving Greece as the odd man out. The central rate for each currency can be "realigned" if necessary by mutual agreement of the participating countries. From the ecu central rate, bilateral central rates are calculated for each currency against each of the other participants. Each currency is allowed to fluctuate by +/–2.25% around these central rates, or by +/–6% in the case of the pound and the peseta. If a currency reaches its "floor" or "ceiling" rate, the central banks are obliged to intervene in the foreign-exchange markets to maintain it within the agreed limits. In practice, this means selling the currency which has reached its ceiling rate and buying the one that is at its floor. When this occurs, various credit mechanisms have been created within the EMS to provide short-term support for countries in difficulties. If a currency stays at its floor or ceiling over a lengthy period, or appears likely to do so, it is a clear sign that it should be realigned. When this happens the finance ministers of the EU meet, normally over a weekend in Brussels, to approve a realignment. This does not normally take the form of a simple up or down revaluation for a particular currency, but the opportunity is taken to make a number of marginal adjustments, in both directions, to other currencies as well. The consequence has been that the sudden, often competitive devaluations of the past have been avoided, and the currencies within the system have fluctuated much less violently than others (including the pound) which have not been included (see Figure 10, page 106).

The value of the EMS was diminished, to some extent, by the fact that the UK held aloof for so long from bringing the pound into the ERM, a perverse decision which most economists feel did more harm

to the UK than to the EC. Nevertheless, even with the UK "quarter
in, three-quarters out", as the former UK permanent representative,
Sir Michael Butler, put it,[3] the EMS brought benefits beyond that of
currency stabilisation. It helped to bring about a greater convergence
in the economies of the member states, and the disciplines built into
the system were credited with playing a part in the marked reduction in inflation in the early 1980s in all the participating states. On
average, inflation fell from 12% in 1980 to 5% in 1985, while the average divergence between countries went down from 6.2% to 2.8%. Other
countries outside the EC recognised the value of the ERM in providing
tighter guidelines for their own economic policies. Three Nordic countries – Finland, Norway and Sweden – each tied their own currencies to the ecu in 1990 or early 1991.

In 1992 the ERM came under great strain, partly because of the
recession and partly because the removal of financial controls
meant that vast amounts of currency changed hands each day,
opening the system to manipulation by speculators. The situation
was exacerbated by the fact that the pound had been brought into
the ERM at an unrealistically high exchange rate and the British
government stubbornly resisted pressure to agree to an orderly
devaluation. Consequently in September 1992 massive speculative
movements led to the forced devaluation of several currencies,
while the pound and the lira were withdrawn from the ERM altogether and allowed to float. A similar speculative attack in July
1993 was fended off by a decision to widen temporarily the fluctua-
tion margin within the ERM to 15% either side of the bilateral central rates. In practice, the currencies did not fluctuate much beyond
the previous more narrow limits, which suggests that, unlike the
previous year, none of the currencies were seriously over- or under-
valued. The mechanism remained in operation, but without the
participation of the UK, Italy and Greece.

The ecu

The ecu (European currency unit)[4] has had several other functions
besides acting as a marker for the national currencies of the EC. It
has taken the place of the former EUA (European Unit of Account),
which was a purely book-keeping measurement for establishing the
relative value of payments into and out of the EC accounts. But the
ecu (which has the advantage of euphony, and of having the same
name as a famous pre-revolutionary French coin) has the backing of
a large reserve fund, the European Monetary Co-operation Fund
(EMCF), into which the member states are required to pay 20% of
their gold reserves and 20% of their dollar reserves.

Figure 10 **The European Monetary System, 1980–94**
(currencies against the ecu)

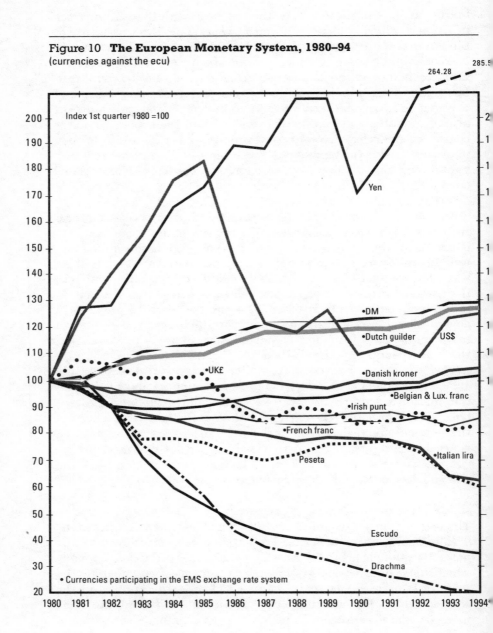

a First four months.

Source: European Commission, DGII.

The result is that there is a great deal of international confidence in the ecu, which is now used for many dealings quite unrelated to the funds of the EU (by 1986 it was the third most common currency used for international bond issues, after the dollar and the Deutschemark). More and more companies and individuals are using the ecu for denominating their bank deposits and travellers' cheques, or for commercial invoices and payments. This is quite an achievement for a currency which does not exist, in so far as neither coins nor banknotes are normally issued in ecus.[5] Its utility for private and commercial financial transactions lies in the fact that its value is unlikely to fluctuate by as much as any individual national currency.

Economic and monetary union

Although anything approaching total convergence (or "cohesion" as it is now known in Eurojargon) between the national economies is unlikely to come about for very many years – in the absence of massive financial transfers from north to south within the Union – the institution of the EMS has proved to be at least a step on the way. It was undoubtedly the most significant move towards the long-term objective of an economic and monetary union (EMU) that the EC had made until June 1988, when the Hannover summit determined that the time had arrived to give a new impetus in this direction. It commissioned a report by a committee of European central bankers and some independent monetary experts, under the chairmanship of the commission's president, Jacques Delors, into how EMU might be obtained. The Delors committee reported in April 1989, proposing a three-stage process towards union, but without attaching any timetable.

Stage one. Co-operation and co-ordination in the economic and monetary fields are to be improved. This would lead, among other things, to a strengthening of the EMS, the role of the ecu and the terms of reference of the Committee of Central Bank Governors. The introduction of a multilateral surveillance procedure would pave the way for more effective co-ordination and for closer convergence of national economic policies and performances.

Stage two. This could not begin until a new treaty (or amendments to the Rome treaty) had been agreed, laying down the basic institutional and operational rules necessary for the realisation of EMU. It would consist of consolidating and assessing the measures taken under the 1992 programme (see Chapter 15) and would be a sort of running-in period for the new procedures. During this transitional period a start could be made on gradually transferring decision-making powers from national to Community level. The most important feature of stage two could be the creation of a federal-type European System of Central Banks (ESCB or EuroFed) which, in the light of experience, would become increasingly independent as regards monetary policies and policies on exchange-market intervention. However, the national central banks would still retain ultimate responsibility for decision-making.

Stage three. Commencing with the move to irrevocably locked exchange rates and the transfer of responsibilities provided for in the new treaty, this stage would eventually lead to the adoption of a single currency.

The general approach of the Delors committee was acceptable to 11 of the 12 member states, but the UK government, under Mrs Thatcher's leadership, reacted coolly and was particularly hostile to the concept of a single currency, even though authoritative studies showed that this would bring major economic benefits, estimated at 15 billion ecus per year, or 0.4% of GDP.[6] Although it was agreeable to stage one of the process beginning on July 1st 1990, it emphatically reserved its position regarding stages two and three.

Despite Mrs Thatcher's objections, the EC heads of government decided at the Strasbourg summit in December 1989 that the requisite majority existed to convene an inter-governmental conference (IGC) to decide on the treaty changes which stages two and three would necessitate. It was subsequently agreed that two IGCs, one on EMU and one on political union, should be held, both convening in Rome in December 1990 and completing their work in time to report to the Maastricht summit, scheduled for December 1991.

Before then, the first Rome summit of October 1990 agreed – against Mrs Thatcher's strong objections – that stage two of EMU, with the creation of the EuroFed, would begin on January 1st 1994. It was her intemperate reaction to this decision which set off the chain of events leading to her resignation a month later. The UK government agreed to take part in the two IGCs, and its attitude became a great deal more conciliatory following Mrs Thatcher's departure. Within the IGC on EMU, it put forward a plan for a 13th currency, or "hard ecu", which would take the place of the single currency advocated by the Delors report. Although aspects of this proposal were sympathetically received by some other member states the prevailing view was that a single currency was necessary if the main benefits of EMU were to be obtained. It was anticipated that John Major, who had launched the "hard ecu" proposal when he was still chancellor of the exchequer, would eventually withdraw it and would agree to a compromise under which treaty changes permitting a single currency would be accepted, but that the UK parliament would retain the right to decide if and when this currency would replace the pound.

Treaty on European Union

This is effectively what was decided at the Maastricht summit in December 1991, when the Treaty on European Union was agreed. The treaty included four chapters relevant to the creation of EMU: those on economic policy, monetary policy, institutions and transnational provisions. The chapter on economic policy requires member states to conduct their economic policy in such a way as to achieve the objectives of EMU and "in accordance with the principle of an open market economy with free competition". Member states are to regard their economic policies as a matter of common concern and are to co-ordinate them through the Ecofin Council. The broad guidelines of economic policy are to be defined by the European Council (that is, by EU summit meetings) and are then to be adopted within the Ecofin Council by qualified majority vote.

A multilateral surveillance procedure has already been instituted under which, in order to ensure closer co-ordination and sustained convergence in the economic performance of member states, the Ecofin Council, on the basis of reports submitted by the commission, monitors economic developments in each member state. Where it considers that economic policies are not consistent with the broad guidelines agreed, the council is entitled, by qualified majority vote, to make policy recommendations to a member state which it may choose to make public. If, in the future, a member state persists in applying policies inconsistent with the guidelines, and in particular if it persists in incurring excessive budget deficits, it may lay itself open to a range of sanctions culminating in a freeze on lending from EC institutions, a requirement to make non-interest bearing deposits and, ultimately, the imposition of "fines of an appropriate size". The treaty makes clear that there is no question of the EC "bailing out" a member state that gets into financial difficulties, although financial assistance may be available in the event of "natural disasters" or other problems not caused by the improvidence of the member state concerned.

On monetary policy, it is laid down that the primary objective "shall be to maintain price stability", that is, a minimal level of inflation. For this purpose a European System of Central Banks (ECSB) is to be created, made up of the national central banks (NCBs) of the member states, all of which should become independent of their national governments, and a new European Central Bank (ECB), to be established at the beginning of the third stage of EMU.

The treaty confirms that the second stage of EMU would commence on January 1st 1994, by which date all member states were expected to have implemented measures to provide for the free movement of capital, and to have adopted multi-annual programmes to ensure lasting convergence necessary for EMU, in particular with regard to price stability and sound public finances. At the beginning of stage two, the European Monetary Institute (EMI) was set up as the forerunner of the ECB. Its members are the various national banks, and it replaces the Committee of Governors and the European Monetary Co-operation Fund, which has ceased to exist. Its task is to prepare the way for stage three and to strengthen co-operation between the NCBs, on whose behalf it may hold monetary and foreign exchange reserves.

The EMI, together with the commission, will report to the Ecofin Council on the progress of member states in making their national legislation compatible with EMU, and will provide information on their record concerning price stability, budget deficits, exchange rates, convergence indicators and long-term interest rates. The council will assess which member states fulfil the four conditions for adoption of a single currency, which are defined in a protocol to the treaty.

- Its inflation should, over the previous year, not have exceeded by more than 1.5% that achieved by an average of the three best performing states.
- Its currency has been within the narrow band of the ERM for at least the preceding two years and has not been devalued during that period.
- Its long-term interest rates have not exceeded by more than 2% over the preceding year the average of the three best-performing states so far as price stability is concerned.
- It is not subject to a decision of the council that it is running an excessive budget deficit.

No later than December 31st 1996 the European Council, acting by qualified majority, will decide whether a majority of member states meet these criteria and whether it is therefore appropriate to enter the third stage of EMU. If so it will set the date for the beginning of the third stage. If by the end of 1997 the date has not been set it will definitely begin on January 1st 1999. Before July 1st 1998 the Ecofin Council will repeat the earlier process in order to decide which member states fulfil the conditions for adoption of a single currency. A special protocol to the treaty gives the UK the right to opt out, even if it fulfils these conditions. It stipulates that the UK should not be obliged to enter the third stage without a separate decision to do so by its government and Parliament.

At the beginning of the third stage the EMI will be replaced by the ECB, whose executive board will be appointed by the member states which are ready to participate in a single currency. The Ecofin Council, acting by unanimity of the participating states, will adopt the conversion rates at which their currencies will be irrevocably fixed, at which rate the ecu will be substituted for their currencies and become a currency in its own right.

The ECB, in conjunction with the NCBs with which it will make up the ESCB, will be responsible for managing the new currency, but the Maastricht treaty stipulates that:

Member states may issue coins subject to ECB approval of the volume of the issue. The council may, acting by a qualified majority on a proposal from the commission and after consulting the ECB and in co-operation with the European Parliament, adopt measures to harmonise the denominations and technical specifications of all circulation coins to the extent necessary to permit a smooth circulation of coins within the Community.

1 The accepted abbreviation for Economic and Financial Affairs Council.
2 Including the Luxembourg franc, which is at parity with the Belgian franc.
3 Michael Butler, *op. cit.*, page 69.
4 The value of the ecu is determined by a weighted "basket" of currencies, which since September 21st 1989 has been composed of DM30.1, FFr19.0, £13.00, L10.5, BFr7.6, Ptas5.3, DKr2.45, IR£1.1, Dr0.8, Esc0.8, LFr0.3. The composition is reviewed every five years and, in the event of a request, whenever the weight of a currency has changed by 25% or more. The most recent periodic review was in September 1989, when the peseta and escudo were included for the first time.
5 But Belgium issued 5 ecu and 50 ecu coins in 1987, in silver and gold, to commemorate the 30th anniversary of the Rome treaty. They are legal tender in Belgium.
6 See *The ECU Report* by Michael Emerson and Christopher Huhne, Pan Books, London, 1991.

18

TAXATION

Taxation has been regarded from the outset as a subject reserved to the sovereignty of the member states, except in so far as its incidence may distort competition within the Union or discriminate against nationals of other EU countries. Accordingly, except on such matters as the avoidance of double taxation, EC decisions on tax matters have been concerned almost exclusively with indirect taxation: customs duties (see page 8) on the one hand, and VAT and excise duties on the other. Virtually every decision relating to taxation requires unanimous agreement in the Council of Ministers, and this requirement was not relaxed in the Single European Act which substantially widened the range of decisions subject to decision by qualified majority vote. The incidence and range of taxation varies enormously within the Union, with Denmark and the Netherlands being the highest taxed countries and Spain the lowest.

General application of VAT

The main taxation change which has occurred has been the general application of value-added tax (VAT), replacing a variety of different indirect taxes in the member states. Two directives adopted in 1967 provided for those countries not already applying VAT to introduce it within a specific timetable, and new applicant countries have also been required to change their tax systems accordingly. Spain agreed to apply VAT from its entry in 1986, Greece applied it in 1987 and Portugal brought its system into line by 1989. VAT commended itself to the Community because of its economic neutrality. At each stage in the making or marketing of a product, the tax paid at the preceding stage is deducted from that paid by the vendor. In this way the tax remains proportionate to the value of the goods and services, no matter how many transactions they have been through.

The member states reached agreement in 1977 on a common basis for assessing VAT, although it was subject to many exceptions. It was, however, enough to enable the Community to collect on this basis part of its "own resources", subject to a maximum rate of 1%, raised from 1986 to 1.4%. However, the member states continued to differ enormously as to the level at which VAT was charged, the

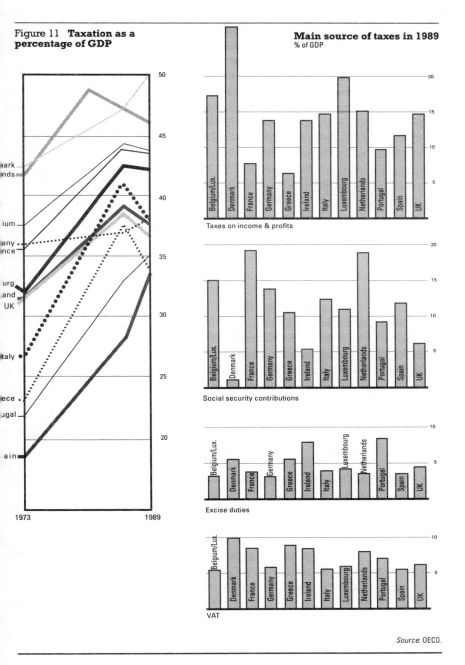

Figure 11 **Taxation as a percentage of GDP**

Main source of taxes in 1989
% of GDP

Taxes on income & profits

Social security contributions

Excise duties

VAT

Source: OECD.

number of different rates and the goods and services which were excluded or were subject to a zero rate.

Table 13   **Convergence of VAT rates, 1987–94**

	1987		1994	
	Maximum	Standard	Maximum	Standard
Denmark	22	22	25	25
Ireland	25	21	21	21
Belgium	33	19	20.5	20.5
Italy	38	19	19	19
France	33.3	18.6	18.6	18.6
Greece	36	18	18	18
Netherlands	20	18.5	17.5	17.5
UK	15	15	17.5	17.5
Portugal	30	17	16[a]	16
Germany	14	14	15	15
Luxembourg	12	12	15	15
Spain	33	12	15	15

[1] Portugal sought to continue an increased rate of 30%, which is contrary to EU law since January 1st 1993. It is the subject of infringement procedures taken by the commission against Portugal.

Excise duty

The other form of indirect taxation which member states have continued to levy is excise duty on certain specific products, such as alcoholic drinks, manufactured tobacco and fuels. Despite numerous proposals by the commission, the only common regulations adopted before July 1991 related to the structure of duty on cigarettes. Acting on complaints from the commission the Court of Justice, however, delivered judgments which have made several member states modify their range of duties in order to prevent them favouring home-produced beers, wines or spirits to the detriment of imported products.

The commission has also established a common basis for duty-free allowances for travellers between member states. In principle duty-free allowances should have been phased out altogether after January 1st 1993 when the EU's internal market was completed. It was decided, however, that until June 30th 1999 duty-free sales could continue at airports, on planes and on ferries for travellers going from one member state to another. The quantitative limits are shown in Table 14. Specific allowances have also been established for:

- small postal consignments;
- temporary importation of certain means of transport; and
- final importation of personal property in case of removal of residence, marriage or inheritance.

Table 14 **Duty-free allowances for travellers within the EU to June 30th 1999**

Item	Allowance per person
Cigarettes	300
or Cigarillos	100
or Cigars	50
or Tobacco	250 grams
Spirits	1 litre
or sparkling or fortified wines	2 litres
Still wines	2 litres
Perfume	50 grams
Toilet water	0.25 litre
Other purchases	Maximum value 90 ecus

Note: Travellers under 17 do not qualify for duty-free purchases of tobacco products and alcohol.

Harmonisation of indirect tax rates

A strong impetus to harmonising indirect tax rates was given by the adoption in 1985 of a specific target for completing the Community's internal market. Lord Cockfield argued strongly when presenting his white paper in June 1985 (see pages 93–94) that these rates would have to be "approximated" if the objective of removing all internal frontier controls was to be achieved. By approximation he meant bringing them so closely together that no significant distortion of trade was likely to be produced. He took as his model the USA, where the different states levy varying rates of sales tax, but the difference between them is seldom great enough to attract much cross-border trade merely for the benefit of paying a lower rate of tax.

In July 1987 the commission produced its proposals which it said should be implemented by member states no later than December 31st 1992.

VAT.   Two rate bands were proposed: a standard rate of 14–20%, and a reduced rate "for items of basic necessity" of 4–9%. The items suggested for this reduced rate were foodstuffs, energy for heating and lighting, water, pharmaceuticals, books, newspapers and periodicals, and passenger transport. Member states would be free to fix their national rates at any point between these 5–6 percentage point margins. "However," said Lord Cockfield in introducing the proposals, "in view of the inclusion of certain sensitive sectors, such as the cultural sector, the commission recommends that member states fix the applicable rate in the lower half of the band for the reduced rate."

Excise duty.   The commission proposed a complete harmonisation, arguing that since VAT was applied in addition to excise duties, it would widen the effective range of the VAT bands even further if a similar degree of flexibility was allowed. It therefore specified a precise amount of duty for all products attracting excise duty.

Commission's proposals intended to cause least disruption ...
The commission's proposals, which needed the unanimous agreement of the Council of Ministers after it received the opinion of the European Parliament, were drawn up with the intention of causing the minimum possible disturbance to member states. Although all countries would need to make some adjustments, the commission considered that three member states (Belgium, Italy and the Netherlands) would be able to continue to obtain the same level of total tax revenue from the VAT and excise-duty rates proposed as they currently receive. One member state (France) would suffer a slight budgetary loss, while three member states (Germany, Greece and the UK) would obtain small or moderate increases in budgetary receipts. Two member states (Denmark and Ireland) would suffer pronounced budgetary losses, while the other member states (Luxembourg, Spain and Portugal) would obtain substantial increases in budgetary receipts.[1]

Apart from Denmark and Ireland, which would have to compensate for "pronounced budgetary losses", the country which would have had the greatest difficulty as a result of these proposals is undoubtedly the UK, which currently levies a zero rate on many items including food, children's clothing and books (as does Ireland). In the 1987 election campaign Margaret Thatcher said that she would "veto" any attempt to prevent zero-rating being applied in the UK in the future.

... but agreement took time

Although the Cockfield proposals contained no provision for the continuation of zero-rating, they did recognise that several member states were likely to be faced with considerable "political, social or budgetary" difficulties in implementing the proposals in full. The commission therefore invited the member states, after having studied the difficulties involved, to make proposals for "derogations" (exceptions to directives or regulations which may, in principle, be only temporary, but which in practice may continue indefinitely) to allow them not to apply certain parts of the proposals.

It took four years, and a great deal of horse-trading, for the member states to reach any sort of agreement on the Cockfield proposals. In June 1991 a political agreement was reached in the Council of Ministers that they should be adopted, though in a greatly amended and watered-down form.

VAT proposals amended

The amended proposals stipulated that, from January 1st 1993, the standard rate of VAT should be set at a minimum of 15% in all member states; no maximum was suggested. In addition, for a list of 20 or so goods and services, regarded as essential and not extensively traded across national borders (including food, domestic heating and lighting, passenger transport, and books and newspapers), one or more reduced rates of at least 5% could be applied. In a major concession to the UK it was agreed that zero and other rates less than 5% could continue if they were already in effect on January 1st 1991. Special derogations were allowed for Luxembourg, Portugal and Spain, which would have had to make especially large changes in order to comply. In the case of the UK no actual changes would have to be made as a result of this agreement. The amended proposals were finally approved in July 1992, in a directive which stipulated a minimum standard VAT rate of 15% for a four-year period. All the arrangements were linked to a transitional period, due to end no later than January 1st 1997, during which VAT on goods exported within the Community would be taxed in the country of destination rather than of origin. After that date all goods should be taxed on the same basis, irrespective of where they were sold. The commission was told to come up with proposals for a permanent system, which would make this possible by the end of 1994. As Table 13 shows, there was a considerable convergence of VAT rates between 1987 and 1994, partly due to market forces but also as a consequence of the adoption of the 1992 directive. The range of maximum rates between member states was later reduced from

Table 15 **Minimum excise duties**[a]

Mineral oils	ecus/'000 litres
Leaded petrol	337
Unleaded petrol	287
Diesel fuel	245
Heating oil	0
Heavy fuel ('000kg)	13
LPG & methane	
fuel	100
industrial use	36
heating	0

Alcoholic beverages	ecus/'000 litres
Beer[b]	0.748 per Plato degree
	1.87 per degree of alcohol
Still wine	0
Sparkling wine	0
Intermediate products	450

Manufactured tobaccos	Duty
Cigarettes (100), global excise duty (specific & ad valorem without VAT)	57% of retail sale price (all taxes included) of most popular type of cigarette
Other manufactured tobacco	20%

Note: Greece and Luxembourg were granted a transitional period of two years until the end of 1994 during which the minimum rate of excise duty on diesel fuel will be 195 ecus/'000 litres. Luxembourg was also allowed minimum rates on leaded petrol (292 ecus/'000 litres) and unleaded petrol (242 ecus/'000 litres).

[a]As agreed in a directive adopted in 1992.
[b]For small independent breweries (producing under 200,000hl per year) these minimum rates are reduced by 50%.

Sources: EU Council of Ministers; European Commission.

26% to 10% and that of standard rates from 9% to 6%, with the exception of Denmark, which continued to levy a single rate of VAT markedly higher than in any other member state.

Excise duty proposals virtually abandoned

If the approximation proposals on VAT were severely modified, those on excise duties were virtually abandoned. In place of the complete harmonisation proposed by Lord Cockfield, the Council of Ministers agreed in June 1991 that minimum duties, for the most part well below those actually paid in most member states, should be agreed for after January 1st 1993. It had been impossible to reach agreement between the northern member states, which applied high duties on both revenue and health grounds for alcohol and tobacco, and the Mediterranean countries, large producers of wine and tobacco, which traditionally applied nil or low duties. Table 15 sets out the minimum rates that were agreed.

Other forms of taxation

The commission had been concerned that certain other taxes have a bearing on the competitive position of companies based in different member states, and it seems likely that it will at some stage produce proposals for harmonising company taxation, though probably not income tax, at least for the foreseeable future. In 1989, at the behest of the French government, it attempted to secure the introduction of a common "withdrawal tax" on investment income, but the proposal was withdrawn when it became evident that most other member states would not agree. In 1990, however, it succeeded, after a lengthy delay, in persuading the Council of Ministers to adopt three directives which would provide for a common system of taxation applicable to mergers, and to subsidiary or associated companies when these were based in different member states.

1 *Abolition of Fiscal Frontiers: Summary of the Commission's Proposals*, July 1987.

19

AGRICULTURE

CAP was first common policy implemented

The common agricultural policy (CAP) of the EC was, together with the customs union, the objective spelled out in the greatest detail in the Treaty of Rome. It was, indeed, for a long time virtually the only common policy that the Community was able to implement. From the point of view of European farmers it has been a spectacular success, but that success has caused enormous problems to the Community. On the one hand the CAP has absorbed such a high proportion of the budget that the development of other policies has been aborted. On the other hand the subsidised export of a number of products in which substantial surpluses have built up has distorted world trade, bringing the EU into conflict with the USA and other traditional food exporters, as well as with developing countries whose agricultural economies risk being undermined by those exports.

Effect on EU agriculture

The aims of the CAP, as set out in Article 39 of the treaty, are as follows.

1 To increase agricultural productivity.
2 To ensure a fair standard of living for the agricultural population.
3 To stabilise markets.
4 To guarantee regular supplies.
5 To ensure reasonable prices in supplies to consumers.

The CAP has greatly contributed to the transformation of the structure of the Union's agriculture. Generous price support has combined with technological innovation to generate massive increases in production and productivity. The EU is virtually self-sufficient in all but tropical foods and a number of vegetable proteins and starches for animal feed. Thanks to a two-thirds reduction since 1958 in the number of people living off the land, the average standard of living of those remaining has risen sharply.

While the policy has helped to realise the first four objectives listed above, this has tended to be at the expense of the fifth. EU farm support prices are almost invariably higher than world prices, often substantially so. The EU consumer has therefore had to pay for the success of the farming sector not only through higher prices but through taxes, which have contributed to an EU budget predominantly devoted to farm support.

The CAP has three main elements.

- A single market for farm goods (free movement throughout the Community and common prices).
- Community preference (a common tariff barrier against imports from outside the EU).
- Common financial responsibility (costs are paid from a common fund to which all members contribute).

Monetary Compensation Amounts

Common prices were introduced for the principal farm products between 1962 and 1967, but exchange rate modifications since then have obliged the Community to employ so-called "green currencies" in order to maintain this common price structure. For the main product groups the difference in value between "green" and real currencies is covered by Monetary Compensation Amounts (MCAs) applied on intra-Community and third-country trade. In countries with a negative MCA prices paid to farmers are lower; in those with a positive MCA prices paid are higher than they would otherwise be. As most EC exchange rates have tended to be more stable in recent years (in part due to the introduction of the European Monetary System, see pages 103–105) the importance of MCAs has declined, and farm prices have consequently varied less from country to country than during the 1970s. The commission would like to abolish "green currencies" altogether, but has had great difficulty in persuading the member states (Germany in particular, where their abolition would involve a cut in prices in national currency terms) to do so.

European Agricultural Guidance and Guarantee Fund

The common fund, known as the European Agricultural Guidance and Guarantee Fund (EAGGF, generally known as FEOGA, from its French acronym) is the most controversial aspect of the CAP. Its guidance section, which pays for modernisation and improvement, now accounts for less than 10% of the total, and its activities excite little opposition. It is the guarantee section which has absorbed the

Table 16 EC agriculture: basic data, 1990

	1	2	3	4	5	6	7	8	9	10	11
EC 12	127,499[d]	8,682[d]	6.6[d]	8,644	13.3	202,012	3.1	12.1	8.5	-20,704	20.3[d]
Belgium	1,363[b]	101[b]	2.8[b]	93	14.8	6,370	2.4	10.1[e]	5.6[e]	-1,640[e]	19.9
Denmark	2,799	158	6.0	87	32.2	6,851	4.2	17.3	22.4	955	21.8
France	30,581	1,325	6.1	982	28.6	46,648	3.3	10.9	12.1	607	19.5
Germany[f]	11,868	961	3.4	705	16.8	28,928	1.7	9.5	3.8	-6,204	16.4
Greece	5,741[c]	930[b]	25.3[b]	953	4.0	8,332	16.5	15.5	27.8	-244	37.8
Ireland	5,697	167	15.0	217	22.7	4,331	10.5	9.2	23.7	649	39.0
Italy	17,215[b]	1,895	9.0	2,784	5.6	36,567	4.0	14.0	5.5	-5,395	22.3
Luxembourg	127	6	3.3	4	30.2	191	2.4	10.1[e]	5.6[e]	-1,640[e]	20.3
Netherlands	2,019[c]	289	4.6	132	15.3	15,687	4.6	15.4	22.8	-1,061	18.7
Portugal	4,532[c]	795	17.8	636	5.2	3,535	5.5	26.8	10.5	-1,275	31.4[d]
Spain	27,110[c]	1,486	11.8	1,792	13.8	25,215	4.7	18.1	15.3	-2,501	22.4
UK	18,447	569	2.2	260	64.4	19,357	1.5	10.8	6.9	-4,594	21.7

1 Utilised agricultural area ('000ha)
2 & 3 Employment 2 ('000) 3 (% working population)
4 No. holdings ('000)
5 Utilised agricultural area per holding (ha)[a]
6 Final production (m ecus)[b]
7 % agriculture in GDP[b]
8 % food & agricultural products in all imports
9 % food & agricultural products in all exports
10 External trade balance in food & agricultural products (m ecus)
11 % household expenditure on food, beverages & tobacco as proportion of total consumer expenditure[c]

[a]1987. [b]1989. [c]1988. [d]Estimate. [e]Belgium/Luxembourg Economic Union. [f]Excluding eastern Germany.

Source: European Commission.

lion's share of the expenditure and whose activities have led to severe strains on the Union's finances.

The guarantee section's main purpose is to support, wherever necessary, the prices of the main European agricultural products to ensure the maintenance of farmers' incomes. This is done through four different mechanisms, depending on the product involved. These mechanisms together cover 94% of all European farm produce, the remainder being left to free-market operations.

1 About 70% of products (including wheat, barley, rye, maize, rice, sugar, dairy products, beef and sheepmeat) enjoy support prices which carry either a permanent or conditional guarantee of price and sale. When market prices fall below a certain level and other conditions are fulfilled, the intervention authorities buy up any produce offered to them, stock it and eventually resell it according to Union rules. The market can also be supported by more flexible means, such as storage aids for pigmeat, subsidies for distillation of table wine and aids to the buying-in of surplus fruit and vegetables by producer organisations.

2 About 21% of produce (minor cereals, quality wines, certain fruits and vegetables, as well as pigmeat, eggs and poultry) are protected only by measures to prevent low price imports from outside the Union.

3 Direct subsidies of one kind or another apply to most other products (durum wheat, olive oil, oil seeds and tobacco). In the case of products predominantly imported by the Union, prices are kept down for the consumer while guaranteeing a minimum income for the producer. In the case of oil seeds, which are subject to variable import duties, a deficiency payment bridges the difference between the world market price and the price guaranteed to the producer.

4 Flat-rate aid according to hectares planted or quantity produced covers less than 1% of production (cotton seed, flax, hemp, hops, silkworms, seeds and dehydrated fodder).

The CAP's controversial elements

Guaranteed price system. This forms the core of the CAP. The prices are set each year by the EU farm ministers, all of whom are under pressure from their own farming communities to set the price at the highest possible level. The result has been a constant stimulus to over-production, together with from time to time enormous stocks of one product or another ("butter mountains", "wine lakes") building up, the cost of storing and disposing of which has placed an added burden on the fund. The worst offenders were the dairy farm-

Table 17   **EAGGF guarantee appropriation by product group, 1994 (% of total)**

Arable crops	37.0
Beef, sheepmeat, goatmeat & pigmeat	18.0
Fruit & vegetables, wine, tobacco	12.4
Milk & milk products	11.8
Sugar	5.8
Olive oil	5.5
Processed products	1.6
Other sectors	5.3
Other expenditure	2.6

Source: European Commission.

Table 18   **EAGGF guarantee expenditure, 1973–94 (m ecus)**

1973	3,928
1977	6,830
1980	11,315
1985	19,744
1989	25,873
1990	26,522
1994	36,465[a]

[a]Appropriation.
Source: European Commission.

ers, whose surpluses in 1980 absorbed 43% of the guarantee fund even though milk products amounted to less than 20% of total agricultural production. Cereals (15.8%) and sugar (10.2%) also absorbed disproportionate amounts of the fund. Since then these products have been treated more stringently in the annual price fixing exercises, and by 1985 their average shares were down to 29.3% (milk products), 12.2% (cereals) and 8.8% (sugar).

Export subsidies.   The other expensive and controversial element in the CAP is the payment of export subsidies (known as "restitutions" or so-called refunds) to enable European produce to compete in world markets. Exporters are refunded the difference between the internal prices at which they purchase their produce and the lower price at which they must sell it on the world market. In 1986 the cost of export restitutions amounted to 8,600m ecus, nearly 40% of the total expenditure from the guarantee fund.

This form of dumping has led to much protest from the USA and other competing exporters such as Argentina, Australia and New Zealand. There is also a widespread feeling that subsidised sales, and even EU gifts of food aid to poorer developing countries, inhibit those countries from developing their agricultural economies.

Budgetary pressures ...

The commission has been acutely aware for several years of the need to cut back on agricultural expenditure which was rising at a much faster annual rate than the total resources of the Community. Its favoured tactic has been to attempt to make the farmers pay for their own unwanted surpluses by means of levies on surplus production (particularly on milk). Initially their attempts to secure economies were largely frustrated by the farm ministers, but the EC's budgetary crisis and the determination of several member states, particularly the UK, to curb the overall level of expenditure led to the decision at the Fontainebleau summit of June 1984 that farm spending should henceforward increase at a slower pace than the budget as a whole. This intention proved impossible to adhere to in the face of the rapidly declining value of the dollar during 1986–87, which automatically increased the cost of export restitutions (it was estimated that each 1% fall in the value of the dollar cost the Community budget 150m ecus).

... led to a few modifications ...

Quite apart from the budgetary pressures, there is now a growing realisation that the CAP is in urgent need of modification. It has engendered structural surpluses of a large number of products, and drastic changes are now necessary if production is to be aligned more closely with market demand. Ideally, these changes should concentrate on eliminating marginal production by concentrating more resources into the guidance section of FEOGA, and taking large areas of relatively infertile land out of production. Unfortunately the economic crisis since 1973 has meant that few alternative sources of employment have been available for people leaving the land and this process has been deliberately slowed down, although the agricultural labour force is still declining by about 2.5% a year.

The open-ended production subsidies provided by the system of guaranteed prices have been attenuated to some extent by the introduction of guarantee thresholds and co-responsibility levies for some products; in particular, by the application of milk quotas since 1986. In August 1987 the commission published proposals to apply a system of "stabilisers" to every product. That would involve the automatic cutting of price support whenever any crop exceeded a fixed ceiling. The imposition of such stabilisers for cereals and a long list of other products was endorsed at the Brussels summit of February 1988, as part of the overall budgetary reform settlement. New rules were also approved for restricting agricultural expenditure, so that its annual growth rate should not exceed 74% of the growth in GDP. The objective was to ensure a progressive reduction in the proportion of EC expenditure going to the CAP.

... but major reform is likely during 1990s

In 1990–91 the EC's agricultural budget came under fresh pressure, partly because of the cost of incorporating East German farmers into the common agricultural policy. This was compounded by the demands of other farm-exporting countries for the EC to agree on sharp cuts in all its subsidy programmes. These demands came to a head in December 1990 at what was supposed to be the final phase of the Uruguay round of GATT trade talks, which were held in Brussels. Led by the USA, the other farm-exporting states proposed that the EC should make cuts of 75% in all three areas of farm support: domestic subsidies, market access and export competition. The best that the EC could offer, after prolonged wrangling between the farm ministers of the member states, was a 30% cut over ten years, backdated to 1986. This deadlock was the principal reason for the collapse of the GATT talks, which were only re-started with great difficulty in the summer of 1991.

Meanwhile the European Commission came forward with farm-price proposals for 1991/92 which just succeeded in remaining within the budget guidelines, through a mixture of quota cuts and price freezes. The farm commissioner, who was Ray MacSharry, subsequently produced firm proposals for a major reform of the CAP, which would replace price guarantees by direct income support for less prosperous farmers. This, it was hoped, would not only curb EC expenditure in the future, but would help to reduce the gap between EC and world prices, while making it easier to secure agreement in the agricultural sector of the resumed Uruguay round GATT negotiations.

The MacSharry proposals were amended, partly to satisfy UK objections that they discriminated against larger, more efficient farmers, and were ultimately adopted in May 1992. The centrepiece of the package was a 29% cut in cereal prices spread over the following three years. This should lead to cheaper feeds for livestock, enabling price cuts of 15% for beef, 20% for pork and poultry, 7–8%

for butter and around 3% for bread.

Farmers will be compensated for their loss of income by direct income payments. These will, however, be dependent on their "setting aside" 15% of their productive land in order to ensure a sharp fall in Europe's overcapacity. The original MacSharry plan restricted these payments to small farmers, but now they are available to all farms irrespective of their acreage. The effect of these price cuts should be largely to remove the differential between internal EU prices and those charged on the world market. This would mean that by 1996 or 1997 the export subsidies the EU uses to dump its surplus production should virtually have ceased. This should remove the grievance of other major farm exporters, such as the USA and the Cairns group of 14 countries (including Argentina, Australia and Canada), that the EU has been stealing their markets. The new reform programme enabled the EU to agree with the US government, under the Blair House agreement of November 1992, on a joint approach to the difficult agricultural sector of the Uruguay round of GATT world trade negotiations. Despite some backsliding by the new French government elected in March 1993, the agreement held and enabled the round to be successfully concluded in December 1993.

Further modifications to the CAP will result from the enlargement talks with Austria, Finland, Sweden and Norway, which concluded in March 1994. All four countries provided more financial support to their farmers than the CAP would have allowed, justifying this by the harsh climatic conditions (Arctic or Alpine) under which much of their agriculture was produced. The EU insisted that prices in all four countries should immediately be aligned with those within the Union, but agreed that direct compensation could be paid to the farmers provided that it was at the expense of the national government concerned.

The adaptation of the CAP will not be readily achieved because of the variety of national and sectional interests involved, and because of the great strength of the farming community as a pressure group, even in countries such as the UK where only a small proportion of the population is directly dependent on agriculture. Nevertheless, it would be surprising if over the next few years significant progress is not made towards matching agricultural supply more closely with actual demand, both within the Union and in world markets. It goes without saying that such adaptation would be less painful in the context of renewed economic growth.

20

RESEARCH AND NEW INDUSTRIES

The industrial policy of the EU has had two main prongs: to help older, declining industries such as textiles, shipbuilding and steel (see Chapter 24) restructure themselves in such a way as to minimise the inevitable pain and disruption; and to assist in the development and spread of new technologies which provide the foundation for future economic growth.

EC's industrial research began in 1980s

Although the Community had for many years been heavily involved in fundamental and applied research in the nuclear industry, its involvement in industrial research began only in the early 1980s with the growing realisation that the EC was falling seriously behind the USA and Japan, and was also in danger of being outstripped by thrusting new economies such as those of South Korea, Singapore and Taiwan. The European Commission reported that over half the EC's needs for microprocessors, 75% of its video recorders and 80% of microcomputers were being met by imports.

European co-operation had already borne fruit in a number of areas where a very large capital investment and the capture of a significant slice of the world market were necessary conditions for success. Examples included Airbus and Ariane in the aerospace sector, which received loans from the EIB, and JET, in the thermo-nuclear fusion sector, a powerful experimental research institution built and operated by the EC (see pages 162–163). Yet the commission was worried about the wasteful duplication of research expenditure which, collectively in the EC, compared favourably with both the USA and Japan, but which was too fragmented to produce comparable results.

The commission's objective has been to stimulate co-operation between businesses, laboratories and universities throughout Europe in the development of new technologies and new products fulfilling existing or potential market needs. What needed to be stimulated, in its view, was not so much basic research as joint action in the pre-competitive stage of technological development. It would be up to business to take over at the production and marketing stage, taking advantage of the more competitive and dynamic commercial environment created by the planned completion of the internal market.

Forecasting and assessment in science and technology (FAST)
An early initiative to discover the areas in which a Community effort would be most appropriate was the establishment of the FAST programme in 1978. With a small budget of 5.6m ecus, including 1.2m ecus contributed by associated bodies, a ten-strong team organised and co-ordinated a mass of multi-disciplinary research, both technical and socio-economic, covering 36 subjects and involving 54 research centres in Community countries. The FAST team explored, in the greatest detail, three areas where EC involvement could prove crucial:

● information technology;
● biotechnology; and
● the transformation of work and employment.

In June 1983 a second four-year FAST programme was launched. Costing 10.5m ecus, including 2m ecus from associated bodies, it was staffed by 12 researchers, assisted by another ten seconded from member states for periods of 1–2 years. FAST II centred on four major research themes.

● Relations between technology, work and employment.
● The development of integrated systems for renewable natural resources.
● The emergence of new industrial systems in the communications and food-processing sectors.
● Transformation of service activities and technological change.

Prompted by the FAST findings, the commission proposed a series of programmes to the Council of Ministers designed to encourage transnational co-operation in research and development.

European strategic programme for information technology (ESPRIT)
ESPRIT was a five-year programme (1984–88) designed to help Europe respond to the challenge of foreign competition in information technology. The Community financed up to 50% of the pre-

competition research and development work, undertaken jointly by enterprises from at least two member states, universities and research institutes. Areas covered included:

- advanced micro-electronics in high-integration circuits;
- software techniques;
- advanced information processing;
- the computerisation of offices;
- computer-controlled production techniques.

There was also an "infrastructure" side to the programme, which ensured its effective implementation through a system of information exchange between participants, co-ordination of work, consideration of standards problems and the dissemination of the results of the research. By the end of the ESPRIT I programme in 1988 a total of 227 projects had been implemented. These involved 536 participating companies, universities and research institutes, and some 3,000 full-time researchers. Of the 327 companies which participated, almost 45% were firms employing fewer than 500 people (and two in five of these employed fewer than 50). The total cost of the ESPRIT I programme was 1.5 billion ecus, of which 750m ecus was paid for by the EC.

The budget for ESPRIT II, covering the years 1989–93, was more than doubled to 3.2 billion ecus, once again financed on a 50:50 basis by the Community and the programme participants. The ESPRIT strategy in the second five years was concentrated on three major technological areas:

- micro-electronics and peripheral technologies;
- the creation of technologies and tools for the design of information processing systems;
- enhancing the capacity for using and integrating information technology, principally with a view to extending the scope of its applications.

Research and development in advanced communications technologies for Europe (RACE)

The RACE programme is intended to help Europe remain in the forefront of the telecommunications industry. Its principal objective is to develop the technology needed for wide band fibre-optic networks capable of transmitting simultaneously sound, pictures and computerised information, thereby allowing the multiplication of new integrated telecommunications services. Some 44m ecus were spent on the definition phase of RACE, and the total cost of the programme proper (1987–91) was 1.5 billion ecus, half of it from the EC budget. In 1990 it was agreed to extend the programme for another five years to 1995. By then it involved more than 400 organisations in the member states as well as in five EFTA countries. These included 11 telecommunications network systems, 260 businesses (including 130 small and medium-sized ones), 85 research centres and universities and 60 miscellaneous bodies, such as user groups.

Basic research in industrial technologies for Europe (BRITE)

BRITE was a four-year programme (1985–88), organised and financed on the ESPRIT model, to encourage the development and spread of new technologies, new processes of manufacture and new products in the "traditional" sectors, which still account for three-quarters of industrial employment. The programme had two sections covering the following:

- basic technologies applicable to various industries (assembly techniques, improving product reliability, reducing wear and tear, new computerised testing methods, membrane and particle technology, and so on);
- flexible materials and products, especially those in use in the textile, leather and household goods industries.

The cost to the EC budget over the four years was 125m ecus. It was followed by a second four-year programme of research and technological developments, to run from 1989 to 1992.

Biotechnology research

The five-year biotechnology research programme (1985–89) covered a key sector, 40% of all manufactured goods being biological by nature or by origin. Many new applications are foreseen in agriculture, chemicals, pharmaceuticals and environmental protection. The aim of the programme was to stimulate research and also training in areas such as bioinformatics, the collection of biotic materials, the basic technology of cells and cultivated live tissues, and the evaluation of toxicity and other risks which could flow from the development of biotechnology. The budget cost of the programme was 55m ecus.

In 1990 the commission adopted a new proposal for a specific research and development programme in the field of biotechnology (Biotech) which is divided into three parts:

- molecular approaches;
- cellular and organism approaches;
- ecology and population biology.

The cost of a five-year programme (1990–94) was set at 164m ecus.

The Eureka programme

A large number of EC firms, universities and research institutes are also benefiting from the Eureka programme, which was proposed by President Mitterrand in 1985 partly as a European alternative to President Reagan's star wars initiative. Eureka is not an EC programme, however, and it is open to participation by other West European countries, including the members of EFTA.

Five-year framework research programmes

Despite these increased efforts, the European Commission remained dissatisfied by the degree of commitment of the member states to the co-ordination of their research programmes. In 1986 the president of the commission, Jacques Delors, proposed that the research share of the Community budget (including the amount spent on nuclear research, see pages 162–163) should be more than doubled, from 3% to 8% of the total. As a first step the commission proposed a five-year framework programme for 1987–91, with a total budget of 7,735m ecus. Despite favourable opinions from the European Parliament and the Economic and Social Committee, the member states (particularly the UK) were unwilling to make provision on this scale, and it was not until July 1987 that a slimmed-down programme costing 5,396m ecus was eventually approved. A mid-term evaluation of the 1987–91 framework programme, drawn up in 1989 at the commission's request by five eminent figures from science and industry, recommended that it should be replaced by a rolling five-year programme revised every year. This suggestion was subsequently adopted, and a much simplified framework was approved for 1990–94, with the total being increased to 5.7 billion ecus.

The European Council, at the Edinburgh summit in December 1992, stressed the need for the EU's R&TD activities to continue to focus on generic, pre-competitive research with a multi-sectoral

Table 19   **Fourth framework research programme, 1994–98 (m ecus)**

	ecu mn
First activity (research, technological development demonstration programmes)	10,686
Second activity (co-operation with third countries and international organisations)	540
Third activity (dissemination and optimisation of results)	330
Fourth activity (stimulation of the training and mobility of researchers)	744
Maximum overall amount	12,300

Source: Council of Ministers.

Table 20   **Indicative breakdown between themes in the first activity of the fourth framework programme (m ecus)**

Information and communication technologies	3,405
Industrial technologies	1,995
Environment	1,080
Life sciences and technologies	1,572
Energy	2,256
Research for a European transport policy	240
Targeted socio-economic research	138
Total	10,686

Source: Council of Ministers.

impact. At the same time it set the financial perspective for 1993–99 and laid down the general framework for EU funding allocated to research. Subsequently the fourth framework programme (1994–98) was proposed by the commission, for a total of 13.1 billion ecus, including nuclear research. However, although the Council of Ministers approved the programme in December 1993, it agreed only to 12.3 billion ecus being met from EU funds (see Table 19).

Developments in telecommunications

One field in which the EU has sought to play a particularly active role is telecommunications. The commission has made repeated efforts to achieve the opening-up of public procurement policies in member states and a harmonisation of technical rules, with so far only mixed results. It has had more success with the development of infrastructure projects and the co-ordination of development programmes.

Euronet Diane. Set up in 1980, Euronet Diane was the first European information network created by the Community and the national postal and telephone authorities. It allows users in member states to consult about 600 databanks and databases by means of a computer and a telephone.

Apollo. The Apollo programme was set up so that the commission and the European Space Agency (ESA)[1] could co-operate on high-volume data transmission by satellite. This project will facilitate the development of experimental equipment and will stimulate the creation of a European market for ground stations and receiving antennae.

Insis and Caddia. These two programmes have been established within the EU to pursue exchanges of information through an integrated network of services including:

- transmission of written documents;
- electronic mail;
- access to statistical databases;
- video conferences;
- videotex.

The commission is also taking the lead in efforts to secure a common European approach to the planning and development of a second-generation system for cellular mobile telephones, integrated services digital networks (ISDN) and transnational broad-band communication channels.

---

1 A non–EC body, based in Paris, to which Sweden and Switzerland belong as well as most of the member states of the EC.

21

REGIONAL POLICY

The regional policy of the EC was not originally directly based on the Rome treaty, though the preamble to that treaty refers to the need to "reduce the differences between the various regions and the backwardness of the less favoured regions". (The Single European Act incorporated regional policy into the treaty, and formally recognised it as one of the means of strengthening the Community's economic and social cohesion.) The impetus for developing a regional policy came from the first enlargement, in 1973, when Denmark, Ireland and the UK joined the Community. One of the new British commissioners, George Thomson (now Lord Thomson of Monifieth), was given the specific responsibility of overseeing EC policy towards the regions.

Great disparity between regions

He found that there was a very considerable disparity between the poorest and most prosperous regions, both within countries and within the Community as a whole. According to figures published some years later by the commission, the ratio varied from 1:1.4 in West Germany, 1:2.4 in France, 1:3.1 in the UK, 1:3.8 in Italy and 1:5.1 in the Community as a whole (the overall range became greater still with the admission of Greece, Spain and, especially, Portugal).

The less privileged regions, which taken together now comprise more than a quarter of the population as a whole, may be divided into two principal groups.

- Underdeveloped rural areas, whose economy mostly depends on agriculture. These regions have low levels of income, high levels of unemployment and, frequently, poorly developed infrastructures. They include most of Greece and Portugal, southern Spain, the Italian Mezzogiorno, Ireland, Northern Ireland, Corsica and the French overseas departments.
- Areas whose former prosperity was founded on industries now in decline, and which are characterised by ageing plant and high unemployment. Most of these are in Belgium, France and the UK.

Aims of regional policy

The main objectives of the Community's policy for the regions are as follows.

- To ensure that regional problems are taken into consideration in other EC policies.
- To attempt to co-ordinate the regional policies of the member states.
- To provide a broad range of financial support for the development of the Community's poorer regions.

In order to facilitate the first objective, the commission regularly monitors the economic and social conditions of all the regions and studies the regional consequences of all EC policies. The common agricultural policy, for example, was found to be strongly geared towards helping the more prosperous agricultural areas, and modifications have been introduced which have reduced, but by no means completely removed, this anomaly. The Social Fund (see Chapter 22) has been sharply oriented towards the needy regions and special regional programmes have been designed to back up other Community policies.

So far as co-ordination of national efforts is concerned, an important aim has been to ensure that member states do not indulge in the ultimately self-defeating practice of outbidding each other by increasing the level of aid. Common rules allow the Community to avoid wasting scarce resources and to ensure a more coherent pattern of regional development. The commission has fixed upper limits on the state aids which can be offered to would-be investors in the underdeveloped regions. They range from 10% to 100% of the cost of investments, on a sliding scale according to the gravity of the problems in the particular regions.

ERDF is central element of regional policy

The central element in the Community's regional policy is, of course, the European Regional Development Fund (ERDF), set up in 1975. As it was already clear that the UK risked becoming a heavy net contributor to the EC budget (see page 17) unless it could find ways of attracting Community expenditure within its own borders, the UK government made exceptional efforts to avail itself of ERDF funds, as did Ireland and Italy, the then two poorest members of the EC. Yet from the outset it was accepted that there was no question of channelling the entire fund towards the neediest regions of the neediest countries. Each member state was awarded a quota, and its poorer regions were entitled to assistance even if they were far more prosperous than depressed or even average regions in other countries. Nevertheless, the poorer countries rightly got the larger quotas and in the first decade, up to the end of 1984, more than 91% of ERDF spending went to five countries: France, Greece, Italy, Ireland and the UK.

In terms of spending per head of population, Ireland gained most, followed by Greece, despite having joined the Community only in 1981; Italy was in third place. Half of all ERDF grants were spent in priority regions: the Mezzogiorno, Greece (except Athens), Ireland, Northern Ireland, Greenland (which left the EC following a referendum in 1985, but previously absorbed the entire Danish quota) and the French overseas departments. During its first ten years the budget of the ERDF increased eightfold, reaching 2,140m ecus (7.8% of the budget) in 1984, which was, however, only about one-eighth of the Community's spending on the CAP.

ERDF allocation rules changed

In 1985, after a prolonged negotiation between the commission and the member states, the rules governing the ERDF were changed in order to make them more flexible and more directed towards the least-favoured regions. Instead of fixed national quotas, each country was allocated a percentage range. These were revised in 1986, to take account of Spanish and Portuguese membership, and are now as shown in Table 21.

Table 21 **ERDF allocation (%)**

	Lower limit	Upper limit
Belgium	0.61	0.82
Denmark	0.34	0.46
France	7.47	9.96
Germany	2.55	3.40
Greece	8.35	10.64
Ireland	3.81	4.61
Italy	21.59	28.79
Luxembourg	0.04	0.06
Netherlands	0.68	0.91
Portugal	10.65	14.20
Spain	17.95	23.93
UK	14.48	19.31

Source: European Commission.

The lower figure represents the minimum of each year's ERDF budget guaranteed to each member state, always assuming that a sufficient volume of eligible applications for aid are sent to the commission. The variation each year in allocations within the range depends on the extent to which projects presented by member states are considered by the commission to be significant in Union terms.

ERDF expenditure programmes

Expenditure by the fund is divided between programmes, projects and studies. In each case the ERDF meets 50% or 55% of the total cost, the balance being contributed by the member state or states involved. In exceptional cases the ERDF may now assume 75% of the total cost, and 80% in Greece, Portugal, Ireland and Spain. Programmes may consist, either jointly or separately, of infrastructure development, grants to industry, crafts or services, or measures to exploit the potential for internally generated development of the regions themselves. There are two kinds of programme.

European Union programmes. Undertaken at the initiative of the commission, these programmes aim to help to solve serious social and economic difficulties in one or more regions. They consist of coherent groupings of projects, spread over a number of years, aimed specifically at Union objectives and the implementation of Union policies. In general, Union programmes will affect several member states with their agreement (for example, the Lorraine iron making area which includes parts of France, Belgium, Germany and Luxembourg).

National programmes of Union interest. These are proposed to the commission by national governments and pursue national objectives while contributing to the achievement of Union policy goals. The ERDF can only finance programmes of this kind in areas or regions designated by member states for the purpose of their regional aid schemes. One particular type of programme is intended to exploit the indigenous potential of regions by mobilising small-scale local resources, including for the development of tourism. Much the largest amount of money is expended, however, on individual projects put up by member states, often on behalf of local authorities, other public bodies or commercial firms, in their own countries.

Table 22 **Structural funds commitments, 1993 (ecu m")**

Objective

1 Regions lagging behind in development	12,175
2 Regions in industrial decline	2,052
3 & 4 Long-term unemployment & vocational integration of young people	1,779
5a Adaptation of agricultural structures	1,649
5b Development of rural areas	1,174
Total	18,829

Source: European Commission.

Other EU grants and loans

Apart from the ERDF funds, the regions also benefit from a range of other EU sources, including the following.

- Grants and loans to coal and steel areas from ECSC funds.
- Loans from the European Investment Bank and other EU funds.
- Soft loans under the European Monetary System for projects in Ireland and Italy.
- Grants from the European Social Fund and from the guidance section of the European Agricultural Fund (EAGGF).

The Regional Fund, the Social Fund and the guidance section of the EAGGF are known collectively as the structural funds of the Union, and under the Single European Act it was agreed in February 1988 that they should be doubled, in real terms, by 1993. An extra amount of 3 billion ecus was committed in 1990 to provide for regional assistance in eastern Germany in the period 1991–93. By 1993 it was envisaged that the structural funds would account for a quarter of the EU budget.

Over the five years 1989–93 a total of 73 billion ecus was allocated by the structural funds. In the years 1994–99 this figure will rise to 141 billion ecus (at 1992 prices). The division of this money between the various objectives of the funds during 1993, when nearly 19 billion ecus were committed, is shown in Table 22. The division between member states of the amount actually spent in 1992 is shown in Table 23.

Integrated Operations

Mention should also be made of the Community's Integrated Operations which are intended to focus assistance upon limited areas suffering from multiple deprivation. The first two integrated

Table 23 **National shares of payments made by the structural funds, 1992**

	1	2	3, 4	5a	5b	Total	%
			Objectives				
Belgium	–	64.65	68.04	10.77	4.61	148.07	1.0
Denmark	–	2.86	21.30	12.94	3.29	40.39	0.3
France	198.03	258.39	424.83	58.76	262.94	1,202.95	8.3
Germany	1,237.05	167.55	268.43	34.55	141.71	1,849.29	12.7
Greece	1,595.47	–	–	63.62	–	1,659.09	11.4
Ireland	945.72	–	–	35.08	–	980.80	6.8
Italy	1,452.30	49.86	123.19	76.62	40.68	1,742.65	12.0
Luxembourg	–	3.17	2.61	0.27	0.03	6.08	0.1
Netherlands	–	39.05	52.32	8.41	12.00	111.78	0.7
Portugal	2,097.53	–	–	62.30	–	2,159.83	14.9
Spain	2,741.22	278.88	166.71	88.45	85.38	3,360.64	23.2
UK	153.28	476.68	485.59	32.37	98.42	1,246.34	8.6
Total[a]	10,428.51	1,341.46	1,613.20	479.20	649.06	14,508.14	

[a]Totals do not add exactly since they include small amounts not distributed to member states.
Source: EC Commission.

operations were launched in Naples and Belfast, in 1979 and 1981 respectively, and others have since been established in four other areas of the UK, as well as others in Belgium, France, the Netherlands, Portugal and Spain.

Integrated Mediterranean Programmes

On a much larger scale are the Integrated Mediterranean Programmes, eventually agreed by the Council of Ministers in 1985 as a result of pressure from Greece during the closing stages of the enlargement negotiations with Spain and Portugal (see page 20). Over seven years the Community was to spend 4.1 billion ecus in grants and provide 2.5 billion ecus in loans for programmes intended to improve the socio-economic structure of the southern parts of the EC in order to facilitate the adjustment of those regions to the enlargement. The regions selected by the commission to benefit from these programmes were Languedoc-Roussillon, Corsica, Provence-Côte d'Azur, Aquitaine and Midi-Pyrénées in France, the Mezzogiorno, Latium, Tuscany, Umbria, the Marches, Liguria and part of Emilia-Romagna in Italy, and the whole of Greece.

Regional expenditure to increase

In February 1992 the commission published proposals for expenditure over the five years 1993–97. It did not, as had been predicted, propose a further doubling of overall regional spending, but it did provide that expenditure should be doubled in regions in the four poorest member states: Greece, Ireland, Portugal and Spain. It also provided for the creation of a Cohesion Fund, as agreed at the Maastricht summit, from which expenditure principally on transport, energy and telecommunications in the poorest member states could be met. In total the amount proposed for the three EC structural funds and for the Cohesion Fund was to increase from 18.6 billion ecus in 1992 to 29.3 billion ecus in 1997.

22

SOCIAL POLICY

ESF is centrepiece of social policy

At the centre of the EU's social policy is the European Social Fund (ESF), established under Article 123 of the Rome treaty. The purpose of the fund was defined as:

> To improve employment opportunities for workers in the common market and to contribute thereby to raising the standard of living... it shall have the task of rendering the employment of workers easier and of increasing their geographical and occupational mobility within the Community.

In its early years the ESF operated on a very small scale, providing assistance for the retraining of workers displaced through structural changes. With the sixfold increase in unemployment between 1970 and 1986, when it reached the record level of 16m people or 12% of the working population, both the finances and the scope of the fund were greatly increased. During 1986 nearly 2.5m people (85% of them under 25 years of age) benefited from the ESF, whose financial commitments for the year amounted to more than 2,500m ecus, or 7% of the total EC budget. By 1994 the amount committed had increased to 6,460m ecus, or about 8.8% of the EU budget.

Main priorities of ESF

In 1983 the Council of Ministers decided that the ESF should henceforth have two overriding priorities, and since then the greater part of its resources has been focused on these two (overlapping) priorities.

Young people. The ESF is now required to spend the bulk of its resources on the training and employment of the under-25s. The objective is to help fulfil an undertaking made by the Council of Ministers to ensure that new training opportunities will be provided for all young people who desire them, and in particular for those with reduced employment possibilities due to the lack or inadequacy of their education or vocational training.

The most disadvantaged regions. Some 44.5% of the ESF's expenditure is concentrated in seven "absolute priority" zones, containing altogether about one-sixth of the Union's working population (23m people). These are the whole of Greece, Ireland and Portugal, the Italian Mezzogiorno, the Spanish regions of Castilla y León, Castilla-La Mancha, Extremadura, Andalucía, Murcia, the Canaries, Galicia and the towns of Ceuta and Melilla, Northern Ireland and the French overseas departments. Moreover, while expenditure from the fund normally covers a maximum of 50% of the eligible costs, and does not exceed the total financial contribution made by the public authorities in the member state concerned, in the case of "absolute priority" regions, ESF aid can be increased to 55% of eligible expenditure.

ESF support for youth training programmes ...

Much of the aid earmarked for young people is channelled through major schemes undertaken by several of the member states. For example, in France tens of thousands of young people have benefited from employment/training contracts, enabling them, with the ESF's assistance, to work in a business while continuing their training. In Ireland significant support has been given to the Industrial Training Authority to help set up extensive youth training programmes.

On the other hand, through national governments, the commission receives thousands of applications each year to support small-scale schemes. Normally around half of these applications are approved.

... certain categories of adults ...

In addition to its efforts on behalf of young people, the ESF gives priority to adults in the following categories.

- Unemployed or underemployed workers, and especially the long-term unemployed.
- Women who wish to resume work.
- Handicapped people capable of joining the labour market.
- Migrant workers from within the EU and immigrants who have settled there in order to work, together with their families.
- Workers, particularly in small and medium-sized firms, faced with the problem of retraining due to the introduction of new technologies or the improvement of management techniques.
- People working in the field of employment promotion; experts in vocational training or recruitment, or development agents.

... and other specific operations

Finally, specific operations under the ESF, for which 5% of the budget must be reserved, include the following.

- European Union-type operations which are part of integrated programmes involving assistance from other EU funds (see page 140).
- Operations to help vocational training and youth employment.
- Operations linked to industrial or sectoral restructuring and the introduction of new technologies, or to the development of the labour market
- The employment of women where they are under-represented in the workforce.
- Assistance to handicapped and migrant workers and the training of instructors, vocational guidance or placement advisers.
- Specific innovatory operations involving fewer than 100 people.

ECSC support

In addition to the schemes supported by the ESF, some 261m ecus was expended under the ECSC budget during 1993 to assist workers in the coal and steel industries. This took the form of income-support allowances in the event of early retirement, unemployment or redeployment, as well as financial contributions towards expenditure relating to vocational training and mobility, and allowances for the reintegration of workers in new jobs. A special programme, known as Rechar, was launched in 1990 to provide financial help for the economic conversion of coal mining areas where the pits were being closed down. Altogether, ECSC provided loans worth over 7.8 billion ecus between 1975 and 1993 to finance conversion schemes in the two industries, creating new jobs for over 500,000 workers (see Table 24).

The Social Charter of Workers' Rights ...

The other principal element in the Community's social policy is the Social Charter of Workers' Rights, signed at Strasbourg in December 1989 by 11 of the 12 heads of government. Margaret Thatcher, who was then the UK prime minister, refused to sign on the grounds that the proposals foreshadowed by the charter would reverse the measures which her government had introduced to deregulate the labour market and would lead to higher unemployment by deterring employers from creating new jobs.

The Social Charter was originally conceived by Jacques Delors, who argued that the implementation of the 1992 programme would

Table 24 **ECSC conversion loans, 1975–93**

	Total loans granted (m ecus)	Jobs created (no)
Belgium	349.16	22,845
Denmark	11.70	854
France	913.46	66,747
Germany	2,395.80	171,041
Greece	5.00	375
Ireland	4.40	420
Italy	926.73	63,070
Luxembourg	25.80	2,100
Netherlands	37.80	2,696
Portugal	48.43	3,632
Spain	217.77	10,394
UK	2,723.51	151,134
Transborder operation 'Saar-Lor-Lux'	190.00	11,750
Total	7,849.55	507,058

Source: European Commission.

chiefly benefit European companies whose profits would rise as barriers to their operating on a Europe-wide basis would disappear. He successfully persuaded all the governments except that of the UK that the 1992 programme should be buttressed by parallel measures which would improve the working and social conditions of employees.

The charter itself had no more than a declaratory effect, but it was to be followed by a Social Action programme, containing 47 pieces of legislation which, if adopted by the Council of Ministers, would be binding on the member states including the UK.

... meets opposition from the UK ...

The UK government let it be known that it would consider each of these 47 proposals on their merit and would not offer a blanket opposition. In the spring of 1991 the then employment minister, Michael Howard, said in an interview that about one-third of the proposals would be acceptable to the government without any serious amendment, another third would be capable of amendment to meet UK objections, but that the final third would be unacceptable.

In fact the UK government's verbal opposition to the programme became more muted after the replacement of Mrs Thatcher by John Major. Nevertheless, the UK opposed most of the first batch of legislation to be tabled in late 1990 and in 1991. This included a draft directive to protect the employment rights of pregnant women. They would be guaranteed 14 weeks of paid leave and the right not to be dismissed, or lose seniority, on account of the pregnancy. A second directive, also opposed by the UK, sought to restrict the maximum number of hours which employees could be required to work within a fixed period, with special provisions for restricting night work. A third would require subcontracted workers from other countries to have the same rights – on health and safety, equal opportunities and dismissal – as local workers.

A fourth directive, which would give part-time workers the right to have a written contract provided that they were employed for more than eight hours per week was adopted in May 1991 with UK support. Further proposals expected during the first stage of the Social Action programme were directives giving workers a statutory right to paid leave for training courses and increasing the work protection for children and adolescents. A non-binding code of conduct on sexual harassment at work was also being planned by the European Commission.

... but could be adopted anyway

Much of the Social Action programme could be approved by qualified majority voting and would therefore be adopted despite UK opposition. The draft Treaty on European Union, presented to the Maastricht summit in December 1991, would have made the remaining proposals also liable to majority voting rather than unanimity. However, John Major refused to accept this and consequently the other 11 member states signed a Protocol on Social Policy which provided that they could decide these matters by qualified majority voting among themselves, but that the UK would not take part in the deliberations nor be bound by the outcome. This extraordinary decision, whereby 11 member states use the institutions, procedures and mechanisms of the EC for the taking of decisions which do not apply to the 12th member, was an unprecedented development and many observers doubted whether it would last long. The UK Labour Party immediately announced that it would sign the protocol if it won the forthcoming general election. In the event the Conservatives won, albeit with a much reduced majority, though it was widely believed that the government would shift its position within a very few years as the influence of the former prime minister, Margaret Thatcher, grew fainter.

This belief proved to be unfounded as the Major government hardened its attitude towards EU-sponsored legislation in a wide variety of fields, in the face of fierce pressure from "Euro-sceptic"

Conservative MPs. It now seems that the UK is set to remain the odd man out, in the social field, until and unless there is a change of government.

23

WORKERS' RIGHTS

Under Article 117 of the Rome treaty the member states agreed on the need to promote improved living and working conditions for workers, while Article 118 gave the commission the task of promoting close co-operation between member states in the social field, particularly in matters relating to:

- employment;
- labour law and working conditions;
- basic and advanced vocational training;
- social security;
- prevention of occupational accidents and diseases;
- occupational hygiene;
- the right of association, and collective bargaining between employers and workers.

In practice, the impact of the Community has been most marked in relation to the rights of migrant workers, equal pay for men and women (see pages 188–189), and safety factors. Despite the activities of the European Social Fund (Chapter 22) and the European Regional Development Fund (Chapter 21), relatively little has been achieved in terms of assuring employment for the workers of the Community, unemployment having risen to 15m, or around 11% of the labour force by the end of 1986. It subsequently fell to 12m (8.3%) in 1990, but by February 1994 it was over 16m (10.7%) and rising. Attempts to harmonise social security systems have enjoyed only very partial success, while commission initiatives to provide a wider framework for worker participation in management decisions have been blocked by the unwillingness of some member governments (notably that of the UK) to agree to legislation in this field.

Rights of migrant workers

Nearly 5m EU citizens are now living in Union countries apart from their own (together with nearly 8m migrants from non-EU countries). Under Union law, EU migrants must be treated like nationals of the host country. Their right of free movement from one member state to another is guaranteed, and all discrimination on national grounds is forbidden, whether relating to employment, social security, trade union rights, living and working conditions, housing, education or vocational training. Union migrants going to jobs in another EU country do not need a work permit and can claim a five-year residence permit which is automatically renewable, even after their retirement.

The right to work is, in theory, subject only to two restrictions:

- for "justified reasons" of public order, health or safety; and
- for certain forms of public administration work.

In practice member states have tended to try to shut off all public administration jobs from foreign applicants, but a series of decisions by the Court of Justice has gradually reduced the range of posts which can be reserved to nationals of the host country.

Mutual recognition of professional qualifications

It has taken a long time for the member states to agree on the mutual recognition of professional qualifications, so that for many years it was not possible for many workers to practise their professions in EC countries other than their own. However, doctors, nurses, veterinary surgeons, dentists and midwives are now able to do so, provided that they are nationals of an EU country and have obtained their qualifications within the EU. Lawyers established in one member state are able to offer their services in another, as are architects and pharmacists, but only since 1987 as it took the best part of 20 years for agreement to be reached in the Council of Ministers.

Improvement of working conditions

Somewhat more urgency has been shown in dealing with proposals for the improvement of working conditions. In 1975 the European Foundation for the Improvement of Living and Working Conditions was established in Dublin, and since that date it has helped to formulate EC policy in this area. The major emphasis has been on safety and health in the workplace, where more than 100,000 people are killed in accidents each year and millions injured. The ECSC was involved from the outset. It established the Mines Safety and Health Commission, a body composed of government representatives, employers and workers, to help prepare proposals for coal mines and other mining industries. A similar body with a more general remit, the Advisory Committee on Safety, Hygiene and Health Protection at Work, was set up in 1974.

In its second action programme on work safety, adopted in 1984, the EC concentrated on:

- rules for the use of dangerous substances;
- ergonomic measures and principles for preventing accidents and dangerous situations;
- improvements in organisation, training and information;
- problems posed by new technologies.

Several directives have been adopted on safety signs, on electrical equipment used in mines with firedamp, and on protection against chemical, physical or biological agents such as lead, asbestos, noise and vinyl chloride monomer. Under the Single European Act, agreement on new directives or regulations on improving the working environment and on health and safety provisions will no longer require unanimity within the Council of Ministers. This should lead to a speeding-up of decision-making in this area.

Workers' rights in companies

Since the mid-1970s the European Commission has made vigorous efforts to promote the protection of workers' interests in other areas, notably by safeguarding their rights in companies. Directives have been in force since 1977 establishing minimum requirements with regard to mass redundancies, since 1979 guaranteeing established rights in the event of transfer, and since 1983 ensuring payment of salary and other claims when an employer goes out of business.

Three major commission initiatives, however, ran into determined opposition, provoking expensive, provocative but ultimately successful lobbying campaigns by employers' organisations. These involved not only the main European employers' association UNICE, but also large US-controlled multinational companies and the Japanese employers' association Keidanran. The European Trade Union Confederation (ETUC) attempted to rally support for the commission's proposals, but all three have become firmly stuck in the Council of Ministers (where they need unanimous approval). There seemed no prospect of any of them being adopted in the foreseeable future, despite the fact that all three have been welcomed by a majority of member states, several of which had already adopted domestic legislation along similar lines.

The three proposals were as follows.

European company statute. This draft statute set out an industrial relations framework for European companies which might be formed, for example, as a consequence of cross-border mergers. The original draft, which was put forward in 1975, was largely based on German experience, and contained the proposal that companies should have a two-tier board structure, a board of management and a supervisory board, with direct worker representation on the supervisory body.

Fifth Directive on the structure of limited companies. Originally tabled in 1972, this directive was intended to apply to any firm in the EC employing more than 500 people. It also provided for compulsory worker representation on supervisory boards.

The Vredeling Directive. Named after the former Dutch commissioner for social affairs, Henk Vredeling, whose proposals the commission approved in 1980, this draft directive related to "complex" companies (those having more than one branch), although its evident target was multinational companies whose very nature made them difficult to control on a purely national basis. The purpose of the directive was to require managements to provide general information about the company to employees and, in particular, to consult them on any decisions which would have consequences for their jobs (closures, redundancies, plant reorganisation, and so on).

Charter of the Fundamental Social Rights of Workers

A widespread view that the benefits of the 1992 programme would accrue mainly to the business community led to demands that it should be balanced by a comparable programme designed to enhance the rights of workers. The commission consequently produced a draft Community Charter of the Fundamental Social Rights of Workers (Social Charter), which was signed by 11 heads of government with the exception of Mrs Thatcher in Strasbourg in December 1989 (see also pages 145–146). The charter has no legal force in itself but it foreshadows the introduction of a series of directives designed to entrench workers' rights with regard to such matters as:

- labour mobility;
- employment;
- social protection;
- collective bargaining and freedom of association;

- vocational training;
- health and safety;
- equal opportunity;
- consultation and participation; and
- measures to protect women workers, young people, the elderly and the disabled.

Revised European company statute

In 1989 the commission also tried to refloat its earlier proposal for a European company statute. In its revised form this would be a voluntary option for companies, but sweetened with the possibility of more favourable tax treatment. The proposals for worker participation were made a great deal more flexible, with three alternative systems on offer based respectively on French, German, and UK practices. Despite this new flexibility the UK government remained firmly opposed. It is now probable, however, that part of the statute will be adopted under the Protocol on Social Policy (described on pages 145–147) which would mean that, initially at least, it would be applicable only in the other 11 member states. The commission approved such a proposal in April 1994, under which European Works Councils will be established in multinational firms within the EU so that employees may be informed and consulted about strategic decision-making by their companies. This proposal, which was expected to be adopted by the Council of Ministers later in 1994, will not apply to workers in the UK, but British firms with employees in other EU countries will be required to comply. The expectation was that other multinational companies would not wish to discriminate against their British employees and would therefore include them on a voluntary basis, while British trade unions would apply direct pressure on British companies to introduce works councils along similar lines.

24

STEEL

When the European Coal and Steel Community (ECSC) was established in 1951 the coal and steel industries, which were regarded as the "basic industries", held a dominant place in the West European economy. This is now much less true, though both industries remain significant factors. The steel industry, in particular, has been transformed in the past three decades, and the Community was largely instrumental, first in its rapid growth and subsequently in its sharp decline.

Strong Community influence on steel industry

The Community was able to have such a strong influence over the steel industry because the Treaty of Paris gives the European Commission (the successor body to the High Authority) much stronger actual and potential sway over the coal and steel industries than the Treaty of Rome accords it over other industries. It has considerable powers over investments by companies, state aids, production levels and selling prices, and it has the financial means to give concrete, though limited, aid where necessary. Under Article 58 of the Paris treaty, with the assent of the Council of Ministers, it may declare a state of "manifest crisis" which gives it even wider powers, including the right to impose production quotas on individual companies and to inflict prohibitive fines if these are exceeded.

Period of expansion is followed by a sharp decline

The establishment of the ECSC heralded a period of continuous expansion in the steel industry. The abolition of customs barriers led to a rapid increase in internal trade, which increased by 129% in the first five years. By expanding the markets the ECSC also fostered company mergers and encouraged the rationalisation of production and increased productivity. Year-on-year world demand for steel grew by 6%, and EC production rose accordingly, from 93m tons in 1962 to 156m tons in 1974, 22% of total world production.

After 1974 the situation changed completely. Following the first "oil shock" world demand for steel fell abruptly in 1975, and was still severely depressed ten years later. Although EC steel capacity continued to rise, reaching 200m tons in 1980, production declined to 110m tons in 1983, when the industry was working at only 57% capacity compared with 87% in 1974. Prices quickly fell to the point where companies were no longer profitable, dropping in three years by an average of 45%. The substantial financial losses forced many firms to scale down or abandon investment plans. Governments intervened on a large scale to write off losses and public subsidies spiralled out of control.

Eurofer cartel fails to solve the problems

In 1977 the commission persuaded the major producers to form a voluntary cartel, called Eurofer, which ordered production cuts and set minimum "guide prices" for virtually all steel products, which were reinforced by fines against companies that broke the rules. A reference price was set for imports, and an anti-dumping duty was levied on all imports at prices below that level.

For some three years Eurofer worked quite well; price cutting ceased, the market improved and some surplus plants were closed down. In the summer of 1980, however, Eurofer collapsed as prices slumped yet again. The relatively profitable West German firms, Klockner and Thyssen, began to cut prices and boost production; others, including the nationalised British Steel Corporation, plunged deep into the red. The EC commissioner responsible for industry, Viscount Etienne Davignon, responded by asking for a state of "manifest crisis" to be declared, and then imposing a much more stringent cartel. Under this, over 80% of steel output was placed under compulsory controls, while the remainder (mainly special steels) was subjected to voluntary quotas. Companies which exceeded these quotas were subjected to heavy fines which proved a sufficient deterrent to bring them back into line.

A drastic slimming down ...

The price that the industry and the member governments were required to pay for the protection afforded to them was a drastic slimming down of the industry, accompanied by a phasing out of state subsidies. Each member state was asked to make an equivalent effort, and collectively they proposed capacity cuts totalling 19m tons. In the commission's view this was insufficient and eventually in November 1982 the member states agreed in principle on cuts of 30m–35m tons. By the end of 1985 some 32m tons of capacity had, in fact, been shed. State aids, forbidden in principle by the ECSC treaty, were permitted on a temporary basis but only on condition that they contributed to the restructuring of the industry, were limited in duration and did not create unacceptable distortions of competition. At the same time a specific timetable for the abolition of aids was established. All subsidies were supposed to cease after December 31st 1985. In fact, from that date no more investment aid and no more operating aids to steel making were allowed. But, for a further three years, subsidies could continue to be granted for anti-pollution or research and development schemes, together with closure aids granted under very strict conditions.

It had been hoped that at the same time production quotas would be removed and that full competition would be restored to the steel sector. But demand for steel remained low, and it was clear that further restructuring would be necessary before a slimmed down industry was in a position to become fully competitive. Moreover, the important North American market was increasingly being sheltered from EC exports by protective measures. It was therefore decided in December 1985 that deregulation would be implemented on a step-by-step basis during a three-year transitional period, rather than being introduced overnight. The proportion of steel output subject to the quota was accordingly reduced to 65% during 1986, and to 45% in 1987.

... led to a healthier industry

The reshaping of the steel industry had cost governments around 33 billion ecus up to the end of 1985 while the Community spent more than 5 billion ecus to help alleviate related social problems: retraining, alternative job creation, early retirement, and so on. Meanwhile 152,000 jobs were shed. The industry was now in a healthier state with some major loss-makers, such as British Steel, returning to profitability. But it was not yet out of the wood, and it was not until June 1988 that the commission was able to declare that the state of "manifest crisis" was over and to put an end to the production quota system which had been in force since 1980. The industry's finances were by then much improved, although this had been achieved only through shedding a large proportion of the workforce.

Renewed difficulties appeared in the early 1990s with the economic recession and fierce competition from foreign suppliers, particularly from Eastern Europe. In November 1992 the Council of Ministers adopted a proposal from the commission on a further restructuring of the industry, foreshadowing a production cut of more than 20m tons, compared with the 1991 level of 137m tons. Subject to the establishment of a closure programme, the council approved a series of social support measures to cushion the further contraction of the industry, as well as the imposition of tariff quotas to curb the level of imports from non-member states.

ECSC treaty will not be renewed

The ECSC treaty is due to expire in 2002, and in 1991 the commission initiated a debate as to whether this date should be brought forward so that the coal and steel industries would henceforth be treated in the same way as other industries within the EC, without any special provisions. In the event the commission recommended that the treaty should be allowed to run its full term but that no attempt should be made to renew it. This recommendation was supported by the Council of Ministers and by the ECSC Consultative Committee. It seems likely that well before the treaty runs out the levies imposed on coal and steel production will be phased out, or sharply reduced, as they currently yield far more than is needed to meet the social costs of the run-down of the two industries.

25

ENERGY

Common energy policy slow to evolve

The coal industry has been subjected to detailed supervision under the ECSC since 1951, and the civil nuclear industry, particularly with regard to research and development, under Euratom since 1958, yet the Community has been much slower to evolve a common energy policy which would enable it to plan and implement a joint strategy to meet all its energy needs. Since the first "oil shock" of 1973, which caught the EC woefully unprepared, there has been a certain convergence in policy and common objectives have been defined without, however, a central machinery being established to ensure that they are pursued in a co-ordinated manner. The result is a "semi-common" policy, with agreement in principle on most objectives, but a patchwork division of responsibility between the different sectors.

This is undoubtedly a significant improvement on the situation in the early 1970s, but the EC remains particularly vulnerable in the energy field where, in 1991, external sources of supply still accounted for 50% of total consumption, compared with a mere 18% for the USA. Moreover, its internal energy production is likely to remain stable or even to decline, while its demand would surely grow in the event of renewed economic growth. Of the 12 member states only the Netherlands and the UK are net exporters of energy.

A programme is finally adopted in 1974

The 1973 crisis, which saw the quadrupling of oil prices virtually overnight, was followed by the fiasco of the December 1973 Copenhagen EC summit, which singularly failed to produce a joint response to the Arab oil producers, France and the UK in particular preferring to pursue bilateral deals with oil suppliers rather than to present a united front with their EC partners. It was only in September 1974 that the Council of Ministers adopted a programme drawn up by the European Commission called "Towards a New Energy Policy Strategy". This programme, adapted in 1980 and again in 1986, has formed the framework for most subsequent discussions on energy policy.

The overriding priority laid down was the importance of reducing dependence on imported oil supplies and the desirability of diversifying the sources of supply. This objective was pursued with considerable success. Over ten years the Community cut its oil imports by half. By 1983 it was estimated that the equivalent of 250m tons of oil annually was being saved due to more efficient use of energy: an economy of more than 20%. North Sea production had been built up to nearly 130m tons, and the same amount was being saved in imports by greater use of nuclear energy. The 1986 update of the 1974 report defined new energy policy aims for the period to 1995 and listed both sectoral and horizontal targets.

Sectoral targets

Efficiency. Efforts must be intensified to ensure a further improvement of at least 20% by 1995, despite the fall in oil prices. The commission was asked to prepare programmes for all sectors of the economy – services, industry, agriculture and transport – and to disseminate the results of national and Community demonstration projects which tested the industrial and commercial viability of new equipment. The EC spent around 150m ecus 1978–85 in support of more than 370 energy-saving demonstration projects, while the EIB lent 3.3 billion ecus for similar projects, mostly small and medium-sized, in industry and infrastructure. In June 1990 the Community adopted a five-year programme entitled Thermie, with an annual budget of 350m ecus, to provide financial support for projects that promote energy technology in the rational use of energy, renewable energies, solid fuels and hydrocarbons.

Oil. Over 12 years the EC had reduced the share of imported oil in its gross energy consumption from 62% to 31%, but this had crept back up to 35% by 1991. The level of net imports must be maintained at below one-third of total consumption by continued encouragement for economy and substitution, and promotion of internal exploration and production. More assistance for the development of innovatory technologies in the hydrocarbon field is envisaged, as well as the possibility of EU assistance in prospecting.

Natural gas. The market share of natural gas, some 19.3% in 1991, had grown by 50% since 1973. With the prospect of a possible fall in European production, there should be greater incentives for gas exploration and for diversifying supplies from third countries. EIB loans for the construction of gas pipelines should help to achieve these objectives.

Solid fuels. A determined effort has been made to increase the market share of coal, lignite and peat (22.4% in 1991). Despite a doubling of coal imports since 1973, consumption slightly declined, due to a 16% fall in Community coal production in the mid-1980s. Since 1989 it has been rising. The transformation of power stations from oil to coal and the use of coal for district heating schemes is encouraged by EU grants and loans, and the Union is also backing efforts to standardise and perfect technologies that cause less pollution.

Electricity generation. The drive to replace oil by coal and, above all, nuclear fuel, which had already reduced the share of oil from 50% to 25%, should be continued, with the objective of bringing it down to less than 15% by 1995. The aim was to increase the nuclear share (then approaching 30%) to 40% by 1995 and 50% by the end of the century. As a longer-term objective, the commission envisaged investment in a network of fast breeder reactors (which would multiply by 50 times the energy potential of uranium) and would be economically competitive by 2005. The Chernobyl accident in 1986, and mounting public anxiety about the operation of nuclear power stations, convinced the commission that further progress could only be made if the public concern could be allayed. In June 1986 it proposed to the Council of Ministers an action plan which placed heavy emphasis on safety measures. Nevertheless, there was a virtual halt in new nuclear energy projects and by 1991 the nuclear share in total EC energy production had fallen to 25.8%.

New and renewable energy sources. Greater financial support should be provided for the development of new technologies, such as mini-hydro plants for electricity generation, the use of biomass and waste, solar, geothermal and wind energy. These could together account for nearly 5% of consumption by the end of the century, in the view of the commission, which had by 1985 already provided grants to assist more than 500 demonstration projects, while EIB loans had been made available for the development of 100 of them. In 1991 a new research and technological development programme was launched with a budget of 157m ecus over five years.

Horizontal targets
Completion of the internal market. The market for oil products is already largely open, and little more can practically be done to open up the coal market any further, given the high cost of internally produced coal in relation to imports from countries such as

Poland and the USA. There is, however, scope for increasing internal trade in the gas and electricity sectors through the encouragement of long-term contracts, cross-border investment and interconnections between national systems, such as France–UK and France–Italy, both of which have been assisted by EIB loans. In 1990 a more comprehensive programme was adopted for linking up energy networks throughout the Community.

Common pricing.   The EC has been increasingly active in ensuring that all energy sectors should follow common pricing principles which are transparent and realistic and should not distort competition between industries. For example, the Dutch gas industry has been prevented from supplying cheap gas to horticulturalists which allowed them to heat their greenhouses more cheaply than their competitors in other EC countries. In 1990 a directive was adopted enforcing transparency in the pricing policies of electricity and gas suppliers.

Improved security of supply.   This is to be achieved by the development of competitive European production, diversification of imports, greater flexibility of consumption and effective contingency measures. Community legislation provides for the compulsory stocking of fuel at electricity plants, equal to 30 days' consumption and for oil stocks to be maintained at a minimum level equivalent to 90 days' consumption.

External relations.   The EU is seeking to capitalise on its bargaining power as a major customer of energy supplies, the Union absorbing some 14% of the world market. In 1989 the EC negotiated an economic co-operation agreement with the Gulf states, which have the world's largest oil reserves, and it maintains close relations with OAPEC, the Organisation of Arab Petroleum Exporting Countries. In the nuclear field long-term agreements with the principal uranium suppliers (Australia, Canada and the USA) assure a certain stability of supply. The commission is seeking to secure a greater degree of co-operation between member states on gas supply contracts. In the developing countries the Union is helping to disseminate new technologies (solar energy, energy saving, and so on) through some 60 aid programmes. (See also European Energy Charter, page 164.)

Environmental protection.   Since 1989 the EC, in response to strong pressure from public opinion, has adopted a series of measures designed to reduce environmental damage caused by the energy sector. They concern the introduction of lead-free petrol, the reduction of toxic emissions from automobiles and large combustion plants, and the reduction of the sulphur content of heating oil and diesel fuel.

Regional development. In addition to the grants and loans offered by the ECSC, the ERDF and the EIB for regional development projects, many of which are concerned with the energy sector, the special five-year Valoren programme for improving the efficiency of energy resources in the less-favoured regions was launched in 1986. This programme, which has been allocated 400m ecus, will seek to exploit the use of indigenous fuels (such as small peat and lignite deposits) as well as to promote the efficient use of energy.

Technological innovation. The EU is pursuing a major research, development and demonstration programme focusing on:

- nuclear safety (reactor security, waste management, control of fissile materials, protection against radioactivity, and so on);
- controlled nuclear fusion;
- solid fuels;
- new energy resources; and
- the efficient and environmentally friendly use of energy.

Much of the research is being pursued by firms and institutes in the different member states. In 1993, for example, under its Thermie programme (for the promotion of energy technology), the commission gave financial support amounting to 129m ecus to 137 different projects. The four research centres directly established by Euratom, at Karlsruhe in Germany, Ispra in Italy, Geel in Belgium and Petten in the Netherlands, now known collectively as the Joint Research Centre (JRC), do important work mainly in the field of nuclear safety and environmental protection. The most ambitious undertaking by the EC, however, was the establishment at Culham in the UK of the Joint European Torus (JET), where all West European research into nuclear fusion is now concentrated. This is one of only four major programmes in the world, the others being in Russia, the USA and Japan. Co-operation and exchange of information agreements have been reached with both the US and the Japanese programmes, and hopes of worldwide co-operation, also involving Russia, have been encouraged following the 1985 US-Soviet summit at Geneva. The construction of an experimental fusion reactor, within a framework of international co-operation, is seen as the next major step in a programme whose ultimate objective is the generation of electricity by more economic, cleaner and safer means than those provided by nuclear fission.

Meanwhile, in 1991 the SAVE programme (Specific Actions for Vigorous Energy Efficiency) was launched, with the objective of reducing energy intensity per unit of GNP by 20% over the following five years. A series of actions to limit carbon dioxide emissions by improving energy efficiency was launched under this programme in 1993.

Trans-European Networks. A programme of Trans-European Networks (TENs) – in transport, telecommunications, training and energy – was announced by the commission in 1990. In particular, it contained proposals for energy interconnections in natural gas and electricity. Financial measures were proposed to promote private funding (particularly by meeting the costs of prior feasibility studies) and to ensure that higher priority is given to TENs in the future operation of the EU's budgetary and lending instruments. While the commission's intention is that, as far as possible, funding should come predominantly from the private sector, public funding, which might include Union support, will be required in certain cases. The Cohesion Fund, set up as a result of decisions taken at the Maastricht summit in December 1991, will be able to provide some funding for TENs in the poorer Union states.

Among the more interesting projects so far as electricity is concerned are the following.

● Interconnections between Greece and Italy (1993) and between Ireland and the UK (1995).
● The reinforcement of a series of interconnections (1991–95) within certain countries (Belgium, France, Germany and the Netherlands) or between member states: from France to Spain and Portugal in one direction and to Belgium, Germany, Italy and Switzerland in the other; from Italy to Austria and Switzerland; from Germany to the Netherlands, Denmark and Austria.

For natural gas a complex network is planned. Particular projects already given the go-ahead include the following.

● The Midal project between Emden and Ludwigshaven (Germany) and the Zeepipe project (Belgium), which should open up ways of bringing in Norwegian gas (1991–93).

- The introduction of natural gas in Greece (1993) and Portugal (1994), three German projects (1991–93) to link up the eastern *Länder* and the interconnection of mainland Italy, Corsica and Sardinia.
- A series of interconnections between member states: Ireland– UK (1993), France–Spain–Portugal, Belgium–Germany, Germany– Denmark, and UK–continent.
- Some projects concern non-member countries: reinforcement of the Italy-Tunisia Transmed gas pipeline (1992), and inter-connections between Denmark and Norway and between Spain and Morocco (1995).

European Energy Charter

A major initiative towards international co-operation in energy sup-plies was launched by the Dutch prime minister, Ruud Lubbers, who, in 1989, proposed that an energy charter should be signed between the EC and the Soviet Union, under which Western know-how and investment would be made available to the Soviet natural gas and oil industries in exchange for the Soviet Union guarantee-ing supplies to Western Europe over a lengthy period. The Euro-pean Energy Charter was eventually signed in The Hague in December 1991 by the EC, 37 European and OECD states and 12 for-mer Soviet republics. Its objective is to create a climate favourable to the operation of enterprises and to the flow of investment and technology by applying market-economy principles to the field of energy. Concrete co-operation will focus specifically on:

- access to and development of energy reserves;
- market access;
- liberalisation of trade in energy;
- energy efficiency and environmental protection;
- safety principles and guidelines;
- research, technological development, innovation and dissemination;
- education and training.

During 1994 it was hoped that the signatory countries would sign a legally binding Basic Agreement setting out the general rules on trade in energy, conditions of competition, access to capital, transmission and transit, transfers of technology, environmental protection, intellectual property, conditions for investment and the procedure for settling disputes.

26

TRANSPORT

Slow progress on common transport policy ...
The Rome treaty, in Article 74, envisages the creation of a common transport policy, but for the first 24 years of the EC's existence progress in this direction was so slow that in September 1982 the European Parliament brought proceedings against the Council of Ministers in the Court of Justice for failing to carry out its obligations under the treaty. The action was partially successful. The court held that the council had infringed the treaty by failing to ensure freedom to provide services in international transport and to lay down conditions for the admission of non-resident carriers to national transport in the member states. The court declined, however, to take cognisance of the absence of a common transport policy as such, since the treaty did not define that policy with sufficient clarity to enable the court to pronounce on it. It did, however, recommend the council to work continuously towards the progressive attainment of a common transport policy.

... speeds up after court ruling
Following the court's ruling there was a significant acceleration of council decision-making in the transport field, partly in the context of the adoption of a timetable to complete the EC's internal market by 1992. In 1991 a report entitled "Transport 2000 and Beyond" was adopted, setting objectives for an integrated continent-wide transport system, involving EC assistance in linking national networks and in improving links with central and Eastern Europe. Transport is estimated to provide 6.5% of the EU's gross national product, and it employs more than 6m people. Its importance in the economic integration of Western Europe can hardly be overestimated. In 1983 the European Commission established a series of broad policy targets.

- Greater integration of national transport policies.
- A better climate of competition between and within different forms of transport.
- Greater productivity and efficiency in the European transport system, partly through eliminating bottlenecks and bureau-

cratic restraints.
- Financial support for a series of major infrastructure projects of Union-wide importance.
- A co-ordinated Union approach to safety, technical harmonisation, environmental protection and working conditions in the transport industry.

Although the commission has sought to implement a global policy, applying common principles to the different forms of transport – all of which compete with each other to a varying degree – it has for the most part had to adopt a sector-by-sector approach.

Roads

It is in road transport that the commission has made the most persistent attempts to secure the adoption of EC policies, and it has often had to wait for many years before the Council of Ministers was able to agree on the proposals which it had put forward. Its main concerns have been the following.

Road safety. Some 50,000 people are killed and 1.5m injured each year in road accidents. A string of directives has harmonised standards for brakes, lighting, windscreens, sound levels, and so on. After a 20-year delay, agreement was reached in 1984 for common standards on weights and dimensions of commercial vehicles. The maximum lorry weight was then set at 40 tons (38 tons in the UK and Ireland). A further agreement on maximum axle weights for articulated lorries was reached in 1986 (11.5 tons, but 10.5 tons in the UK and Ireland). In addition, 1986 was declared Road Safety Year and the commission drew up an action programme including infrastructure improvements and measures relating to road signs, vehicle safety and the behaviour and training of drivers. By the end of 1991 directives had been adopted on:

- technical vehicle inspection;
- lorry suspension systems;
- the fitting of speed limitation devices in lorries and coaches;
- limiting the risks involved in the carriage of dangerous goods.

Frontier crossing. Delays and bureaucratic checks at internal frontier crossings had been a major source of expense and an undoubted barrier to inter-EC trade. Under the 1992 programme, progressive steps were taken to remove this barrier. From January 1st 1988 a single administrative document (SAD), also valid for crossing into EFTA countries, replaced up to 70 different forms previously required for lorries crossing internal EC borders. On January 1st 1993 the SAD was withdrawn and frontier controls on all internal EU borders ceased.

International transport of goods. This has traditionally been restricted by quota and by licence. Up to 1985 only some 40% of road freight was liberalised, but under an agreement reached by the Council of Ministers in June 1986 the remainder of the trade is being progressively opened up to free competition. By 1993 all quota restrictions ended, but it will only be by June 1998 that full freedom to operate transport services in other member states (cabotage) will be granted. Meanwhile the commission has established a more rational pricing system, publishing a scale of reference tariffs which is periodically revised.

Employment in road transport industry. Since 1974 the Community has established conditions for employment in the road transport industry, notably in terms of professional ability and training. Maximum driving periods have been established for each day and each week as well as obligatory periods of rest. Observance of these rules is controlled by a tachograph (known pejoratively as "the spy in the cab") which records the driving and resting time and speeds of heavy goods vehicles.

Railways
Community action regarding the railways has mainly focused on their troubled finances, which have steadily deteriorated in the face of increasing competition from road, air and waterway transport. The gap between revenue and costs has caused large deficits, bridged by subsidies which have placed considerable burdens on national budgets. In many cases these subsidies are a recognition of non-commercial duties imposed by the state, such as low fares and the continuation of loss-making lines in thinly populated areas.

Since the early 1960s the Community has tried to balance competition between rail and other forms of transport. Rules on financial competition have been harmonised to take account of public service obligations, capital and operating subsidies. The financial involvement of governments has been made more transparent without being generally reduced. In 1975 the Council of Ministers laid down guidelines for financial recovery and a clearer definition of relations between the railway companies (almost all of which were publicly owned) and government authorities.

To boost the productivity, efficiency and quality of rail services, the commission suggested in 1981 the laying down of multi-annual programmes, notably for investment in infrastructure and rolling stock, the re-examination of public service obligations and the extension of combined rail-road services under the umbrella of a specialised international company with considerable independent powers. This suggestion has not, so far, been adopted by the Council of Ministers. The commission has since tabled further proposals for an improved capital structure for rail companies and a better sharing of infrastructure costs (those for roads and waterways are normally financed by national budgets).

Transport infrastructure

The EC has played an important role in helping to finance transport infrastructure projects, ranging from roads and motorways to bridges and tunnels, ports and airports, canals, the upgrading or electrification of railways and the purchase of more comfortable and economic equipment (aircraft, high-speed trains, and so on). Nearly 20 billion ecus had been loaned by the EIB up to 1993 and a comparable amount had been expended in grants by the European Regional Development Fund. Projects in the UK which have benefited include Manchester and Birmingham airports, the Tyne-Wear metro, the Manchester light railway, the second Severn bridge and the ports of Ramsgate and Harwich.

Trans-European Networks (TENs). In 1990 the commission published proposals for assisting the development of TENs in transport, energy and telecommunications. So far as railway development is concerned, a master plan was published for a high-speed network by the year 2010, including 9,000km of new lines, 15,000km of modified track and 1,200km of links between main lines. In addition, it identified 15 key links, often frontier links, where implementation essential to the smooth operation of the European network presents a number of difficulties. It also anticipated rapid progress in the technical compatibility of equipment. The priorities adopted by the commission were are follows.

- A study of the problems raised by the 15 key links mentioned.
- Major links: the northern route, Paris–London–Brussels– Amsterdam–Cologne, with connections to other member states; the southern route, Seville–Barcelona–Lyon–Turin–Milan–Venice, with onward connections to Tarvisio and Trieste, and from Madrid to Lisbon and Oporto.

- Improved communications with Ireland: the Dublin–Belfast–Crewe and Dublin–Belfast routes.

The EU, through the EIB, had already assisted in the financing of the Channel Tunnel, which will be a crucial element in the high-speed rail network.

The commission has initiated a parallel study on future prospects for a Union motorway network and is advocating EU financial support for three types of project.

- Linking up existing networks: the Brenner route across the Alps from Italy to northern Europe; links across the Pyrenees: Toulouse–Barcelona (through the Puymorens tunnel, to be completed in 1994), Toulouse-Madrid and Bordeaux–Valencia (through the Somport tunnel, to be completed in 1995).
- Improving communications with outlying regions: the road link to Ireland (between Crewe and Holyhead), the Brindisi–Patras–Athens route and the Madrid–Lisbon link.
- Other links to improve communications with the EU's neighbours: the Athens–Evzoni–ex-Yugoslavia route (held up due to war), and connections with Scandinavian countries via the Aalborg–Fredrikshavn motorway and Fehmark link.

Inland waterways
Inland waterways play an important role in heavy industrial trade in several parts of the EU, the most notable of several large waterway systems being formed by the River Rhine and its tributaries. Since 1976 member states have agreed to a mutual recognition of each other's decisions on the navigability of waterways, and since 1982 the Council of Ministers has laid down technical specifications for waterway craft. In 1991 the council adopted a directive liberalising cabotage (international competition for the carriage of goods or passengers within other member states) and others on the mutual recognition of boatmasters' certifications, cockpit crew licences and driving licences.
The commission has taken the initiative in:

- moves to scrap overcapacity, financed by national governments;
- setting up a market monitoring system;
- drawing up an international agreement securing free competition once the Rhine–Main–Danube canal is completed and mutual access is provided for vessels from East European waterways.

Shipping

Few Community agreements had been reached on sea transport before 1986, despite the importance of this sector to the EC's trade. Around 95% of its external trade is carried by sea, which also plays an important part in intra-EU trade, in part because three member states do not have a common land frontier with the rest of the Union. It is strongly in the interests of the EU to keep the shipping industry open to international competition, but it was only in December 1986 that the Council of Ministers agreed most of the elements of a common shipping policy which should enable the EU to use its collective bargaining power in such a way as to strengthen its opportunities to compete on the world market. Four regulations were then approved, which came into effect in July 1987.

Competition.   This regulation set out precise directions as to how the EC's general rules of competition should be applied to the maritime transport sector. Transport had previously been excluded from a 1962 regulation which had defined competition rules for most other economic sectors.

Predatory pricing by third countries.   This provided for a co-ordinated response, allowing the EC to take anti-dumping measures against the countries or companies concerned. A complaints investigation procedure was instituted, and provision made for the imposition of provisional or definitive duties on the country's vessels.

Cargo reservations.   This regulation provided for a co-ordinated EC response to third countries which reserve a portion of their trade to their own vessels. Countermeasures which may now be applied include the imposition of permits for loading, carrying or discharging, the introduction of quotas or the imposition of taxes or duties.

Freedom to provide services.   Community vessels are now free to ply between member states and between member states and third countries. Member states are forbidden to enter agreements with third countries which would restrict access for the vessels of other member states.

A fifth regulation which would allow vessels from member states to compete for the coastal trade of other member states (cabotage), and would effectively have completed the common shipping policy, was, however, shelved. This opened up a division between the more northerly EC countries which are strongly in favour and certain southern states which would like to continue with their national restrictions. In particular, Spain was reluctant to allow other member states to compete for trade between mainland Spain and the Canary Islands, and Greece wished to remain in a position, in the event of Turkish accession to full membership of the EC, to exclude its ships from plying between the Greek islands. Agreement in principle on the liberalisation of cabotage was eventually reached in 1991, but it will be several years before full international competition becomes a reality.

In the wake of the tanker disasters at La Coruña and the Shetland Islands, the European Commission and the Council of Ministers mapped out, in 1993, an EU policy on safety at sea to underpin the work of individual member states, and to ensure more effective implementation of international regulations. The commission prepared directives or regulations to:

- lay down common rules for ship inspection;
- enforce a minimum level of training for crews;
- regulate the ballast requirements for oil tankers;
- set up a European vessel reporting system;
- regulate the carrying of dangerous or polluting goods.

Airways

Air transport was for many years the sector on which the Community had the least impact, and where its competition rules remained largely a dead letter. The entire system was controlled by a series of inter-governmental and inter-airline agreements which effectively excluded competition, and led to some of the highest air fares in the world, very substantially greater, in particular, than on routes of comparable distance in North America. Before 1986 EC action had been largely restricted to the adoption of directives on co-operation in accident inquiries, the reduction of noise from aircraft and helicopters and the opening of routes between certain regional centres in the Community.

In April 1986 a ruling from the Court of Justice gave the commission the green light to force the pace. In a case involving the French travel firm Nouvelles Frontières, which had challenged price-fixing regulations under the French Civil Aviation Code, the court ruled that the EC general competition rules were applicable to air transport and that member state governments have an obligation under the Rome treaty not to approve air fares if they know that they result from an agreement or concerted practices between airlines. In the absence of a specific regulation applying the competition rules to air transport, the competence for deciding whether an air fares agreement contravenes the treaty's competition rules rests with the commission (under Article 89) and the anti-trust authorities of the member states (Article 88). Subsequently the then competition commissioner, Peter Sutherland, threatened legal action against ten leading European airlines if they did not terminate or drastically amend their price-fixing agreements. After having stalled for several months, the ten airlines indicated in April 1987 that they were willing to comply. The introduction of competitive fares, however, still depended on the abrogation or amendment of bilateral agreements between the airlines and their own national governments, only a minority of which were prepared to contemplate such a radical departure.

Simultaneously with its legal initiative, the commission sought to secure a political compromise which would enable at least a partial liberalisation of fares to be implemented. After lengthy and tortuous negotiations such a compromise – involving discount fares, capacity sharing, the entry of new competitors on established routes, regional to hub airport connections, the right to pick up and put down passengers at intermediate points, and the conditions under which block exemptions to EC competition rules should be granted – was agreed in principle by the Council of Transport Ministers in June 1987. It was, however, immediately vetoed by Spain, on the ground that the inclusion in the agreement of Gibraltar as a UK regional airport compromised the Spanish claim to sovereignty over the Rock.

The Spanish veto was lifted in December 1987 following a bilateral deal with the UK over the use of Gibraltar airport. The compromise agreement came into force in January 1988. In 1991 the commission adopted a third liberalisation package designed to introduce full competition between European airlines after 1993. The principle that airlines should be allowed to set their own prices on international routes was agreed by the EC in March 1992, but there was a virtual impasse on timing with the UK and the Netherlands demanding free markets from the end of 1993 while France and the others held out for a six-year "transition period". A four-year compromise was finally agreed in June 1992.

The principal beneficiaries of the agreement will be the Union's fast-growing private airlines which have lower overheads and can charge lower prices than most state-owned organisations. The opponents of liberalisation, however, have won enough "safeguards" to keep new competitors out. In an attempt to prevent a fall in profitability such as hit US airlines following deregulation in the 1980s, EU governments will be able to object to the commission if an airline proposes to charge too little for tickets.

27

FISHERIES

A common fisheries policy was envisaged by Article 38 of the Rome treaty, on similar lines to the common agricultural policy. Yet no proposals for such a policy were produced before 1966, and it was another 17 years before the policy was finally put into place.

Initial fisheries policy causes problems

In 1970 an attempt was made by the six original member states to assert the principle of free access to Community fisheries, but the decisions taken then by the Council of Ministers were limited in scope. A common market organisation for fish was created, including price-support mechanisms and measures to protect the Community market. To modernise the sector and ensure equal terms of competition within it, the Community was given the task of co-ordinating the structural policies of the member states and of supplementing them with financial interventions of its own.

The timing of these decisions was unfortunate, as they occurred during the closing stages of the entry negotiations with Denmark, Ireland, Norway and the UK, all important fishing nations. It appeared that the original six members had determined to settle the issue to their own advantage before the new member states had a chance to exert their own influence. Consequently Norway turned down the entry terms its government had negotiated in a closely fought referendum. Many observers regarded the fisheries policy as a decisive factor which swung the vote against membership. Opinion was appeased in the other three applicant states by a last-minute agreement that all members could, until the end of 1982, restrict fishing within a six-mile coastal limit, and in certain areas a 12-mile limit, to vessels which traditionally fished in those waters.

Exclusive fishing zones extended

Well before the 1982 deadline was reached it became apparent that a much more comprehensive approach would be necessary if fishing resources in EC waters were to be conserved. From 1975 onwards a number of countries on the Atlantic coastline, including Iceland,

Norway and Canada, extended their exclusive fishing zones to 200 nautical miles. These limits were subsequently to be endorsed by the new international Convention on the Law of the Sea. The effect was to turn out of these waters many EC boats and also trawlers from third countries, many of which now concentrated their efforts on the North Sea, which was seriously threatened with overfishing. In 1977, in self-defence, the Community also extended its fishing limits to 200 miles, leaving itself in charge of a huge expanse of sea, in which competition between member states' fishermen was becoming intensified. Within these limits there was intense argument, particularly involving the UK, over the extent to which member states could claim permanent and exclusive rights in their coastal waters.

Common fisheries policy agreed

The European Commission tabled proposals as early as 1976, but it was only at the beginning of 1983, following hard fought negotiations in which Denmark, in particular, had found great difficulty in reaching agreement with its partners, that a common fisheries policy (CFP) was finally concluded. Its main provisions are as follows.

Fishing zones. In principle the Union's waters are open to all EU fishermen within a 200-mile limit from the Atlantic and North Sea coasts, but within narrower limits in the Mediterranean and Baltic seas. Member states are, however, allowed to retain limits up to 12 miles from their shores, within which fishing is reserved for their own fleets and for boats from other member states with traditional rights. In addition, fishing in an area beyond 12 miles around the Orkney and Shetland islands, for potentially endangered species, is subject to a system of Union licences. These measures will apply for 20 years, but may be reviewed after ten.

Fish stocks. These are conserved and managed by fixing total allowable catches (TACs) which are agreed annually by the Council of Ministers for all species threatened by overfishing. They are divided into quotas for each member state.

Conservation. Based on scientific advice, conservation measures consist mainly of limits on fishing in certain zones, minimum mesh sizes for nets and, in certain cases, minimum sizes for fish landed. With the agreement of the commission, member states may apply extra conservation measures of their own, but these must not discriminate against other member states.

Surveillance.   Measures such as obligatory logbooks, port inspections, aerial controls, and so on, are applied by the member states, under the supervision of the commission, which has a team of inspectors for this purpose.

Marketing.   Standards as regards quality, size, weight, presentation and packing are applied throughout the Union, largely through the agency of producer organisations, but subject to inspection by the commission. Guide prices are set by the Council of Ministers with "withdrawal" prices set at 70–90%, the Union compensating fishermen for catches withdrawn from the market. Export refunds are available when, as is usually the case, the guide and withdrawal prices are higher than world prices. If European supplies prove insufficient, customs duties on imports can be suspended, as has happened in recent years with tuna and cod.

International relations.   Reciprocal agreements, permitting limited access to each other's waters and markets have been made with several other countries, such as Norway, Sweden, the Faeroes, Canada and the USA. Other agreements with developing countries in Africa and the Indian Ocean permit EU vessels to fish in their waters in exchange for financial and technical assistance.

EU is world's fourth largest producer

The accession of Spain and Portugal in 1986 doubled the number of fishermen in the Community (now about 300,000), and increased the tonnage of the fishing fleet by about 65% and total catches by 30%. The EU is now the world's fourth largest producer. Spain and Portugal were required to adapt their fishing policies to the CFP, with mutual access being provided to several fishing zones, the number of which was to be reviewed by 1995. During the negotiations for Norwegian membership of the EU in March 1994, it was however agreed that Spain and Portugal should have full access to EU waters as from January 1st 1995.

At the same time the Community stepped up its financial aid for restructuring the fishing fleets – with grants available for the scrapping of surplus capacity, the construction and modernisation of boats, the development of aquaculture and improvements in processing and marketing. The CFP is based to a large extent on the model of the CAP, but it is far less expensive. The total cost for 1994 was around 445m ecus, or about 0.6% of the entire budget.

28

ENVIRONMENT

There was no legal provision in the Rome treaty for a common EC policy on the environment, other than the general authority given by Article 235 enabling the Council of Ministers, acting unanimously, to take appropriate measures to achieve any of the objectives of the Community. This evident gap – which reflects the relative lack of interest in environmental matters in the 1950s – was remedied by the Single European Act, which in Article 25 set out a threefold aim for Community action on the environment:

- to preserve, protect and improve the quality of the environment;
- to contribute towards protecting human health;
- to ensure a prudent and rational utilisation of natural resources.

Programmes adopted from 1973

It is not surprising that, in the absence of any earlier definition of EC competence in this area, the Community's environment policy evolved in an ad hoc and incremental manner. It was not until 1985, for example, that the Council of Ministers drew up a work programme for obtaining information on the state of the environment and natural resources in the Community. Nevertheless, from 1973 onwards the council adopted a series of five-year action programmes which gradually broadened out from immediate responses to serious pollution problems to an overall preventive strategy for safeguarding the environment and natural resources. The main areas in which EU measures have so far been adopted include the following.

Water pollution. A number of directives have been approved dealing with the protection of water, surface and underground, fresh and salt. Quality standards have been set for bathing water, drinking water, fresh water suitable for fish life and water used for rearing shellfish. The discharge of toxic substances is strictly controlled, with limits set for mercury, cadmium, lindane, DDT, pentachlorophenol and carbon tetrachloride, and specific rules for the control and gradual reduction of dumping of titanium dioxide, which causes "red sludge". The Union is a participant in several conventions designed to reduce pollution in international waterways such as the River Rhine, the North Atlantic, the North Sea and the Mediterranean.

Atmospheric pollution. Despite the adoption of a series of directives on such topics as the discharge of sulphur dioxide, the use of chlorofluorcarbons (CFCs) in aerosol cans and the control of pollution from certain industrial premises, progress has been slow in what are widely regarded as the two key areas: pollution from large combustion plants, particularly power stations, and the emission of gases from motor vehicles. Both of these are blamed for widespread damage to forests through acid rain and for a variety of threats to public health. In March 1985 the council reached agreement concerning the lead content of petrol (which provided that unleaded petrol would be generally available in the Community from October 1st 1989), but it was only in July 1987, that – under the majority voting provisions of the Single European Act – a series of regulations on automobile exhaust emission was adopted. A substantial work programme has been initiated by the European Commission to study the greenhouse effect and to find ways to limit the heating-up of the atmosphere. Specific measures are also envisaged to reduce pollution by such substances as photochemical oxidants.

Noise. Directives have been adopted fixing maximum noise levels for cars, lorries, motorcycles, tractors, subsonic aircraft, lawnmowers and building-site machinery. The noise level of household equipment must be stipulated on its packaging, and proposals are under consideration concerning helicopters and rail vehicles.

Chemical products. Particularly since the Seveso accident in northern Italy in 1977, which resulted in the contamination of a large area by a highly toxic dioxin, increasingly stringent measures have been taken to reduce the risks arising from the manufacture and disposal of chemical substances. As long ago as 1967 a directive was adopted relating to the classification, packaging and labelling of dangerous substances. Two 1973 directives control the composition of detergents, while since 1986 there has been a European Inventory of Existing Chemical Substances, which lists all chemical products on the market, enabling them to be subject to a general procedure for notification, evaluation and control. Other measures ban the use of certain substances in pesticides, and strictly control the manufacture and use of PCBs and PCTs (the substances involved in the Seveso accident), and of asbestos. In an attempt to prevent further major accidents and to limit their consequences, a directive of June 1982 imposes on manufacturers in all member states the obligation to inform the authorities about substances, plants and possible locations of accidents.

Following the Bhopal tragedy in India there has been strong pressure, particularly in the European Parliament, for a further tightening up of control measures. Concern about the depletion of the ozone layer, which protects the earth from ultraviolet rays, led the Community to adopt a series of measures to bring about a substantial reduction of CFCs and other substances thought to be responsible for this phenomenon.

Waste disposal.   Since 1975 Community rules have been in force concerning the collection, disposal, recycling and processing of waste, of which the EU produces more than 2 billion tons every year. Specific measures have also been taken in individual areas, such as waste from the titanium oxide industry, waste oils, the dumping of waste at sea and radioactive waste. Recommendations have been made on the reuse of old paper, cardboard and drinks containers.

Nature protection.   The EU is a member of the 1979 Berne Convention on the conservation of wildlife, and has also recommended member states to adhere to the 1950 Paris Convention on the protection of birds and the 1971 Ramsar Convention on Wetlands. The Council of Ministers has adopted several directives on the conservation of wild birds, on banning the importation of products made from the skins of baby seals (following a mass campaign in which the European Parliament played a crucial role) and on the control and restriction of scientific experiments on animals. Financial support is given to projects to conserve natural habitats, and further proposals were planned under the fourth action programme (1988–92) to protect fauna and flora.

Broadening the scope of environmental policy

By the early 1990s there was a widespread feeling that the EC should adopt a much more determined and systematic approach to environmental management. The June 1990 summit in Dublin called for action by the Community and its member states to be developed on a co-ordinated basis, in keeping with the principles of sustainable development and giving priority to preventive measures. The creation of a European Environmental Agency was agreed, but its establishment was delayed by failure among the member states to agree on where it should be sited.

1991 saw a considerable broadening of the scope of EC environmental policy, which became inextricably linked to overall economic policy-making. Commission initiatives were seen to be necessary to bring about the integration of environmental considerations into other policy areas including agriculture, the internal market, transport and energy. Linked very closely to energy policy issues and in response to the urgent problem of global warming, the commission proposed a package of measures to limit carbon dioxide emissions and to improve energy efficiency and security of supply. It proposed a carbon dioxide/energy tax as a means of attaining the target of stabilising emissions at 1990 levels by 2000. The council approved the commission proposals in principle, but it is far from certain that the energy tax proposal will go ahead. European industrialists believe that they will lose price competitiveness against their main rivals in Japan and the USA unless a comparable tax is also levied in these two countries. This issue was discussed at the UN Earth Summit in Rio de Janiero in June 1992, where the EC took a leading role in proposing a worldwide approach to the reduction of carbon dioxide emissions.

Also in 1991 the Council of Ministers adopted the LIFE programme, designed to provide financial incentives for priority projects in the environmental field. It also adopted measures on:

- the EC Norspa project (to protect the environment in the coastal areas and waters of the Irish Sea, North Sea, Baltic Sea and north east Atlantic Ocean);
- waste water;
- a Community eco-label;
- the protection of natural habitats;
- pollution by lorries.

Finally, the Treaty on European Union agreed at the Maastricht summit in December 1991 incorporated a new section on the environment in the Rome treaty, substantially extending EU competence, although a number of issues were reserved for unanimous decision in the Council of Ministers rather than by qualified majority voting as the commission would have preferred.

29

CONSUMERS

Cinderella of the EU

To some extent consumer policy has been the Cinderella of the EU. It was not mentioned in the Rome treaty, and it took years of campaigning by consumer organisations, often backed by pressure from the European Parliament, before practical steps were taken to ensure that consumer issues were considered on a serious continuing basis. The turning point came at the EC summit meeting in Paris in 1972, when the heads of government decided that economic development must be accompanied by an improvement in the quality of life. This meant that the Community should pursue an active consumer policy. Three important steps followed over the next few years.

- The creation of a service, and then a directorate-general, for the environment and consumer protection, within the commission.
- The creation of a Consumers' Consultative Committee (CCC).
- The adoption by the Council of Ministers, in April 1975, of a first consumer information and protection programme. Five basic consumer rights were enunciated: the right to safeguards for health and safety; the right to economic justice; the right to redress for damages; the right to information and education; and the right to consultation. These rights were to be implemented by concrete measures and also taken into account in other Community policies, such as agriculture, the economy, social affairs and the environment.

Consumers' Consultative Council

The CCC (renamed Consumers' Consultative Council in 1989) is appointed and serviced by the commission. It consists of 39 members, including representatives from each of four major European consumer organisations:

- the European Consumer Bureau (BEUC);
- the Committee of European Community Family Organisations (Coface);

- the European Community Consumer Co-operatives (Euroco-op);
- the European Confederation of Trade Unions (ETUC).

The commission gives annual grants to each of these bodies and tries to bring them into closer contact with equivalent European organisations representing manufacturers, distributors and advertising agencies. The CCC is consulted from the outset on any commission work in areas which touch on consumer interests, and may also give opinions on its own initiative.

Extending consumer choice

An important judgment by the Court of Justice in 1979 had a major significance in extending consumer choice. This was in the "Cassis de Dijon" case, and it reaffirmed in principle that all goods legally manufactured in a member country must be allowed into others. The judgment found that national technical regulations, even if applied equally to domestic and imported goods, must not be allowed to create a barrier to trade except for overriding reasons such as the protection of public health or consumer interests.

It was not until 1983 that EC ministers responsible for consumer affairs met for the first time. They are now established participants in the Council of Ministers, meeting several times each year and addressing themselves to a steady stream of proposals put up by the commission. Decisions taken so far in the consumer field can be divided into three broad categories:

- the health and safety of consumers;
- protecting consumers' economic interests;
- consumer information and education.

Health and safety

It is in this category that most progress has been made. Measures adopted have covered the following areas.

Foodstuffs.   European lists of permitted substances and purity standards have been established for foodstuff additives, such as colourings, anti-oxidants, preservatives, emulsifiers, stabilisers and gelifiers. Pesticide residues in fruit and vegetables and erucic acid in oils and fats for human consumption have been limited to maximum levels. Regulations also govern the production of honey, fruit juice, tinned milk, cocoa and chocolate, coffee and chicory extracts, mineral waters, jams and marmalades and chestnut purée, and specialist foodstuffs such as products for special diets. Directives are in force relating to the labelling of foodstuffs, specifying ingredients, quantity and the date by which they should be consumed. A ban has been imposed on the use of animal growth promoters which contain certain substances with hormonal or thyrostatic effects.

Dangerous substances. Directives control the classification, marketing and labelling as well as the use of many toxic substances such as pesticides, solvents, paints, varnishes, printers' ink, glues and asbestos.

Pharmaceuticals. The testing, patenting, labelling and marketing of pharmaceutical products are all controlled by EU directives.

Other products. EU directives regulate, for safety reasons, such products as cosmetics, textiles (where the main concern is to prevent the use of inflammable material), toys and a number of other manufactured products. Several hundred directives have been approved for the purpose of standardising tools, component parts and finished products in manufacturing industry, with a view to increasing the efficiency and competitiveness of European firms, but since 1985 a new approach to standardisation has been adopted. Since then new directives have concentrated only on laying down safety specifications and have relied on the mutual recognition of national standards where no European standards exist. The commission does, however, give financial support to the two bodies responsible for setting European standards, CEN and Cenelec, and has given them remits to draft European standards concerning, in particular, toys, pressure vessels, gas appliances and information technology.

Warning system. In March 1984 the Council of Ministers established a Community system for the rapid exchange of information on dangerous products. This warning system allows the authorities of one member state rapidly to draw the attention of all the others to serious incidents and allow action to be taken to protect the health and safety of consumers. A pilot project is also in operation monitoring accidents caused by consumer goods in order to reduce or prevent accidents of this type which cause more injuries than either road or work accidents.

Protection of consumers' economic interests
Action to protect the economic interests of consumers has been slower because of difficulty in achieving agreement within the

Council of Ministers on proposals put forward by the commission. A number of directives have, however, been adopted in recent years on the following.

Misleading advertising.   Consumers can complain to the courts, which are empowered to require advertisers to prove the accuracy of their claims.

Consumer credit.   All credit agreements are to be made in writing, be easily understandable and clearly indicate the real interest rate charged.

Door-to-door sales.   This directive is designed to protect consumers against hard selling techniques, and allow them time to have second thoughts.

Airlines.   A regulation which came into force in April 1991 requires airlines to pay financial compensation to passengers who are delayed through being "overbooked" on commercial flights.

Product liability.   Potentially the most important EC decision affecting consumers was the adoption in August 1985 of a directive on product liability, which came into force in 1988. It imposed a strict liability on producers for damage caused by defects in their products, and it was adopted only after several years of campaigning on behalf of the victims of unforeseen side-effects of pharmaceutical products. Under the directive member states may impose a limit to the liability, but this must be at least 70m ecus.

Consumer information and education
In addition to the directives controlling the labelling of foodstuffs and dangerous substances, others require electrical household equipment to be marked with its estimated energy consumption and food to be marked with unit prices (by the kilogram or litre). Measures are also proposed to extend price marking to goods other than food. A three-year action plan, adopted in 1990, comprised 22 further measures in four main areas:

* consumer representation;
* health and safety of consumers;
* commercial transactions involving consumers;
* consumer information and education.

A second three-year plan, launched in 1993, focuses on two important areas:

- consolidation of EU legislation, with the adoption of directives on cosmetic productions and on unfair terms of trade;
- selective priorities designed to raise the level of consumer protection and to make consumers more aware of their rights, notably by encouraging access to justice, by creating a European guarantee and after-sales service scheme, and by adopting trans-frontier financial services.

The plan also aims at better integration of consumer policy within other EU polices.

The commission is active in promoting a wider awareness of the results of comparative tests on consumer goods, better co-operation between the testing organisations and more information for consumers on the action taken on their behalf. It sponsors frequent conferences on consumer issues, supports experiments on consumer education in schools and gives subsidies to national consumer groups to support local consumer information programmes.

30

EDUCATION

Education has always been regarded as an area where national traditions and methods – which are extremely varied – should be respected and, indeed, fostered. Any attempt to standardise teaching, structures, methods or syllabi, it is accepted, would be misplaced. There was little reference to education in the Rome treaty, except for the need for mutual recognition of diplomas (Article 57) and vocational training (Articles 41 and 118).

Six-point programme adopted in 1976

Since 1974, however, there has been increasing recognition of the need for closer co-operation between the member states in educational matters. Accordingly, in February 1976 the Council of Ministers adopted a six-point Community programme which covered the following.

1 Improved cultural and vocational training for migrant workers and their children.
2 Better mutual understanding of the different European educational systems.
3 The collection of basic documentary information and statistics.
4 Co-operation in higher education.
5 The improvement of foreign-language teaching.
6 The equality of opportunity of access to all forms of education throughout the Community.

Since then the programme has been extended to include measures to improve the vocational training of young people and to ease the transition from school to workplace, while from 1980 onwards there has been increasing concern about youth unemployment resulting, for example, in the decision in 1983 to earmark 75% of the Social Fund for measures aimed at improving job opportunities for young people under 25 (see pages 143–145).

Policy mostly takes form of recommendations

With a few notable exceptions EC policy has taken the form of recommendations to member states rather than of legislation requiring action by them. The main exception has concerned efforts to ease freedom of movement in jobs and professions with training and other requirements, where a long series of directives has ensured that by the beginning of 1993 a comprehensive formula existed for the mutual recognition of educational diplomas and the right to practice any trade or profession in all member states. Another directive, adopted in 1977, concerned the schooling of the children of migrant workers within the Community. It required member states to set up reception classes, specialised training for teachers and education in the language and culture of their country of origin.

More typical, however, was the Community's approach to promoting a wider knowledge of EC languages. In June 1984 ministers from the member states committed themselves to a programme that aimed at encouraging a working knowledge of two languages apart from the mother tongue before the statutory leaving age. There is no guarantee, however, that all member states will make an equivalent effort to achieve this clearly desirable objective. Similar agreements have been reached to promote:

- student and teacher mobility;
- education in European current affairs;
- the transition from school to working life;
- education for the handicapped;
- literacy campaigns; and
- new information technologies.

Eight important projects

Direct action by the Community itself has been limited, but there has been a marked increase in activity over recent years. Eight projects, in particular, are worthy of mention.

Eurydice.   This information service network has been in operation since 1980, with access to educational administrators in all member states, and to a wider public since 1982. It consists of a computer-based databank, containing a mass of information about educational developments throughout the EU.

Erasmus (European Community Action Scheme for the Mobility of University Students).   A project first proposed by the European Commission in 1985 which foresaw that by 1992 some 10% of the student population (that is 150,000 students) should spend an integrated period of study in another EC country. A slimmed-down version was eventually approved by the Council of

Ministers in 1987, which meant that fewer than 45,000 students benefited during the first three years. In 1990 the budget was more than doubled, and the programme is now steadily building up. A parallel programme called Science encourages the mobility of research workers. In 1990 a trans-European mobility scheme for university students called **Tempus** was established to extend the benefits of the Erasmus programme to students from the new democracies of central and Eastern Europe. **Tempus II** will provide support for the restructuring of the higher education systems of these countries, and will allow states from the former Soviet Union to participate. It will run from 1994 to 1998.

Comett.   A programme, since 1990 also open to EFTA countries, to stimulate and strengthen co-operation between universities (including all post-secondary training establishments) and industry.

Lingua.   Started in 1990, Lingua contributes to the financing of scholarships, exchanges and teaching materials in order to promote the training of teachers in foreign languages as well as the learning of languages in higher education, vocational training and industry.

Eurotechnet.   This programme encourages the exchange and dissemination of experiences, the creation of European networks of demonstration projects and co-ordination of research on vocational training for new technologies.

European University Institute.   This post-graduate institution, set up in Florence in 1976, offers courses in history and civilisation, economics, law and political and social sciences.

European Centre for the Development of Vocational Training.   Established in Berlin in 1975, the purpose of this centre is to foster the development of vocational training and in-service training of adults at Community level.

The European Schools.   Nine schools offer an international syllabus, in which part of the teaching is in a language other than the pupil's native tongue, leading to a European baccalauréat which provides admission to universities throughout the EU. Mainly intended for the children of people working in EU institutions, the schools are open to other pupils. The schools are in Luxembourg, Brussels (2) and Mol in Belgium, Varese in Italy, Karlsruhe and Munich in Germany and Culham in the UK.

31

WOMEN'S RIGHTS

The position of women within the Union has substantially improved in the nearly 40 years since the EEC was first established, although they are still some way from removing all the disadvantages from which they suffer, and from achieving full equality with men. By the end of 1991, of the EC's estimated total working population of 146m, some 58m were women (73% of these were in services, 20% in industry and 7% in agriculture). Over the preceding 20 years the proportion of women in the workforce had steadily risen, from under 35% to 40%, but women were still heavily concentrated in certain sectors and job categories that were often vulnerable, less highly qualified, lower paid and with fewer promotion prospects. Above all, women predominated in part-time employment (82%, although this had come down from 90% six years earlier), and there is a higher proportion of women among those unemployed than among the working population as a whole.

EU has helped improve women's status

There can be little doubt that the Union itself has been instrumental in improving the status of women. Article 119 of the Rome treaty stipulates that "each member state shall ... ensure and subsequently maintain the application of the principle that men and women should receive equal pay for equal work". It goes on to spell out the principle in some detail, stipulating that "pay" means "the ordinary basic or minimum wage or salary and any other consideration, whether in cash or in kind, which the worker receives, directly or indirectly, in respect of his employment from his employer".

The article goes on to state that: "Equal pay without discrimination based on sex means:

- that pay for the same work at piece rates shall be calculated on the basis of the same unit of measurement;
- that pay for work at time rates shall be the same for the same job."

Despite the seeming lack of ambiguity in these provisions, it was necessary for the Council of Ministers to adopt several further measures before all the member states took adequate action to ensure their implementation. Five directives in particular have been adopted.

Main directives concerning women's rights

February 1975.   Member states are obliged to revise their laws so as to exclude all discrimination on grounds of sex; particularly in systems of occupational classification. Under this directive, all workers believing themselves to be victims of discrimination must have the right and the possibility to take their case to a tribunal, and be protected against any wrongful dismissal if they do so.

February 1976.   Member states are obliged to ensure equal treatment in regard to working conditions and access to employment, training and promotion. Here, too, provision was made for individuals to have recourse to justice without putting their jobs at risk. Any person believing themselves to be wronged can lodge a complaint with a national tribunal or other competent body. In the event of a dispute over the interpretation of Community law the European Court of Justice will decide the question. In one important case brought by a Belgian air stewardess, the court ruled that women employees could not be compulsorily retired at a lower age than men.

December 1978.   Any discrimination in statutory social security schemes covering risks of illness, disability, old age, accidents at work, occupational illness, unemployment and family allowances is rendered illegal.

July 1986.   Discrimination in occupational pension schemes to be eliminated by 1993.

End 1986.   Direct or indirect discrimination against independent women workers (including agricultural workers) was to be eliminated by the end of 1989 (or 1991 in some cases). The directive also included further provisions regarding maternity and social security.

Series of action programmes put forward

In addition to these directives, the European Commission has put forward a series of action programmes to the Council of Ministers, which have been adopted in the form of recommendations (that is they are not mandatory on the member states). The third of these, covering the years 1991–95, has three priority areas:

- the application and development of the legal framework;
- the promotion of occupational integration of women;
- the improvement of women's status in society.

The programme also provides for specific measures for certain categories of people who come up against particular problems: women who are alone or who have charge of single-parent families, immigrant women, handicapped women, women working in the home, and so on.

NOW project

As part of its programme under the European Social Fund, the commission is funding a project known as NOW, for promoting equal opportunity in the field of employment and vocational training. It also tabled two directives to improve the position of pregnant women at work. The first of these, adopted in September 1990, laid down minimum health and safety standards, while the second (which was expected to be adopted in 1992 – see page 147) guarantees 14 weeks' maternity leave and protects pregnant women against dismissal or the loss of promotion rights.

Educational initiatives to encourage equal opportunities

In the belief that the roots of sexual discrimination may lie in the educational system, the commission has launched several initiatives to encourage sexual equality by removing elements which tend to stereotype the sexes from an early age and to cut off girls from career choices more readily open to boys. In June 1985 the EC's education ministers approved an equal opportunity programme, concerned mainly with:

- training those in charge of education and increasing their awareness;
- getting a better mix of men and women in teaching jobs;
- improving career guidance;
- eliminating stereotypes from educational material.

In vocational training, the European Centre for the Development of Vocational Training (Cedefop) is increasing its research and promotional activity, much of which focuses specifically on problems facing women; for example, those seeking to return to work after a long period. National governments are encouraged to make use of possibilities offered by the European Social Fund, which co-finances numerous programmes for training, re-employment and first-time employment that are open without discrimination to men and women. It also helps to finance specific training programmes for women, particularly for non-traditional occupations.

Specialist services

The commission maintains two specialist services which enable it to monitor the development of women's issues on a continuing basis and to produce a steady stream of policy proposals.

The Women's Employment and Equality Office. Responsible for drawing up and implementing Union policy, and for seeing that equality problems are taken into account in devising and implementing programmes in other policy areas.

The Women's Information Service. Maintains constant contact with women's groups, associations and movements and informs them about Union activities.

A dearth of women commissioners

Given the apparent devotion of the EU to sexual equality, it is surprising that no women members at all were appointed to the European Commission until 30 years after its creation. The second Delors Commission, which took over in January 1989, did have two women members – Vasso Papandreou and Christiane Scrivener – as well as 15 men. The two-year commission appointed for 1993–94, however, included only one woman – Mrs Scrivener – and 16 male members. Cynics might conclude from this disproportion that the commitment of the member governments, which appoint the commissioners, is no more than skin deep.

32

CULTURE AND THE MEDIA

The work of the EU in the cultural sphere was for many years minimal, partly because of a desire to avoid duplicating the activities of the Council of Europe,[1] which has always seen the protection and development of the European cultural heritage as one of its principal functions. The development of new technologies, which are revolutionising the television and film industries and making a mockery of purely national boundaries, has caused a reassessment to be made, as very substantial economic and social interests are involved which largely transcend the limited and purely voluntary framework of the Council of Europe. The commission has concluded that it must henceforward play the pivotal role in marshalling a European response to the commercial and cultural challenge in this sphere, which is spearheaded by US and Japanese interests.

Areas of concentration

The EU's budget for cultural affairs is small (about 13m ecus in 1993, apart from assistance for the development of advanced television services). Since 1973 a small unit within the commission has been responsible for producing proposals and for implementing those which the Council of Ministers approve. There are four main areas:

- free trade in cultural goods;
- the improvement of conditions for artists;
- widening the audience for culture; and
- the conservation of the Community's architectural heritage.

Support and training for artistic workers

Apart from films and television programmes, the EU has been mainly concerned with removing barriers to artistic workers exporting their talents and output from one EU country to another. The temporary tax-free export of the tools of an artist's trade (musical instruments, cameras, and so on) has been facilitated, and the commission is drawing up proposals to ensure the free export of works of art, except for strictly defined "national art treasures" which would be exempted. It is also seeking to establish a European information centre to keep a record of stolen works of art, making it more difficult for thieves to dispose of stolen items.

Research sponsored by the commission has revealed that a large number of cultural workers are unemployed, and that many others earn less than they need to live. They are forced to take a second job or abandon their art. It has proposed a number of measures to strengthen their economic position. These include:

- the harmonisation of national laws governing copyright to creative artists and performers;
- a share in public subsidies for playwrights and composers;
- "resale rights" to artists guaranteeing them a percentage of the proceeds every time their works are sold;
- the payment of royalties on works in the public domain to funds which could be used for welfare payments to artists or for arts sponsorship.

Specific social security and tax improvements have also been proposed, but member states have been reluctant to agree to directives in this field, and so far the Council of Ministers has confined itself to making recommendations to member states.

The commission has used the limited funds at its disposal to support a number of schemes for training young artists, including assistance for young musicians in Siena and Dublin, violin makers in Cremona, composers at the University of Surrey and dancers in Brussels. Grants are available to retrain ballet dancers as instructors, while EU support has been available for both classical and jazz youth orchestras and the Wiltz Festival in Luxembourg, which involves actors, singers, musicians and dancers from five member states. Some assistance has also been given for the training of cultural workers and local cultural employment by the ERDF.

Efforts to widen the cultural audience

In recognition of its responsibilities towards a wider Europe, European Cultural Months were held in Cracow (Poland) in 1992 and Graz (Austria) in 1993. The next city chosen is Nicosia (Cyprus) in 1995. The commission also acted as a sponsor of the Quincentenary exhibition held in Seville in 1992. Other efforts include:

- financial support since 1982 for the translation of great works of contemporary literature, mainly from the lesser spoken languages such as Danish, Dutch and Greek;
- sponsorship of the European Theatre in Milan and Paris;

- a European Film Festival held each year in a different city;
- a variety of events held in the city that the commission designates each year as European culture city (Athens 1985, Florence 1986, Amsterdam 1987, Berlin 1988, Paris 1989, Glasgow 1990, Dublin 1991, Madrid 1992, Antwerp 1993, Lisbon 1994, Luxembourg 1995, Copenhagen 1996, Thessaloniki 1997, Stockholm 1998, Weimar 1999).

Conservation of monuments and buildings

Largely as a result of pressure from the European Parliament, funds have been made available, in the form of interest-rate subsidies and capital grants as well as loans through the EIB, for conservation work on monuments of EU-wide importance or buildings in underdeveloped regions whose restoration would bring economic benefits, especially through tourism. The first beneficiaries, in 1982–83, were the Milos Museum in Greece, the Doges' Palace in Venice and the Parthenon in Athens. Twelve more projects were approved in 1984, and a further 13 in 1986. These 13 give a clear indication of the broadening scope of the Community's support in this field, and its extension to important sites in all 12 member states.

- The remains of Greek ramparts behind the Marseille Bourse.
- The Forum in Rome.
- Charlemagne's palace chapel in Aachen cathedral.
- The abbey of Santa Maria do Bouro at Amares (Portugal).
- The Church of St Nicholas at Edam (Netherlands).
- The Stavronika monastery on Mount Athos (Greece).
- The naval arsenal at Rochefort (France).
- The House of the Dukes of Brabant in Grand Place, Brussels.
- The Georgian Castletown House at Celbridge (Ireland).
- The Temple of Piety at Studley Royal Gardens near Ripon.
- The Danish Museum of Decorative Arts at Copenhagen.
- The archaeological and industrial site at Differdange (Luxembourg).
- The Alhambra at Granada.

A number of other sites have subsequently been added to this list. In 1994 four were being directly assisted from the EU's budget: the Acropolis, Mount Athos, Lisbon and Coimbra.

Books and reading

In 1989 the Council of Ministers approved a programme of support for books and reading, which included eight priority measures.

- A guide for authors and translators.
- A programme for the publication of statistics in the book sector.
- A European literary prize.
- A prize for the best translations of literary works.
- Scholarships for literary translators.
- The conservation of books made from acid paper and use of "permanent paper".
- A study of export aid measures for books.
- A campaign for raising awareness of books and reading.

Films and television

The commission's initiatives regarding films and television were prompted chiefly by the prospects offered by the development of direct broadcasting by satellite and the extension of cable networks. In November 1986 the Council of Ministers approved a commission proposal that the member states should adopt the MAC-packet "family" of standards developed by European industry and the European Broadcasting Union. They are compatible with each other and allow better sound and vision reproduction, the simultaneous use of one visual channel and several sound channels (multilingual programmes), and gradual evolution towards high-definition television (HDTV). The adoption of the commission's proposals would, it was hoped, prevent repetition of the PAL and SECAM television receiver fiasco which left EC countries with two incompatible systems.

In 1991 agreement was reached between the commission and all sides of the audio-visual industry (cable and satellite operators, broadcasters, equipment manufacturers and producers) on a five-year programme which should have led to all new television services and any new satellite transmissions using the MAC standard of HDTV. All large television sets produced after 1992 should have been able to receive MAC transmissions, and the commission pledged to spend 100m ecus a year over five years to assist the simultaneous transmission of PAL and SECAM programmes on MAC, and to support the start-up of new MAC broadcasts.

Yet renewed hesitancy by manufacturers, and the development by Japanese and US researchers of new digital systems which threatened to supersede the MAC system, led member states to have second thoughts, and in 1993 the policy was dropped. In its place the Council of Ministers agreed an action plan for the introduction of advanced television services in Europe with a budget of 228m ecus over four years, at least half of which will be spent on programme production. The financial support is intended to compensate for extra costs incurred by the introduction of a new 16:9 format for television, both for new shoots and for reformatting old material. The plan also set standards for digital and non-digital transmissions.

In 1989 a directive entitled "Television without Frontiers" was adopted, which came into force in October 1991. This directive, which is mandatory on member states, made it illegal for them to impede the transmission of programmes from other EC countries provided they conform with the requirements of the directive. The directive covers:

- advertising breaks;
- the duration of advertising;
- ethical questions;
- sponsorship;
- protection of minors;
- the right of reply;
- the production and distribution of European audiovisual works.

The directive, which has been denounced as discriminatory by the US government, also calls on member states to try to ensure that at least 50% of air time is devoted to programmes originating within the EC and that at least 10% of their programming budgets is devoted to European works from independent producers.

The commission also produced an action programme entitled Media (1991–95) to support the European film industry, in relation to both production and distribution. It designated 1988 as European Cinema and Television Year in the hope of stimulating supportive action by the member states, but the results were disappointing.

---

1 The Council of Europe, founded in 1949, brings together 32 European countries (the 12 EC and the six EFTA countries, plus Bulgaria, the Czech Republic, Cyprus, Estonia, Hungary, Liechtenstein, Lithuania, Malta, Poland, Romania, San Marino, Slovakia, Slovenia and Turkey. The Holy See is an observer, while Albania, Belarus, Bosnia-Herzegovina, Croatia, Latvia, F.Y.R. of Macedonia, Moldova, Russia and Ukraine currently have special guest status). Its purpose is to achieve greater unity between its members to safeguard and realise the ideals and principles which are their common heritage and facilitate their economic and social progress. It has produced some 140 conventions and agreements, many in the cultural field, but these are not binding on the member states. Its most significant contribution is in the human rights field, through the work of the European Commission of Human Rights and the European Court of Human Rights, both of which work under its aegis.

33

CITIZENS' RIGHTS AND SYMBOLISM

The European Union continues to be rather a remote concept to most people. In so far as they think about it at all, it is regarded as a matter for governments, specialist committees and for experts. Although there is a fairly general appreciation (which is stronger in the original six member states than in the others) of the economic benefits which the Union has brought, there is little feeling that the EU affects citizens in their everyday life.

Committee for a People's Europe formed

It was in order to help create such a feeling, and to foster sentiments of loyalty and solidarity among the mass of the population in the member states, that the EC heads of government, at the Fontainebleau summit in June 1984, decided on the appointment of a Committee for a People's Europe, which would suggest ways of strengthening the identity and improving the image of the Community. The committee, which consisted of personal representatives of each of the heads of government and of the president of the European Commission, was chaired by an Italian, Pietro Adonnino. It produced two reports, which were approved in principle by further summit meetings in March and June 1985. These contained a series of proposals for actions, some of a largely symbolic character, for protecting and extending the rights of EC citizens. Some of the proposals were new, others were designed to give fresh impetus to ideas which had been languishing, sometimes for many years, in the maw of the Community's decision-making process.

Adonnino reports ...

The first Adonnino report proposed a number of immediate steps on the following:

- the simplification of border formalities;
- duty-free allowances;
- tax exemptions for books and magazines;
- taxation of frontier workers;
- a general system for the recognition of diplomas;

- the equivalence of diplomas;
- the right of abode.

The second and final report put forward both specific proposals and longer-term objectives which would make the Community more real in the eyes of its citizens. These proposals cover special rights for citizens, culture, information, youth, education, exchanges and sport, voluntary work to assist developing countries, health, social security, drugs and twinning schemes. It constituted more of a miscellaneous shopping list of desirable measures than a coherent plan of action.

... call for special citizens' rights

The special citizens' rights which the Adonnino committee called for included the following.

The right to participate in Euro-elections under equal conditions. Electoral procedures should be made uniform, as the European Parliament has requested, and as is required under Article 138 of the Rome treaty. Where Community citizens are travelling or living abroad at the time of the poll, they should have the right to vote in their home country or country of residence.

The right of self-expression and assembly. This should be granted to Community citizens on the same terms as nationals of the host state.

Permanent residents in another member state. Numbering about 5m, these people should have the right, after a period of time, to vote and stand in local elections. They should also have the right to be consulted on issues which affect them, such as housing or foreign language teaching.

Border region residents. Taken in the widest sense, 48m people should have the right to be consulted when the neighbouring country is contemplating developments which could affect them such as major public works, reorganisation of transport or measures affecting ecology, safety or health.

The right of all Community citizens to enjoy full benefits of Community policies. In cases where these conflict with national regulations, the citizen can seek redress in the courts. Things would be easier for ordinary people, however, and their legal rights would be underpinned, if member states ensured the total, straightforward and rapid implementation of Community law. It would also help if this law was itself codified and simplified. In all cases superfluous legal provisions should be abolished.

The right to better access to the administration.   First, the citizen's right of petition should be strengthened and simplified, as the European Parliament has demanded. A European ombudsman or mediator, or, as the Parliament had requested, a mediating commission, would examine citizens' complaints and could help them to obtain redress.

The right to adequate information on efforts to develop the EC.   The Community institutions and member states should cooperate more closely in informing their citizens of the historic reasons for the creation of the Community and the importance of current efforts to develop it further. The same applies to explaining the implications of EC policies and their impact on people's everyday life.

European passport holders.   The holders of EC passports (see below) should have the right to benefit from the assistance of the embassy or consulate of another member state when visiting a foreign country where their own country is not represented.

During 1986 and 1987 the commission tabled legislative proposals to meet most of the points listed in the two Adonnino reports, and the major part of the People's Europe programme was implemented by the target date of 1992 which the Community set for the completion of the internal market.

Areas of particular difficulty

Frontier controls.   Fears about drug peddlers, terrorism and illegal immigrants have made some member states, particularly the UK, reluctant to ease or abolish controls at internal EC frontiers. This led five countries – France, Germany and the three Benelux states – to sign the Schengen Agreement (see page 95) to eliminate their own frontier controls before the 1992 deadline and to align their immigration and visa requirements for citizens of non-EC countries. Italy, Spain, Greece and Portugal subsequently adhered to this agreement.

Euro-election procedures. The demand for a uniform procedure for elections to the European Parliament will not be met unless there is a change of attitude by the UK government, which has firmly resisted all attempts to adapt its first-past-the-post electoral system to conform to the requirements of proportional representation, as practised by the other 11 states. The Labour Party, which had hitherto been as reluctant as the Conservatives to contemplate a change, is now officially reconsidering its position, and the Liberal Democrats, who are strongly committed to PR, will certainly use whatever influence they have to press for its introduction. The Conservative leadership is probably less resolutely opposed than it was under Mrs Thatcher, but it still seems improbable that a common electoral system will be adopted while the UK Tories remain in power.

EU citizenship

Despite the progress made in implementing the Adonnino proposals, the Spanish government argued that a specific treaty commitment should be made establishing the right of all persons holding the nationality of a member state to citizenship of the European Community. The Treaty on European Union, agreed at Maastricht in December 1991, accordingly contained provisions establishing citizenship of the European Union. It guaranteed the rights of free movement and residence, the right of EU citizens to vote and stand as candidates in municipal elections and European Parliament elections, in countries of residence other than their own, and to equal consular protection in third countries where their own countries were not represented. The right of all citizens to petition the European Parliament was also inscribed, and the Parliament was directed to appoint an ombudsman empowered to receive complaints from any citizen concerning alleged maladministration by EC institutions. The commission was instructed to report every three years on the application of this part of the treaty, and the Council of Ministers was empowered, acting unanimously, to adopt provisions to strengthen or add to the rights inscribed therein.

Attempts to introduce common symbolism ...

One factor which has retarded the development of popular loyalties to the European Union has been the absence of common symbolism, a lack which the commission and the national governments have made increasing attempts in recent years to rectify.

... include an EU flag ...

Since 1986 the European Union has had a common flag, which is flown at national and international functions and ceremonies, as well as on other occasions when public attention needs to be drawn to the existence of the Union.

This flag, which contains a crown of 12 five-pointed stars on an azure background, had already been used since 1955 by the Council of Europe. It is pure coincidence that the number of stars is now equal to the number of member states: it will not be increased – unlike in the case of the US Stars and Stripes – if further countries join the EU. The flag will henceforward be shared with the Council of Europe.

... anthem ...

The Council of Europe also shares the European anthem, for which the words of Schiller's Ode to Joy, set to Beethoven's Ninth Symphony, have been chosen. (This is a cut above most national anthems – of which both words and music are almost uniformly banal – but it remains to be seen whether it will catch the public imagination.) May 9th, the date of Robert Schuman's birth in 1886, was also chosen in 1986 as Europe Day, with the hope that it would be celebrated as a public holiday in each member state.

... passport ...

Since 1974 slow progress has been made towards achieving a common European passport. In 1981–82 the member states reached agreement on a uniform model. The format is 88mm x 124mm, the colour is Burgundy red, and the heading is "European Community", followed by the name of the member state. The date set for its introduction was January 1st 1985, but only three countries, Denmark, Ireland and Luxembourg, respected this deadline. Most other member states started issuing the new style passports (which will progressively replace the old national passports on renewal) later on in 1985, but it was not until 1989 that European passports were being supplied in all 12 member states.

... and driving licence

In 1980 the Council of Ministers adopted a directive on the introduction of a Community driving licence which was implemented in two stages. Since 1983 there has been mutual recognition in each member state of each others' licences, which since then have been issued on the basis of theoretical examinations, practical tests and medical requirements conforming to common specifications. Since

January 1st 1986 driving licences issued by member states conform to a Community model, which meets the requirements of the 1968 Vienna International Road Traffic Convention, so that they are also valid in non-EC countries which subscribe to this convention.

Sport

The European Commission, as well as the Adonnino Committee, has focused on sport as a subject which attracts mass interest and often fanatical loyalties. It has attempted, especially since 1985, to introduce a Community dimension into European sport and has spent a trickle of money on sponsoring a number of new and existing sporting events.

European yacht race. In 1985, 23 of the biggest multi-hulls competed against each other on a 3,000 mile course from the Baltic to the Mediterranean. The European yacht race has now been established as a regular two-yearly event.

Cycling. A Tour of the Future of the European Community was sponsored in 1986 and 1987. In 1992 the commission sponsored the Tour de France which, for the first time, covered seven countries in its 3,830km course. It started in Spain, proceeded through France and then passed through Belgium, the Netherlands, Luxembourg, Germany and Italy before returning to its host country.

Tennis. The world's premier indoor tennis tournament, the European Champions' Championship, held in Antwerp, has been re-named the European Community Championship and since 1986 has been sponsored by the commission.

Swimming. The first European Community Swimming Championships were held in Leeds in 1987.

Sail for Europe Association. Since 1976, sponsored by the commission, the Sail for Europe Association has brought together a crew of young sailors from several member states: the first European sports team. It has taken part in two round-the-world races with the yacht "Treaty of Rome", and has twice competed in the Tour de France with a boat called "Europe" (it won in 1984). In 1987 it organised the Constitution Race, commemorating the 30th anniversary of the signing of the Treaty of Rome and the 200th anniversary of the Constitution of the USA, from Nieuwpoort (Belgium) to Philadelphia.

Olympic games. In 1992 the commission acted as a sponsor of the Winter Olympic Games, held at Albertville, and the Summer Olympic Games, held at Barcelona.

34

AID AND DEVELOPMENT

Part Four of the Rome treaty, comprising Articles 131–136, provided for the association with the Community of the former colonial territories of Belgium, France, Italy and the Netherlands. It said:

> This association shall serve primarily to further the interests and prosperity of the inhabitants of these countries and territories in order to lead them to the economic, social and cultural development to which they aspire.

EU–ACP relations are governed by conventions

Initially this provision applied mainly to former French territories in Africa, nearly all of which became independent in the early 1960s; subsequently former UK, Spanish and Portuguese territories also became eligible. At first only 18 countries were involved, and they were known collectively as the Associated African States and Madagascar (AASM). Now 69 in number, they have been known since the mid-1970s as the African, Caribbean and Pacific (ACP) states (see Appendix 7).

Relations between these countries and the EU have been regulated by a series of conventions concluded at periodic intervals. The first two were signed at Yaoundé (capital of Cameroon) in 1963 and 1969, and they set the pattern for the four subsequent ones, signed at Lomé (capital of Togo) in 1975, 1979, 1984 and 1989. On the one hand, provision was made for duty-free access to the EU for almost all the products of the ACP countries, without any reciprocity being required; on the other, development aid was made available, both in the form of grants from the European Development Fund (EDF), which was set up for this purpose, and of low-interest loans from the EIB. About 10% of the total aid programmes of the EU member states is channelled through the Union, and the bulk of it goes to the ACP countries, although India is the largest single recipient.

The EU–ACP conventions have broken new ground in four ways. They have:

- given stability to co-operation links by creating a legal framework, based on a contract negotiated for a fixed period of years between two groupings, each comprising a large number of independent states;

- established a single contract between regional blocs, excluding economic and ideological discrimination and taking account of the special problems of countries which are severely under-developed and those of enclaves and islands;

- created common institutions allowing a permanent dialogue and largely responsible for the implementation of the develop-ment programmes: a joint assembly of MEPs and ACP represen-tatives, an ACP–EU Council of Ministers and a Committee of Ambassadors;

- instituted a global approach covering all aspects of co-operation: financial aid, trade concessions, stabilisation of export earnings, agricultural and industrial assistance.

Altogether some 99.5% of the goods exported to the EU by the ACP countries are admitted free of customs duties, the main exceptions being farm produce in direct competition with EU produced items protected by the CAP. A special deal has been negotiated for sugar, of which the EU has contracted to buy an annual quota of 1.4m tons at high EU prices, despite the surplus production of sugar beet in the Union. This concession was originally made to offset the loss of Commonwealth preferences by several ex-UK colonies. However, ACP textile exports are sharply restricted by the operation of the Multi-Fibre Arrangement (see page 85).

Development aid has grown substantially ...

The amount of development aid has grown substantially from one convention to the next, but so has the number of recipients. Under the fourth Lomé Convention, which covers the years 1990–2000, the total sum available for the first five years is 12,000m ecus, the bulk of which will be in the form of grants and soft loans. A particular feature of the second, third and fourth Lomé Conventions has been the inclusion of a stabilisation fund (known as Stabex), which com-pensates countries heavily dependent on one or more staple prod-ucts for severe fluctuations in their export earnings. Altogether 48 basic commodities are included, and in recent years over 400m ecus have been paid out of the fund annually to more than 30 ACP coun-tries. A similar system, Sysmin, applies to mineral products. It pro-vides finance for the upkeep or reconstruction of mining installations during periods when their operation is curtailed by unforeseen circumstances.

Table 25 **Lomé IV: development expenditure 1993 (m ecus)**

Sector	1993[a]
Trade promotion	81.802
Cultural and social development	334.341
education and training	88.566
water engineering, urban infrastructure, housing	129.155
health	116.619
Economic infrastructure	165.624
transport and communications	165.624
Development of production	816.919
rural production	225.839
industrialisation	142.319
campaigns on specific themes[b]	448.760
Exception aid, Stabex	138.137
rehabilitation	−0.072
disasters	110.103
Stabex	2.465
refugees and returnees	25.640
Other[c]	62.890
Total	1,599.715

[a] Provisional.

[b] Including desertification and drought, disasters, major endemic and epidemic diseases, hygiene and basic health, endemic cattle diseases, energy-saving research, sectoral imports programme and long-term schemes.

[c] Including information and documentation, seminars, programmes and general technical co-operation, general studies, multisectoral programmes, delegations, administrative and financial costs, improvements to public buildings, project-linked multisectoral technical co-operation (all projects).

Source: European Commission.

... but the emphasis has changed

The third and fourth Lomé Conventions changed the emphasis of the EDF by focusing much greater attention on rural and agricultural development, and on the financing of concerted programmes rather than of individual projects. The EDF also supports cross-border regional development projects to assist small and medium-sized enterprises and "micro-projects" of local importance. It aims to take a bigger interest in the restoration of natural equilibria: the struggle against drought and desertification, and so on.

The EIB provides long-term loans from its own resources, with a 3% interest-rate subsidy paid by the EDF. It also finances or part-finances feasibility studies for industrial projects, including those involving small and medium-sized business, agro-industry, mining, tourism and energy; and productive infrastructure such as ports, railways, water supplies and telecommunications.

The EDF has established in Brussels a Centre for the Development of Industry (CDI), which is managed and staffed by nationals of both ACP and EU countries. Its principal function is defined as "to help to establish and strengthen industrial enterprise in the ACP states, particularly by encouraging joint initiatives by economic operators of the European Community and the ACP states". Co-operation is also to be extended in areas such as energy, shipping and fisheries, as well as in social and cultural fields: the development of the human resources and cultural identity of ACP countries and assistance for workers and students from ACP countries in Europe.[1]

Figure 12 **EC Financial aid to developing countries**

In 1992: 4.28bn ecus from the Community budget, European Investment Bank and the European Development Fund

Planned yearly aid to ACP countres, 1990–95
Total 12bn ecus
Average: 2,400m ecus

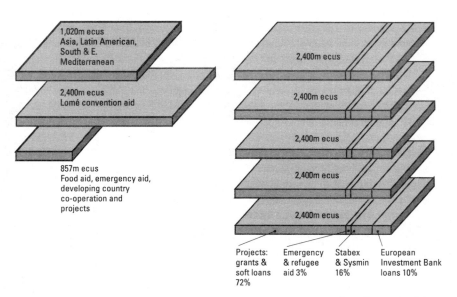

1,020m ecus
Asia, Latin American,
South & E.
Mediterranean

2,400m ecus
Lomé convention aid

857m ecus
Food aid, emergency aid,
developing country
co-operation and
projects

2,400m ecus

2,400m ecus

2,400m ecus

2,400m ecus

2,400m ecus

Projects:
grants &
soft loans
72%

Emergency
& refugee
aid 3%

Stabex
& Sysmin
16%

European
Investment Bank
loans 10%

Source: European Commission.

Other forms of assistance to developing countries

The Lomé conventions are not regarded by the EU primarily as a charitable venture. The self-interest of the Union, which is heavily dependent upon the supply of a host of commodities and raw materials from developing countries, is deeply involved in the maintenance of a stable world economy and the orderly and rapid development of poorer countries. Although it has chosen to give priority to the associated ACP countries through the EDF, the EU also spends an approximately equal amount (rather over 1.6 billion ecus in the 1991 budget) on other forms of assistance to developing countries. Apart from trade concessions under the generalised system of preferences (see pages 84–85), this falls into two main categories.

Food and emergency aid.   The Union sends foodstuffs to countries which request assistance in coping with serious food shortages. Emergency aid is also sent to countries devastated by natural catastrophes or other crises. In 1990 over 500m ecus was expended, largely in supplying over 1.2m tons of grain as well as dairy products and vegetable oils to sub-Saharan Africa, Asia and Mediterranean countries. Numerous emergency aid operations were launched, particularly to assist the victims of famine and civil war in African countries, such as Ethiopia, Sudan, Somalia, Angola, Mozambique and Liberia. The assistance is not entirely disinterested: it helps to reduce the surplus food stocks of the CAP. Funds are, however, also provided for special programmes to help poor countries overcome their food production problems, and to assist the work of non-governmental organisations.

A new departure was marked in July 1989, when EC farm ministers allocated some 110m ecus of food aid to Poland, in response to an appeal from the Western economic summit, which had just been held in Paris, for the European Commission to co-ordinate emergency aid to Poland and Hungary. This assistance was primarily motivated by a desire to encourage these two countries' progress towards democracy. It was followed up by a more comprehensive programme of development aid to the countries of Eastern Europe, administered by the EC on behalf of the OECD countries (the group of 24), and known as the Phare Programme (Poland and Hungary – Aid for Economic Restructuring. Phare in French means "beacon"). Details of help under the Phare programme in 1993 are shown in Table 27.

Aid to non-associated countries.   The EU has concluded a series of agreements with Asian countries, such as India, Pakistan

Table 26 **Allocation of food aid, 1993 (tons)**

Region	Cereals	Milk powder	Butter oil	Vegetable oil	Sugar	Other products[a]
Africa	165,780	927	105	4,900	466	2.615
Caribbean	1,540	–	–	–	–	–
Mediterranean	110,000	3,000	–	8,000	–	1.000
Latin America	66,920	5,945	–	7,345	–	3.380
Asia	155,000	–	–	1,000	–	–
Total direct aid	499,240	9,872	105	21,245	466	6.995
Total indirect aid	845,300	36,890	105	51,639	14,534	39.550
Grand total	1,344,540	46,762	105	72,884	15,000	46.550

[a] m ecus.

Source: European Commission.

Table 27 **Operation Phare: financial aid granted in 1993 (m ecus)**

Beneficiary	Agriculture	Education	Environment	Financial	Civil service	Infrastructure	SMEs	Social	Humanitarian aid	Other	Total
Albania	10.0	2.5	3.3	a	1.2	a	7.0	6.0	10.0	35.0	75.0
Bulgaria	a	15.0	8.6	5.0	8.0	20.9	6.0	10.5	a	16.0	90.0
Estonia	a	1.5	a	a	a	a	a	a	a	10.5	12.0
Hungary	30.5	16.0	a	a	2.5	10.0	31.0	10.0	a	a	100.0
Latvia	a	2.0	a	a	a	a	a	a	a	16.0	18.0
Lithuania	a	2.5	a	a	a	a	a	a	a	22.5	25.0
Poland	30.0	45.0	a	10.0	42.0	55.0	7.0	10.0	a	26.0	225.0
Romania	5.0	18.0	a	a	10.0	a	70.0	a	9.9	27.0	139.9
Slovakia	3.0	5.0	a	a	a	5.0	19.0	3.0	a	5.0	40.0
Slovenia	a	3.5	a	a	a	a	a	a	a	7.5	11.0
Czech Republic	a	8.0	a	a	8.0	9.0	27.0	8.0	a	a	60.0
Other former Yugoslav republics	a	a	a	a	a	a	a	a	a	25.0	25.0
Regional co-operation	a	15.8	20.0	a	10.0	29.0	27.5	10.0	a	a	112.3
Other programmes	a	9.9	a	a	a	a	a	10.0	a	52.2	72.1
Total	78.5	144.7	31.9	15.0	81.7	128.9	194.5	67.5	19.9	242.7	1,005.3

[a] No financial aid granted.

Source: European Commission.

and Bangladesh, as well as with Latin American countries, under which development aid is provided. For the period 1991–95 an aid package of 2,750m ecus was approved, 10% of which is earmarked for the environment, mainly for the protection of the Amazonian forest. Similar development aid is provided to Mediterranean countries in the Maghreb and Mashreq, and to Israel, under financial protocols attached to co-operation agreements with these countries. Altogether some 2,375m ecus have been allocated for 1991–95.

Considerable scope for expansion and improvement

When all the different EU programmes for assisting developing countries are added together they appear to amount to a considerable effort, and it is true that the EU devotes a larger slice of its GDP to development aid than either the USA or Japan. In the early years of the 1990s it was providing 47% of total world aid, compared with 20% by the USA or 17.8% by Japan. On the other hand, it should be emphasised that only two EU member states – Denmark and the Netherlands – have reached the UN target of devoting at least 0.7% of their GDP to aid programmes. Moreover some EU policies, notably the CAP which encourages the dumping of EU food surpluses on world markets, sometimes in direct competition with farmers from developing countries, and even the food aid programme itself, may add considerably to the problems of developing countries. The EU's aid programmes have also been criticised for being geared to the interests of EU firms, which receive the bulk of the contracts awarded, and which may gain more from them than the intended beneficiaries. Despite the real achievements of the EU's development policies, there remains enormous scope for both expansion and improvement before they will come anywhere near to the full realisation of their objectives.

1 Assistance under the Lomé conventions is also available to Overseas Countries and Territories (OCTs) still associated with member states (see Appendix 7 for full list). Overseas territories which have the status of provinces or departments of a member state (such as the Azores, Madeira, the Canary Islands and the French overseas departments) are not eligible. Instead they receive assistance from the European Regional Development Fund (ERDF).

35

FOREIGN, DEFENCE AND SECURITY POLICY

The Rome treaty made no mention of foreign policy, as distinct from foreign-trade policy, and progress towards co-ordinating the foreign policy of the member states has been slow and largely informal. It is, however, one of the relatively few fields where progress, however limited, has been virtually continuous – at least since 1969 – and each year has tended to see somewhat closer co-operation between the member states than the previous one.

Davignon Report provided basic framework
Foreign policy co-operation (known in EU circles as "political co-operation") really dates in an organised sense from The Hague EC summit of December 1969. At this meeting it was decided to ask top national officials to report on the possibilities of achieving a degree of co-operation in foreign affairs. A committee presided over by Viscount Etienne Davignon (then a Belgian foreign office official, later a leading EC commissioner) drew up a report which recommended a system to "harmonise points of view, concert attitudes and, where possible, lead to common decisions".

The Davignon Report was accepted, and with a number of adaptations over the years it provided the basic framework for "political co-operation" by EC countries during the 1970s and 1980s. It proposed that the EC foreign ministers should meet at least twice a year to discuss foreign policy matters. In practice they now normally meet at monthly intervals, and more often at times of crisis. For a number of years, largely due to French insistence during the Gaullist and post-Gaullist period, a sharp distinction was drawn between meetings held on political co-operation (which were normally convened in the capital city of the country currently holding the presidency of the Council of Ministers) and those on "normal" EC business,[1] which were in Brussels or Luxembourg. Over the years this distinction has become looser, and it is now quite common for both types of business to be transacted at the same meeting.

In addition to the foreign ministers, each member state has designated a top diplomatic official, known as the political director, who is specifically responsible for foreign policy co-operation

212

FOREIGN,
DEFENCE
AND
SECURITY
POLICIES

between the 12 member states. The political directors meet every month, and each is assisted by a more junior official, known as the European correspondent, who is responsible for day-to-day communications. They are linked by a special telex system, and exchange upwards of 5,000 telegrams each year. The organisation of political co-operation is assumed by the foreign ministry of the country currently holding the presidency, but under the Single European Act, which formalised "political co-operation" for the first time, a small secretariat was established in Brussels in 1987 to provide back-up support and ensure greater continuity.

Commitment to joint foreign policy formalised ...
The Single European Act formally committed the member states to "endeavour jointly to formulate and implement a European foreign policy" (Article 30). It also (Article 2) regularised the position of the European Council, or the regular series of summit meetings of heads of government, which had been meeting three times a year since 1973, and twice yearly since 1986. The European Council meetings had played a considerable role in promoting "political co-operation", and foreign policy issues invariably occupy a prominent, and sometimes the predominant, place on the agenda. To a significant extent, they have provided an opportunity for the European members of the Western alliance to co-ordinate their positions, and enable them to adopt a more equal posture vis-à-vis the USA, which dwarfs each of them on a one-to-one basis.

... but development hindered by member states' own interests
A number of factors, however, have seriously inhibited this development. One has been the neutrality of Ireland, which has largely prevented the EU from playing the role of the European end of NATO (there is also the fact that three European NATO members – Norway, Iceland and Turkey – are not members of the EU). Furthermore, both Denmark and Greece, although they belong to NATO, have had severe inhibitions about discussing matters of Western security within an EU framework. Denmark, because of its policy of seeking to restrict the EU's authority to those matters specifically referred to in the Rome treaty; Greece, because under the government of Papandreou it adopted a position less critical of the Soviet Union (and of the radical Arab states) than that of its NATO allies.

Three of the larger EU members – Germany, France and the UK – have also on occasion been reluctant to subordinate their independent interests to those of the Union. Before German unification in 1990 the West German government, because of its economic links

213

FOREIGN,
DEFENCE
AND
SECURITY
POLICIES

with East Germany and its desire to keep open doors to closer co-operation with the East German regime and to do nothing to hinder prospects, however remote they then seemed, of eventual unification, often took a slightly softer position in relation to Eastern Europe than the other member states. After unification it continued to be notably more willing than its allies to accommodate the former Soviet Union and to consider economic aid on a large scale. By 1992, however, the cost of unification had become so great that German resistance hardened to paying the lion's share of aid to the rest of Eastern Europe. France and the UK both have worldwide interests, largely arising from their colonial pasts, and each has shown itself rather more nationalistic in its approach than the majority of other member states. France, which since the time of de Gaulle has remained outside the military command structure of NATO, has otherwise shown itself progressively more ready to co-operate with its European partners, particularly since the election of President Mitterrand in 1981. The UK, on the other hand, showed little sign in the Thatcher era of moderating its more independent stance.

For these reasons, the European Council – and the EU foreign ministers' meetings – have not formally assumed the role of the "general staff" of the European end of the Western alliance that might otherwise have been expected. Informally they have come rather nearer to it. For example, defence matters are supposed to be excluded from the agenda (as distinct from the "political and economic aspects of security"), but there is no doubt that they have been discussed several times. On these occasions, the Irish prime minister or foreign minister has kept silent. He might more logically have left the meeting temporarily, but nobody has wished to make an issue of the matter, and in practice the neutral status of Ireland has not been noticeably compromised by the attendance of its ministers. Nevertheless, the Community felt inhibited from shouldering responsibilities in the defence field, and this led in 1984 to an attempt to breathe new life into the moribund Western European Union (WEU) as a forum for discussing defence in a West European context.

Co-operation has been achieved in some respects

In practice foreign policy co-operation within the EU has manifested itself in three main aspects.

Presenting a common EU position.   A serious effort has been made for the 12 countries to speak with one voice in international fora. Thus the foreign minister of the country holding the presi-

214

FOREIGN,
DEFENCE
AND
SECURITY
POLICY

dency now speaks on behalf of all the member states in the general debate which opens every session of the United Nations each September. During the course of the year the 12 EU ambassadors to the UN are in constant conclave and take a lot of trouble to ensure that all the EU countries vote together in divisions in the General Assembly. As well as in the UN, it has become the practice for the country holding the presidency to present a common EU position at other international conferences, notably the Conference on Security and Co-operation in Europe (CSCE), arising out of the 1975 Helsinki agreement.

Imposing sanctions.   Common action has been taken in the imposition of economic sanctions. These have been imposed by all or most EU members, in concert, on eight separate occasions.

- Against Southern Rhodesia in 1965, following a UN resolution.
- Against Iran after the taking of American hostages in 1980.
- Against the Soviet Union and Poland after the imposition of martial law in Poland in 1981 (Greece declined to apply the sanctions).
- Against Argentina during the Falklands War in 1982 (Italy and Ireland discontinued the sanctions halfway through the war).
- Against Israel after the invasion of Lebanon in 1982.
- Against South Africa in 1986 (the UK was initially unwilling to participate, but eventually agreed to do so after the original package of measures had been considerably watered down).
- Against Iraq, following its invasion of Kuwait in August 1990, in accordance with the resolutions of the UN Security Council.
- Against Serbia and Montenegro during the fighting in Croatia and Bosnia-Herzegovina in 1991–94.

It is arguable that none of these attempts at applying the EU's economic clout for a political purpose had the desired effect. What they perhaps did achieve was to cement the EU countries' habit of working together in foreign policy and to strengthen their sense of common purpose.

Taking initiatives.   The EU heads of government have taken a number of initiatives during their periodic meetings in the European Council. Statements and declarations have been made on East–West relations, the Middle East, the Iran–Iraq War, Afghanistan, Poland, Central America and South Africa, with no apparent effect at all, even though some of them (such as the Venice

215

FOREIGN,
DEFENCE
AND
SECURITY
POLICY

declaration on the Middle East which was taken to imply a role for the PLO in the peace process) were widely publicised at the time. A persistent weakness of these statements is that they have tended to be purely declaratory with no serious attempt at a follow-through.

New impetus towards common foreign policy ...

The collapse of communism in Eastern Europe, which had as one of its many consequences the unification of Germany, followed by the Gulf War against Iraq, gave a fresh impetus towards a common foreign policy. On the one hand the German chancellor, Helmut Kohl, felt that it was necessary to tie Germany into a closer European federation if its neighbours' fear of unification were to be allayed. On the other, the serious differences which occurred between the member states before and during the Iraq War emphasised how far the EC had to go before it presented a single face to the outside world.

... reinforced by Maastricht treaty

Steps towards a common foreign, defence and security policy were thus major items on the agenda of the inter-governmental conference on political union, which opened in December 1990 and reported to the Maastricht summit in December 1991. The Treaty on European Union, which was agreed at the summit, did contain far-reaching provisions, although they did not go as far as Germany and most of the other member states would have preferred. A more cautious approach, based substantially on the principle of unanimity rather than majority voting, prevailed, largely at the bidding of the UK government. It was, however, agreed that the whole question should be reviewed at a further conference in 1996, when Germany and its supporters hope that a more thorough-going approach will be adopted.

The Maastricht treaty pledged the "Union and its member states" to put into effect a common foreign and security policy (CFSP). This was to be pursued by establishing systematic co-operation between member states, gradually implementing joint action. The member states are required to inform and consult each other within the Council of Ministers on matters of foreign and security policy, and the council will adopt common positions where necessary. Member states are to ensure that their national policies conform to the common positions, and are to co-ordinate their action within international organisations. The European Council is to define general guidelines for "joint action" and the council will decide, by unanimity, whether an area or issue should be the subject of joint action. The detailed arrangements for the implementa-

216

FOREIGN,
DEFENCE
AND
SECURITY
POLICY

tion of joint action will be decided by qualified majority (that is, 54 votes in favour out of 76, cast by at least eight member states – see page 44).

The treaty states that the CFSP should include all questions relating to the security of the European Union including the eventual framing of a common defence policy, which might in time lead to a common defence. Decisions on security with defence implications would, in the meantime, be implemented on request by the Western European Union. Previously, although there had been a substantial overlapping of membership, relations with the WEU had been complicated by the fact that not all the EC member states belonged to it. At Maastricht a parallel meeting of WEU ministers agreed to admit any EC member states that applied. All except Ireland (which is not a member of NATO) were expected to do so, and it was therefore envisaged that the WEU should henceforth assume the role of the European pillar of the Atlantic alliance. In order to facilitate future co-ordination between the EU and the WEU it was also agreed at Maastricht that the latter's headquarters should be transferred to Brussels.

The treaty specifically gave authority to the country holding the rotating presidency of the Council of Ministers to act on the EU's behalf, which it had often done informally in the past. It effectively gave it the responsibility for organising the CFSP, assisted where appropriate by the preceding and successive presidencies (the so-called "troika") and by the commission. It also laid down that the European Parliament must be kept regularly informed by the presidency, be consulted on broad policy questions and be permitted to question the council and make recommendations. The treaty also provided for co-operation between the member states on the following matters relating to security:

- asylum policy;
- rules governing crossing of member states' external borders;
- immigration policy;
- conditions of entry and movement by third-country nationals;
- conditions of residence including family reunion and access to employment for third-country nationals;
- combatting unauthorised immigration and residence by third-country nationals;
- combatting drugs;
- combatting fraud;
- judicial co-operation in civil matters;
- judicial co-operation in criminal matters;

- customs co-operation;
- police co-operation on information exchange within a European Police Office (Europol).

1 The foreign ministers form the so-called "general affairs council" which is regarded as the most senior of the various manifestations of the Council of Ministers. As such they often meet to discuss matters unrelated to foreign affairs, sometimes arbitrating on issues which overlap the competences of departmental ministers, sometimes discussing particularly knotty problems, sometimes acting as direct deputies to the heads of government.

PART IV

SPECIAL PROBLEMS

36

ENLARGEMENT

It was, from the outset, envisaged that other European countries besides the original six member states would subsequently be admitted into the European Community. Article 237 of the Treaty of Rome stated, in part: "Any European state may apply to become a member of the Community". This general invitation was, however, qualified by the preamble to the treaty which referred to the original members' resolve to strengthen peace and liberty and called upon "the other peoples of Europe who share their ideal to join in their efforts". This wording has subsequently been taken to mean that only countries with a democratic form of government are eligible to join. A further implied condition is that the economies of applicant states should be sufficiently developed to enable them to meet the obligations of membership and to be able to compete effectively within a free market.

Successful applicants

In 1961, and again in 1967, the UK, Denmark, Ireland and Norway made applications to join. On both occasions the UK was eventually vetoed by France, and the other three countries withdrew their applications. In 1969 a third approach was made, and new negotiations began with the four applicants which resulted in treaties of accession being signed in 1972. The three smaller applicant countries submitted the treaties to referenda, which produced majorities in favour in both Denmark and Ireland. France also held a referendum which showed a majority in favour of enlargement, but the Norwegian referendum resulted in a narrow majority against joining the Community (53:47 per cent). Denmark, Ireland and the UK became full members on January 1st 1973, although a transitional period of five years was allowed for adjusting tariffs, and for staggering various other membership provisions regarding, for example, agriculture and budgetary contributions. The UK did not hold a referendum on its entry to the Community, but following the election in 1974 of a Labour government the entry terms were partially renegotiated, and membership was subsequently confirmed by a majority of more than 2:1 in a referendum held on June 5th 1975.

Greece, Portugal and Spain were effectively excluded from membership during the years that they languished under dictatorships. Greece, which had already negotiated associate status with the EC several years before the military coup which overthrew its democratic regime in 1967, lost no time in applying for full membership after democratic government was restored in 1974. Its application was tabled in 1975, and Greece became the Community's tenth member on January 1st 1981. There was a five year transition period for aligning import duties and for most parts of the common agricultural policy. A seven year period, ending on January 1st 1988, was allowed for peaches and tomatoes, and also for the free movement of workers.

Portugal and Spain also applied for membership within a year or two of the Portuguese revolution of 1974, and the death of General Franco in 1975. Their membership negotiations were a great deal longer and more complicated than those with Greece, partly because of initial French reluctance but also because Spanish membership, in particular, was likely to cause greater problems for the existing member states. Agreement was finally reached in May 1985 and treaties of accession were signed on June 12th 1985, to take effect, after ratification by all the existing members as well as by Spain and Portugal, on January 1st 1986. In this case the transitional period was for seven years, ending on January 1st 1993, but for a number of sensitive agricultural products it will last for ten years up to January 1st 1996. Freedom of movement for workers will not come fully into effect for seven years, and in the case of Luxembourg (which already has a large population of immigrant Portuguese workers) for ten years.

Unsuccessful applicants

Turkey, which is recognised as a European state despite having 96% of its land area in Asia, and which signed an association agreement as long ago as 1963, officially applied for membership in April 1987, as did Morocco, which had made an unofficial approach three years earlier, in July 1987. Morocco claimed to be a democratic state with organic links with Europe, but was politely told that it was not eligible. The Turkish application was officially referred to the commission, for an opinion on its acceptability, as provided by the Rome treaty and as had occurred with all previous applications. In the past the commission verdict had always been favourable and membership negotiations had subsequently been opened. In this case, however, the commission reported that Turkey was not yet ready for membership, both because its economy was insufficiently developed and because its democracy had not been fully estab-lished. It was politely suggested to Turkey that its application should be shelved indefinitely. This rebuff did not deter the Turkish government, which in November 1992 announced that it wished to proceed to a full customs union with the EU, as had been foreshad-owed in the original association agreement. The target date that the Turks set themselves was 1995, although the commission has been working on the assumption that January 1st 1996 was more realistic. Setting up the customs union will be a severe test for Turkish industry, which will have to face the full blast of competi-tion from manufacturers within the EU. Yet the Turkish govern-ment welcomes this challenge as it believes that it would give an essential spur to the efficiency of Turkish enterprises. Turkey has attracted a considerable amount of West European investment in recent years, and – since the end of the Cold War – has been seen as an important trading link with the countries of the former Soviet Union and its satellites in the Balkans, the Caucasus and Central Asia. The Turks believe that the more their country becomes eco-nomically involved with the EU the more difficult it will become for the Union to refuse it full membership. In practice, however, Turk-ish accession is unlikely before the beginning of the 21st century.

Two other Mediterranean countries which have association agreements with the EU – Malta and Cyprus – applied for member-ship in 1990. Both could probably have adapted easily enough to the requirements of membership, but they were given no early opportunity to do so. As far as Cyprus was concerned, there was a strong feeling that membership would be inappropriate so long as the northern part of the island continued to be under Turkish mili-tary occupation. Both countries also suffered from EU doubts as to whether very small nations could effectively take on the burdens of membership. The fact that Luxembourg, a founder member, has a similar population to Malta and one which is much smaller than Cyprus's, made it difficult, however, to advance this as an argu-ment against admitting them. The Copenhagen summit, in June 1993, adopted a more encouraging approach, and approved the sending of positive signals to both countries. These foresaw that the membership application of Cyprus would be re-examined in Jan-uary 1995, in the light of the progress made in settling the Turkish Cypriot problem, and that an intensive dialogue would be held with Malta which would help prepare it for integration into the EU. It is conceivable, though far from certain, that the two countries might be admitted to membership in 1998 or thereabouts.

Two events gave a strong impetus to expanding EU membership, which had looked as though it would stabilise for many years after the accession of Spain and Portugal in 1986: the 1992 programme to complete the single European market and the collapse of Soviet communism.

Negotiations with EFTA countries

The launch of the 1992 programme (see Chapter 15) caused immediate ructions in the seven EFTA countries. These had all negotiated industrial free trade agreements with the EC back in the 1960s, but they were afraid that they would be left out of the opportunities which the creation of a single European market would provide.

A two-year negotiation led to an agreement to form a European Economic Area (EEA) due to come into effect on January 1st 1993. Yet in the process of the negotiations most of the EFTA countries concluded that they were being asked to make so many concessions that they might as well go the whole hog and apply for full membership. Austria had already decided to do this before negotiations began and Sweden put in its application in 1991. Finland and Switzerland followed suit early in 1992. Norway still had traumatic memories of the 1972 referendum which narrowly rejected membership at the same time as Danish, Irish and UK entry. Its government, in the face of sharply divided public opinion, hesitated before taking the plunge, but finally put in an application at the end of 1992. Meanwhile, the Swiss voters narrowly rejected membership of the EEA in a referendum in December 1992. This led to a minor renegotiation of the terms of the agreement enabling it to come into effect after a delay of one year, on January 1st 1994, without Swiss participation. Consequently the Swiss application for membership of the EU was put on ice, much to the chagrin of Swiss industry which believed it would have great difficulty in competing if Switzerland remained outside.

This left two EFTA countries: Iceland and Liechtenstein. The latter, with a population of 28,000 (less than one-tenth of Luxembourg's), can hardly aspire to full membership and will probably seek some associate status. Iceland is obsessed with the need to retain full control over its fisheries resources and is not currently thinking of membership. It could well reconsider its position in 2–3 years' time.

Negotiations with Austria, Finland, Sweden and Norway started early in 1993 and were successfully concluded in March 1994. Provided the voters in the four countries endorse the terms of accession in referenda to be held between June and November 1994, the number of member states of the EU will increase from 12 to 16 at the beginning of 1995.

Relatively few problems arose during the negotiating process. Each of the four applicant countries have high per head incomes and all will eventually become net contributors to EU funds. The main contentious issues related to agriculture, the environment, regional policy, transport (in particular the transit of goods vehicles over mountain roads in Austria), alcohol monopolies (in the three Nordic countries) and, in Norway's case, fisheries. Eventually final agreement was reached on the basis that the applicant states would conform to EU legislation, but with varying transition periods and a small number of special provisions to meet specific difficulties.

The problems anticipated by the traditional neutrality policies of Austria, Finland and Sweden largely disappeared with the end of the Cold War. In the event, each of these countries, as well as Norway, declared that, from the time of its accession, it would "be ready and able to participate fully and actively in the Common Foreign and Security Policy as defined in the Treaty on European Union" (the Maastricht treaty).

Obstacles for new members

New members who join the EU are required to accept not only all the provisions of the treaties (see Chapter 3), but also the entire *acquis communautaire* (that is, all the secondary legislation – directives, regulations and decisions – that has already been adopted under the treaties). Consequently membership negotiations, which are nonetheless normally exhaustive and long drawn out, are mostly concerned with the length and nature of the transitional period during which the applicant state will have to modify its existing laws in order to conform, and which provisions shall be included in such transitional arrangements. If an accession treaty is concluded it must then be ratified by the parliaments of all the existing member states before it can come into effect. Since the Single European Act came into force in 1987 it has also been necessary for the European Parliament to ratify new accessions by the vote of an absolute majority of its members. The first time this occurred was on May 5th 1994 when, by a large majority, the membership applications of Austria, Finland, Sweden and Norway were approved.

Eastern Europe

Beyond the immediate future lies the question of extending EU boundaries eastwards. Some voices have been raised against this, but in December 1991 association agreements were reached with

Czechoslovakia, Hungary and Poland which specifically foresaw eventual membership. Similar agreements were later negotiated with Albania, Bulgaria, Romania, Slovenia and the Baltic states of Estonia, Latvia and Lithuania. The agreement with Czechoslovakia was later replaced by separate agreements with the Czech Republic and Slovakia, while the remaining former Yugoslav republics, including what is left of Bosnia-Herzegovina, may qualify for comparable treatment in the future. Some or all of them may later aspire to full EU membership.

At the Copenhagen summit in June 1993 it was specifically affirmed that any central or East European country that so wished could become a member of the EU "once it was able to fulfil the obligations associated with membership and meet the economic and political requirements". The first such countries to apply were Poland and Hungary in March 1994, and it was expected that applications from the Czech Republic and Slovakia would follow soon after. No serious attention will, however, be paid to these applications until after 1996, when the review conference on the working of the Maastricht treaty will take place.

After the central and East European states may come six former Soviet republics in Europe – Armenia, Azerbaijan, Belarus, Georgia, Moldova and Ukraine – all of which have already signalled an interest by applying to join the Council of Europe. It is early days so far as they are concerned, but if by the first decade of the 21st century they have consolidated their democracies and developed their economies – two big ifs – there will be no respectable grounds on which they could be kept out.

Implications of enlargement

The implications of an expansion of membership to the East will be the key subject for discussion at the 1996 review conference. Voting rights within the Council of Ministers will be a contentious issue, with the UK probably arguing in favour of keeping the unanimity rule for a wide range of decisions. On the other side, the view will be forcibly put that the more new members are admitted the more necessary it will be to extend majority voting if any decisions at all are to be taken. Other serious institutional questions will need to be resolved. Could the Union contemplate a European Parliament of 1,000 members, a commission of 24 or more and a substantial increase in the number of official languages, which now stands at nine and will be increased to 12 if Finland, Sweden and Norway join? The answer probably lies in halving the basis of parliamentary representation (which would, for example, give the UK some

40 Euro-MPs instead of 87), and rescinding the rule that each member state was entitled to a commissioner. As for languages, there is an overwhelming case for reducing the number (perhaps just to English, French and German, although the Italians and Spaniards will certainly object). In EFTA there is only one official language – English – which is not spoken in any EFTA state, so there should be few objections from the new EFTA recruits.

There would also be many more difficulties than during past enlargements arising from the relatively poor economic development of the applicant states. It might well prove to be impossible to bring them into the EU as it currently exists without putting intolerable strains upon it. To give only one example: to accommodate the large Polish farm population would totally bankrupt the CAP. So if there is to be any question of early membership, it could only be on the basis of a two-speed Europe, à la carte membership or variable geometry, to cite a number of current metaphors. That means the new members would not be expected to accept all the responsibilities, nor enjoy all the rights, of existing members.

This would be less of a revolutionary development than is sometimes suggested. Already the poorer member states – Greece, Ireland, Spain and Portugal – often win derogations from EU legislative proposals, giving them longer to put them into effect. And the opt-outs which the British government successfully demanded from the Maastricht treaty will produce a two-speed Europe in all but name. Such an approach would not scare away the new Eastern applicants. What they are seeking is a sense of security, of belonging to the West, not a 100% application of EU laws. Yet it would be difficult for many of the existing member states to agree to grant on a wholesale basis what has hitherto been regarded as exceptional.

The Community, which started with six members in 1958, now has a membership of 12 and a population of 345m. The prospect is that by the end of the century this will have grown to 24, with a population of 450m. Ten years later there could well be over 40 members, not including Russia but otherwise embracing the entire continent of Europe, and a total population approaching 700m. This may seem scarcely credible, and many would no doubt deeply regret the sea change in the nature of the Union which such an expansion would imply. Yet the whole logic of the Treaty of Rome and the manner in which the EU has conducted itself so far point inexorably to a gradual but accelerating increase in membership.

37

THE UK AND THE UNION

The UK was a late entrant into the EC, and it has had an uneasy relationship with its partners for much of the time since it became a member state in 1973.

A history of distrust

Even before 1973 there was a long history of distrust and disappointment, despite the evident desire of the original six members of the Community for UK membership. At the end of the second world war the popularity and prestige of the UK was probably higher in Western Europe than at any time before or since, and there was little doubt that had the UK taken the lead in the movement for closer integration it would have had a predominant influence on the shape and form of any association that was formed. In the event, there was widespread dismay and incomprehension at the UK's lack of interest in joining the Coal and Steel Community in 1951 or in attending the 1955 Messina conference which led to the creation of the EEC. The reasons behind this aloofness – the continuing belief that the UK was a global rather than a European power, that it had a special relationship with the USA, and that its major trading as well as political links were with the Commonwealth – were little appreciated beyond the English Channel. Furthermore, the UK initiative in founding the European Free Trade Association (EFTA) in 1959 was widely seen as a spoiling device to reduce the impact of the EEC which had been established the previous year.

Nevertheless, the UK's application to join the EC, when it finally came in 1961, was warmly welcomed, and there was regret in all the member states (including France itself) when President de Gaulle twice vetoed its entry, in 1963 and 1968. It was only at the third time of asking that terms of accession were finally agreed, in June 1971, following renewed negotiations between Edward Heath's Conservative government and the six existing members.

Opposition to EC membership in the Labour Party

The long years of haggling had taken their toll in the UK, and a substantial degree of opposition to membership had built up. This affected both major political parties, but in the Conservative Party, where it was largely confined to a narrow, right-wing, nationalistic fringe, the party leadership had little difficulty in isolating and containing its anti-EC members.

In the Labour Party internal divisions were more serious. The EC was depicted by left-wingers as a capitalist conspiracy opposed to the party's most basic objectives, while many trade unionists feared that food prices would rise as a result of the impact of the CAP. The pro-EC elements in the party, led by Roy Jenkins, held their ground against strong pressure to abandon their own deep convictions; 69 Labour MPs defied the party whip and enabled the membership terms to be approved by a good majority in the House of Commons. The damage done to the Labour Party by this dispute, particularly by the intolerant way in which it was conducted, was considerable, and undoubtedly contributed to the split which occurred a decade later when the Social Democratic Party was formed. Hostility within the Labour Party continued, but it was successfully defused, at least for a time, by the commitment that a Labour government would hold a referendum to determine whether the UK would remain a member. Following Labour's election victory in 1974, the terms of membership were renegotiated, the main change being the institution of a financial mechanism designed to prevent excessive UK budgetary contributions (although in the event it proved to be ineffective, see pages 12–13). A majority of the cabinet led by the prime minister, Harold Wilson, and the foreign secretary, James Callaghan (both of whom had voted against membership in 1971), were able to recommend the acceptance of the revised terms, despite the opposition of a large section of the Labour Party. In the referendum which followed, on June 5th 1975, a majority of just over 2:1 favoured continued UK membership, and the dispute seemed to be over.

It flared up again in 1979 when it was discovered, in the closing months of James Callaghan's Labour government, that – despite the renegotiated terms – the UK, which had now reached the end of its transitional stage of membership, was liable to pay an unacceptably high net contribution to the EC, probably exceeding 1 billion ecus in the following year (see pages 17–18). It fell to Mrs Thatcher's Conservative government, elected in May 1979, to attempt to secure a permanent abatement of the UK contribution. Mrs Thatcher played the leading part in the negotiations, which dominated the life of the Community and particularly the meetings of the European Council until a settlement was reached at the Fontainebleau summit in June 1984 (see page 19). In the meantime Labour Party hostility to UK membership was rekindled, and in the June 1983 general election campaign the party proposed a unilateral withdrawal, without even the possibility of a further referendum. Following Labour's heavy defeat in that election, and the replacement of Michael Foot by Neil Kinnock as party leader, the issue was quietly dropped. There was no mention of withdrawal in the Labour Party manifesto for the 1987 general election.

A year or so later, following a highly successful visit to the Trades Union Congress in 1988 by Jacques Delors, who fired the delegates with a vision of a Europe in which trade unionists would share fully in the fruits of the Community's future development, including the 1992 programme, both the trade unions and the Labour Party finally came round to see the EC in a positive light.

Mrs Thatcher reduced UK influence in the EC ...

This welcome development was balanced by a perverse reaction in the Conservative Party, which, under the leadership of Mrs Thatcher, became steadily more hostile to the EC from September 1988 onwards, when she delivered a widely reported speech at Bruges. This was hailed as a rallying call by all those who looked nostalgically back to the days when the UK was a world power and who were psychologically incapable of adjusting to current realities. Mrs Thatcher became especially hung up over questions of "sovereignty", which she and her supporters saw as a zero-sum concept, assuming that any accretion of power to EC institutions constituted an equal diminution of that of the member states. This ran directly counter to the prevailing view within the Community, which was that national sovereignty had been declining for many years, for reasons which had little to do with the growth of the EC, and that it was only by pooling their resources in a number of fields that the member states would be able collectively to achieve objectives which would be beyond their individual capacity.

In fact it is clear that Mrs Thatcher substantially reduced UK influence within the EC during her final years as prime minister by insisting that the UK took a negative or minimalist position on most proposals for new EC initiatives, even including those, such as the Lingua programme on foreign language teaching (see page 187), which would be of particular benefit to the UK. She seemed to glory in being in a minority of one at meetings of the European Council, and it was her behaviour at and after the Rome meeting in October 1990, which set a date for the beginning of stage two of EMU, that led to her being challenged for the leadership of the Conservative Party and her replacement by John Major.

... and Mr Major has not done much better

John Major evidently did not share Mrs Thatcher's deep distrust of
the Community, and spoke of his desire "to bring the UK into the
heart of Europe". He promptly dropped her abrasive criticisms of
the EC, but, conscious of her continuing influence within the Conservative Party, he continued to approach the proposals for EMU and
"political union" with circumspection. By adopting a more reasonable negotiating approach, he was able to secure considerable
changes in the two inter-governmental conferences, particularly in
that on "political union", and a year after becoming prime minister
he agreed to the Maastricht Treaty on European Union, but only on
the basis of two opt-out clauses. One of these reserved the right of
the UK not to take part in the third stage of EMU, with a European
Central Bank (ECB) and a common currency. Few observers believed
at the time that there was any serious possibility of the UK not participating in stage three, and the only lasting consequence of Mr
Major's obduracy at Maastricht was likely to be the undermining of
the otherwise strong claim of the City of London to house the ECB.
This prediction proved correct when Frankfurt was subsequently
chosen as the site for the European Monetary Institute, which is
the forerunner of the bank. The other opt-out concerned the Social
Charter (see pages 145–148). There is much scepticism as to
whether this will actually prove operative, but if it does it will mean
that the other 11 member states will be legislating for higher levels
of protection for their workers than will be enjoyed in the UK. It is
hard to see how this can be in the UK's interest.

These opt-outs were double-edged so far as Mr Major was concerned. While not really appeasing the Euro-sceptics in his own
party, they were profoundly unwelcome to the Labour and Liberal
Democratic parties which otherwise were enthusiastic supporters of
the Maastricht treaty. It was not, therefore, possible to depend on
wholehearted support from the opposition parties during the long
and difficult process of getting the ratification bill through both
Houses of the UK Parliament. This was completed only in July
1993, after repeated alarms and a real risk that the government,
with its slender parliamentary majority, might be swept away in
the process. Mr Major and his colleagues emerged shell-shocked
from the experience and thereafter seemed to give overriding priority to keeping Tory Euro-sceptics happy. This led to a resumption of
Thatcherite anti-EU rhetoric by ministers, and the UK once again
allied itself with those wishing to obstruct any further progress
towards European integration. Mr Major unwisely attempted to
play to the anti-EU gallery in his party in March and April 1994,

when he sought to maintain the size of the blocking minority in votes in the Council of Ministers at the same level as for 12 member states when the rules were being revised for the extension of membership to 16, with the anticipated accession of Austria, Finland, Sweden and Norway (see page 44). He ran up against determined opposition from all the other member states except Spain, as well as from the European Parliament, and eventually had to make a humiliating climbdown in order not to jeopardise the accession of the four applicants, which had been a long-term UK aim.

An even greater humiliation is likely to face the UK at the 1996 review conference, which is expected to set ground rules for a greatly expanded EU, with the admission of countries from central and Eastern Europe. Unless the Major government can overcome the nationalistic impulses of many of its supporters, or has been replaced by a government more attuned to the aspirations of the leaders and peoples of the other member states, the UK risks being dangerously isolated, and perhaps left behind, while its partners press ahead with new projects from which it would be self-excluded.

UK's hostility has many causes ...

That hostility to the EU and to UK membership has lasted so long cannot be explained by reference to a single cause. The UK's historical experience and the existence of the English Channel, which remained a powerful psychological barrier long after modern transport technology had reduced it to only a relatively minor physical impediment, have undoubtedly had a substantial effect on UK attitudes. The power struggle within the Labour Party between left and right certainly contributed to perpetuating a conflict which might otherwise have been expected to die down much earlier. (Similar divisions in the Conservative Party, at a later period, between Margaret Thatcher and her critics, also contributed to sharpening controversy over Europe.) And it was a cruel stroke of fate that the UK's eventual membership of the EC (which had been delayed for nearly a decade by de Gaulle's intransigence) coincided with the beginning of the economic crisis sparked off by the oil price rises of 1973. By this time the original six members had already enjoyed 15 years of prosperity during which they had been members of the EC, and much of that prosperity was in fact attributed to the effects of membership. By contrast, virtually all the UK experience of membership has been during a period of economic difficulty. Many Britons came to regard the EC as a convenient scapegoat for the lack of economic success.

The UK has also undoubtedly suffered from the fact that it was not a founder member and that several aspects of the Community to which it has most strongly objected, particularly certain procedures within the CAP, were already entrenched by the time that membership came to be negotiated. Although some modifications have subsequently been achieved, there is little doubt that a more acceptable framework, from the UK point of view, would have been adopted had UK influence been brought to bear from the outset. Similarly, many of the working methods of the Community (including the widespread use of French as a working language, which causes more problems for the notoriously monoglot UK than for most of its European partners) might well have evolved differently, making the organisation a more comfortable working environment.

... but it has slowly adapted to EU membership

Yet the very real difficulties encountered at the outset of UK membership have been attenuated with time, and those Britons who have worked for the EU, or who have had professional dealings with it, have mostly shown sufficient adaptability to overcome their initial handicaps.

UK industry, in particular, has progressively adapted itself to membership. Whereas in 1972 only a third of UK exports and imports were with the EC, by 1986 the proportion had grown to half and by 1993 to 55%. Had the UK not entered the EC in 1973, its economy would no doubt have developed in a different direction and sought whatever alternative opportunities, however limited, that might have been available to it. These have now gone, and there can be little doubt that horrendous difficulties would arise if the UK were to leave the EC. Many former opponents of membership tacitly admit that withdrawal would be a virtual impossibility.

For all practical purposes the UK is in the EU to stay, and it would be folly to base national policies on any other foundation than the development of the Union in a manner designed to produce the maximum benefit for its members. The grudging and minimalist attitude still often adopted by UK ministers in their dealings with the EU is in fact highly damaging to UK interests and threatens to reduce the UK's influence within the organisation. This is not a stance which hard-headed French ministers have adopted (at least since the retirement of de Gaulle), and there is no evidence that French interests have suffered in consequence. It is time that UK ministers (and would-be ministers from all political parties) learnt to conduct themselves in a similar way.

38

THE FUTURE

Can the EU become a superpower?

When Paul Kennedy published his highly influential book *The Rise and Fall of the Great Powers* in 1988 he included a long final chapter looking forward to the 21st century. There would not, he concluded, be just one or two superpowers dominating the world scene, but more likely four or five dominant powers, none of which would singly be capable of enforcing its will over the others.

He had no doubt about the identity of four of these powers. They would include both the USA and the then Soviet Union, although each of these would be relatively less strong than in the recent past. China was included because of the immensity of its population and resources and Japan because of the ingenuity of its people. The big question mark, according to Kennedy, was whether these four powers would be flanked by a fifth: the European Community.

On the whole Kennedy thought not. The EC was too divided, too incoherent, to be able to pull its full weight. His measured conclusion was: "If the European Community can really act together, it may well improve its position in the world, both militarily and economically. If it does not – which, given human nature, is the more plausible outcome – its relative decline seems destined to continue."

It may be doubted whether Kennedy would have struck such a sceptical note if he had been writing a few years later. For a whole series of events lent conviction to the view that the EC would indeed fulfil its destiny of becoming a political as well as an economic giant on the world stage, and perhaps a military one as well. Two of these events concern the internal organisation of the EC. The 1992 programme for completing the single market (see Chapter 15) was substantially completed on time, and the bulk of the internal barriers which prevented the EC from operating as a single trading area have either already been removed or will be in the near future. Second, the member states have committed themselves to economic and monetary union, and at the Maastricht summit in December 1992 adopted a series of treaty changes which should increase both the scope and power of the organisation, henceforth to be known as the European Union.

Yet it is by its response to external developments that the EU has shown its readiness to assume the responsibilities of an incipient great power. It has taken the lead in providing moral and material support for the newly free nations of central and Eastern Europe, and it clearly acts as a powerful magnet to them. It was the EU which took the initiative in setting up the European Bank for Reconstruction and Development, and subscribed more than half of its $12 billion capital. In so far as this represents a continuation of the post-war Marshall Plan, which rejuvenated Western Europe, it is the EU and not the USA which will be providing the bulk of the material assistance.

Major expansion is inevitable ...

A major expansion of the membership of the Union, which must have seemed a remote possibility when Kennedy put pen to paper, is now a virtual certainty, with four of the EFTA states set to join in 1995 and several central and East European countries by the end of the century. Beyond that the outlook is more uncertain, but, as explained in Chapter 36, it is not inconceivable that by around the year 2010 there may be as many as 42 member states, comprising the entire European continent apart from Russia.

A large Union is one thing; an effective one is another. Much will depend on the way in which the Maastricht decisions are acted upon, and on the review conference scheduled for 1996, which will assess the workings of the various EU institutions and consider further changes, particularly with regard to the working of a common foreign and security policy and the moves towards achieving a common defence. The uncertain EU response to the break-up of Yugoslavia in 1991–92, when the combatants looked to the EU rather than to the Conference on Security and Co-operation in Europe (CSCE) to broker a peaceful settlement, underlined how unready the Union and its member states were to assume such a role.

... but a United States of Europe is unlikely

What will be the nature of the European Union of the future? Will there, for example, be "an elected president of Europe?", as the author was asked in a recent television programme. "Yes, but probably not for at least another 20 years," he replied, and immediately asked himself whether he was not being unintentionally misleading. For what the interviewer no doubt had in mind, and what most viewers probably took the question to mean, was a presidential election on US lines, with the implication that the EU would evolve into a United States of Europe, with a similar division of powers to the USA.

This does not appear to be a likely, or even desirable, development. The 12 member states of the EU (and even the original six, which formed a more cohesive unit) are far more diverse than the original 13 colonies that came together at the Continental Congress in Philadelphia in 1774. Apart from language and cultural differences they are all sovereign states, several of them with hundreds of years of independence behind them, with distinct political, administrative and legal systems and widely differing historical experiences. It is reasonable to expect that some form of federal government for Western Europe may eventually emerge (and indeed to see the existing European Commission as the embryo of such a government). It is unrealistic to anticipate that it would have powers as extensive as those of the federal authorities in the USA or that France, Italy and Spain should find themselves on a level with Ohio, Pennsylvania or Kansas.

Powers must be appropriately balanced

Compared with past attempts at federation or confederation, and with contemporary efforts to bring neighbouring countries closer together in other parts of the world, the progress made during the 37 years since the EU was founded is remarkable. Yet it is apparent that it will need to proceed further and faster over the next 37 years if Europe is to punch its full weight in a rapidly shrinking but fast developing world. This emphatically does not mean that more and more power should be concentrated in Brussels just for the sake of enhancing the authority of the European Union. An over-centralised Europe is even less desirable than an over-centralised member state, of which there are a number already in the Union. What is required is a clear-headed attempt to identify those powers which, for the common good, can most effectively be exercised at a European level. Those powers, and those only, should be vested in a European authority; all others (including probably some currently exercised from Brussels) should be retained by national governments or, in some cases, devolved downwards to regional or local authorities. This was recognised in the Maastricht treaty, which speaks of "an ever closer union ... where decisions are taken as closely as possible to the citizens".

It goes beyond the scope of this book, and certainly beyond the expertise of the author, to produce a definitive list of which powers are most appropriately exercised at which level. It is indeed evident that the balance will change over time. Already the Union has discovered that both natural and man-made forces have made non-sense out of national sovereignty in areas not originally regarded as appropriate for EU decision-making. Conservation of fish species in the North Sea is one striking example, as it is impossible to prevent the fish swimming round from one country's territorial waters to another. It was only when herrings had all but disappeared that the EU nations were able to agree that if conservation was to be attempted at all it had to be on a Union-wide basis. When trees in the Black Forest started to die in large numbers, partly because of chemical emissions in the UK, the need for an EU environmental protection policy – for which no provision had been made in the Rome treaty – was forcibly brought home to both national governments and public opinion. It is evident that the European Union, as at present constituted, is not attuned to the assumption of some responsibilities now held at national level, but which would certainly be more appropriately exercised on a Europe-wide basis. The existence of national armies in Western Europe (and of so-called "independent nuclear deterrents") is surely an anachronism, but the Maastricht treaty was notably cautious in referring only to "the eventual framing of a common defence policy which might in time lead to a common defence".

The creation of the Eureka programme, which brings together both EU and non-EU countries to promote technological research and development (see page 132), as well as recurrent proposals for a "two-speed" or "variable geometry" Europe (meaning that certain EU programmes or commitments would involve only those member states which wished to participate) indicates a possible way ahead in the military sphere. In the majority of cases, however, the EU, which has proved itself to be a highly adaptable organism, should have little difficulty in absorbing extra capabilities.

To move beyond the immediate programme set at Maastricht will probably require a further significant transfer of power from the member states to the EU institutions. For this to be acceptable the democratic accountability of the Union will also need to be enhanced. This will ultimately involve the direct election of the president of the European Commission, and perhaps of the other commissioners as well, but the more urgent need is to enlarge the role of the European Parliament, which is currently caught in a dangerous power vacuum. The Single European Act and the Treaty on European Union both go some way in this direction, but unless the European Parliament is given a more decisive say in the formulation of EU legislation (at the expense of the Council of Ministers) it risks degenerating into a mere talking-shop.

Progress will be hard but it is essential

Developing the European Union will not be easy, and some painful decisions will need to be taken on the way by the UK and other national governments. Yet the choice facing them is no different from that to which the leaders of the Six far-sightedly responded nearly 40 years ago. As separate nation states they are now condemned to play a constricted role in the world; together they can achieve more, not only collectively but for each national unit individually. This is certain to be even more true in the future, as other, previously relatively backward countries, move forward to fulfil their own potential. Even Europe (or Western Europe) as a whole will find that its relative weight in the world will shrink (the 12 member states made up 6.7% of the world's population in 1984; even by the year 2020 this proportion will have shrunk to around 4.2%; the subsequent fall is impossible to predict with any precision but is likely to be substantial).

The historical achievements of the peoples of Western Europe, their culture, energy, skill and adaptability ought to ensure them a considerable role even in a world in which, quite rightly, other peoples and other regions are aspiring to play their full part. But in order to accomplish all of which they are capable they need a European framework (which ideally would also incorporate the peoples of Eastern Europe) that will give them the best opportunity to deploy their qualities as Britons, Germans, Italians, Dutch, and so on. In the late eighteenth century Edmund Burke described the once mighty Spain as "a whale stranded upon the coast of Europe". If sufficient will is not shown to develop the European Union over the coming decades some future historian may sadly liken Europe to a whale stranded upon the coast of Asia.

1

BASIC STATISTICS OF THE MEMBER STATES

The following table, which has been compiled from information supplied by the Directorate-General for Economic Affairs of the European Commission and by the Union's Statistical Office (Eurostat), contains comparative data on the 12 member states and on the EU as a whole, compared, where the information is available, with the USA, Japan and the world.

	Area ('000km²)	1992 population '000	Density /km²	Projected population in 2000 ('000)
Belgium	30.5	10,022	328	10,274
Denmark	43.1	5,162	120	5,291
France	544.0	57,206	105	59,659
Germany	356.9	80,275	225	82,269
Greece	132.0	10,249	78	10,558
Ireland	70.3	3,542	50	3,577
Italy	301.3	56,757	188	59,065
Luxembourg	2.6	390	151	409
Netherlands	41.2	15,129	367	16,025
Portugal	92.4	9,846	107	10,795
Spain	504.8	39,056	77	40,192
UK	244.1	57,749	237	59,218
EC12	2,363.1	345,383	146	357,326
USA	9,372.7	252,688	27	266,096
Japan	372.3	123,921	328	128,470
World	135,837.0	5,201,000[a]	38	6,251,055

	1991 GDP (bn ecus)	1991 GDP per head at PPP[b] (ecus)	1994[c] inflation (%)	1994[c] unemployment (%)
Belgium	159.2	16,193	2.4	9.9
Denmark	105.3	16,576	1.8	10.3
France	970.3	17,250	2.2	11.2
Germany[d]	1,274.0	18,345	3.5	6.0
Greece	57.1	7,397	11.1	...
Ireland	35.1	10,815	1.5	18.2
Italy	930.9	15,890	4.4	11.2
Luxembourg	7.6	19,636	2.5	3.0
Netherlands	235.2	15,551	2.4	10.0
Portugal	55.5	9,064	6.4	5.7
Spain	426.5	11,964	5.0	22.9
UK	816.5	14,732	2.5	10.3
EC12	5,073.4	15,432	3.4	10.9
USA	4,527.9	20,867	2.7	6.5
Japan	2,720.4	17,932	1.0	2.9
World	–	–	–	–

[a] 1990.
[b] Purchasing power parity.
[c] January.
[d] The figures refer to West Germany as it existed before unification in October 1990.

2
PRESIDENTS OF THE HIGH AUTHORITY AND THE COMMISSION

Presidents of the High Authority of the European Coal and Steel Community (ECSC)
(merged with the European Commission on July 1st 1967)

1952   Jean Monnet
1955   René Mayer
1958   Paul Finet
1959   Piero Malvestiti
1963   Dino Del Bo

Presidents of the Commission of the European Atomic Energy Community (Euratom)
(merged with the European Commission on July 1st 1967)

1958   Louis Armand
1959   Etienne Hirsch
1962   Pierre Chatenet

Presidents of the European Commission
(and since 1967 of the combined European Communities)

1958   Walter Hallstein
1967   Jean Rey
1970   Franco-Maria Malfatti
1972   Sicco Mansholt
1973   François-Xavier Ortoli
1977   Roy Jenkins
1981   Gaston Thorn
1985   Jacques Delors

3
THE COMMISSION AND
THEIR RESPONSIBILITIES

President	**Jacques Delors**	Secretariat-General
		Forward Studies Unit
		Inspectorate-General
		Legal Service
		Monetary affairs
		Spokesman's Service
		Joint Interpreting and Conference Service
		Security Office
Vice-president	**Henning Christophersen**	Economic and financial affairs
		Monetary matters (in agreement with Mr Delors)
		Credit and investments
		Statistical Office
Vice-president	**Manuel Marín**	Co-operation and development: economic co-operation with southern Mediterranean, Middle East, Latin America and Asia; Lomé Convention
		European Community Humanitarian Office
Commissioner	**Martin Bangemann**	Industrial affairs
		Information technologies and telecommunications
Commissioner	**Sir Leon Brittan**	External economic affairs (North America, Japan, China, Commonwealth of Independent States, Europe – including central and Eastern Europe)
		Trade policy
Commissioner	**Marcelino Oreja** (appointed April 1994 in place of Abel Matutes)	Energy and Euratom Supply Agency
		Transport
Commissioner	**Peter Schmidhuber**	Budget
		Financial control
		Anti-fraud measures
		Cohesion Fund: coordination and management

Commissioner   **Christiane Scrivener**   Customs and indirect taxation
Direct taxation
Consumer policy

Commissioner   **Bruce Millan**   Regional policies
Relations with the Committee of the Regions

Commissioner   **Karel Van Miert**   Competition
Personnel and administration
Translation and information technology

Commissioner   **Hans Van den Broek**   External political relations
Common foreign and security policy
Enlargement negotiations

Commissioner   **João de Deus Pinheiro**   Relations with the
European Parliament
Relations with the Member States on transparency,
communication and information
Culture and audiovisual policy
Office for Official Publications

Commissioner   **Pádraig Flynn**   Social affairs and employment
Relations with the Economic and Social Committee
Immigration, home affairs and justice

Commissioner   **Antonio Ruberti**   Science, research and development
Joint Research Centre
Human resources, education, training and youth

Commissioner   **René Steichen**   Agriculture and rural development

Commissioner   **Ioannis Paleokrassas**   Environment, nuclear safety
and civil protection
Fisheries

Commissioner   **Raniero Vanni d'Archirafi**   Institutional matters
Internal market
Financial services
Enterprise policy: small business and distributive trades

Note: a new commission will take office in January 1995.

4

THE DIRECTORATES-GENERAL AND SERVICES OF THE COMMISSION

DG I	External Economic Relations
DG Ia	External Political Relations
DG II	Economic and Financial Affairs
DG III	Industry
DG IV	Competition
DG V	Employment, Industrial Relations and Social Affairs
DG VI	Agriculture; Veterinary and Phytosanitary Office
DG VII	Transport
DG VIII	Development
DG IX	Personnel and Administration
DG X	Audiovisual Media, Information, Communication and Culture
DG XI	Environment, Nuclear Safety and Civil Protection
DG XII	Science, Research and Development; Joint Research Centre
DG XIII	Telecommunications, Information Market and Exploitation of Research
DG XIV	Fisheries
DG XV	Internal Market and Financial Services
DG XVI	Regional Policies
DG XVII	Energy
DG XVIII	Credit and Investments
DG XIX	Budgets
DG XX	Financial Control
DG XXI	Customs and Indirect Taxation
DG XXIII	Enterprise Policy, Distributive Trades, Tourism and Co-operatives

Consumer Policy Service
Secretariat-General of the Commission
Forward Studies Unit
Inspectorate-General
Legal Service
Spokesman's Service
Joint Interpreting and Conference Service
Statistical Office
Translation Service
Informatics Directorate
Task Force for Human Resources, Education, Training and Youth
European Community Humanitarian Office
Euratom Supply Agency
Security Office
Office for Official Publications of the European Communities

5
ADDRESSES OF MAIN EU INSTITUTIONS

European Parliament
Secretariat
Centre Européen, Plateau du Kirchberg
L-2929 Luxembourg
Tel. (352) 43 001

Council of the European Union
General Secretariat
Rue de la Loi 170
B-1048 Brussels
Tel. (32.2) 234 61 11

Commission of the European Communities
Rue de la Loi 200
B-1049 Brussels
Tel. (32.2) 299 11 11

Court of Justice of the European Communities
Boulevard Konrad Adenauer
L-2925 Luxembourg
Tel. (352) 43 031

Court of Auditors of the European Communities
12 rue Alcide de Gasperi
L-1615 Luxembourg
Tel. (352) 43 981

Economic and Social Committee
Rue Ravenstein 2
B-1000 Brussels
Tel. (32.2) 519 90 11

Committee of the Regions
Rue Ravenstein
B-1000 Brussels
Tel. (32.2) 519 90 11

European Investment Bank
100 boulevard Konrad Adenauer
L-2950 Luxembourg
Tel. (352) 43 791

6

PARTY GROUPS IN THE EUROPEAN PARLIAMENT

The Euro-elections have been contested in each member state by the main national political parties. Within the Parliament, however, the elected members have joined together in transnational groups, and they sit in these groups rather than in national delegations, inside the chamber. There are currently eight of these, namely:

Soc	Party of European Socialists
EPP	Group of the European People's Party (Christian Democratic Group)
LDR	Liberal Democratic and Reformist Group
Greens	Group of the Greens in the European Parliament
EDA	Group of the European Democratic Alliance (Gaullists, etc)
ER	Technical Group of the European Right
LU	Left Unity (French Communists and allies)
RBW	Rainbow Group (mainly regionalist parties)
Ind	Non-attached

The membership of these groups in the 1989–94 Parliament is shown on page 50. Following the fourth election to the European Parliament, in June 1994, the membership of the groups, by country, is shown below. The "others" category is largely made up of members from Italian and French parties not previously represented. The majority of these were expected to adhere to the EPP, which also includes the British Conservatives.

Political groups in the European Parliament, July 1994

	Soc	EPP	LDR	Greens	EDA	ER	LU	RBW	Ind	Others	Total
Belgium	6	7	6	2	–	3	–	1	–	–	25
Denmark	3	3	5	1	–	–	–	4	–	–	16
France	16	7	8	–	14	10	6	–	–	26	87
Germany	40	47	–	12	–	–	–	–	–	–	99
Greece	10	9	–	–	–	–	3	–	1	2	25
Ireland	1	4	1	2	7	–	–	–	–	–	15
Italy	19	9	1	3	–	–	–	–	24	31	87
Luxembourg	2	2	1	1	–	–	–	–	–	–	6
Netherlands	8	10	10	1	–	–	–	–	2	–	31
Portugal	10	1	8	–	3	–	3	–	–	–	25
Spain	22	30	2	–	–	–	–	1	9	–	64
UK	63	19	2	–	–	–	–	2	1	–	87
Total	200	148	44	22	24	13	12	8	37	59	567

7
OVERSEAS LINKS WITH THE EU

The 69 ACP states

African
Angola
Benin
Botswana
Burkina Faso
Burundi
Cameroon
Cape Verde
Central African
  Republic
Chad
Comoros
Congo
Côte d'Ivoire
Djibouti
Equatorial Guinea
Ethiopia
Gabon
The Gambia
Ghana
Guinea
Guinea Bissau
Kenya
Lesotho
Liberia
Madagascar

Malawi
Mali
Mauritania
Mauritius
Mozambique
Namibia
Niger
Nigeria
Rwanda
São Tomé & Príncipe
Senegal
Seychelles
Sierra Leone
Somalia
Sudan
Swaziland
Tanzania
Togo
Uganda
Zaire
Zambia
Zimbabwe

Caribbean
Antigua & Barbuda
Bahamas

Barbados
Belize
Dominica
Dominican Republic
Grenada
Guyana
Haiti
Jamaica
St Christopher &
  Nevis
St Lucia
St Vincent & The
  Grenadines
Surinam
Trinidad & Tobago

Pacific
Fiji
Kiribati
Papua New Guinea
Solomon Islands
Tonga
Tuvalu
Western Samoa
Vanuatu

Overseas Countries and Territories (OCTs)

Denmark
Special relationship
Greenland

France
Territorial collectives
Mayotte
St Pierre & Miquelon

Overseas territories
New Caledonia & dependencies
French Polynesia
French Southern & Antarctic Territories
Wallis & Futuna Islands

Netherlands
Overseas countries
Netherlands Antilles (Bonaire, Curaçao, St Martin, Saba, St Eustace)
Aruba

UK
Overseas countries and territories
Anguilla
British Antarctic Territory
British Indian Ocean Territory
British Virgin Islands
Cayman Islands
Falkland Islands
Southern Sandwich Islands & dependencies
Montserrat
Pitcairn Island
St Helena & dependencies
Turks & Caicos Islands

8

THE TREATY ON EUROPEAN UNION

The Treaty on European Union was approved at the Maastricht meeting of the European Council on December 9th and 10th 1991, and signed in Maastricht on February 7th 1992. After ratification by the 12 national parliaments, it came into force on November 1st 1993.

The treaty, which is divided into six parts, and a long list of annexes and protocols, consists principally of amendments to the Rome treaty, in whose text it has been incorporated. The main provisions of the Maastricht Treaty are as follows.

1 The commitment of the Community to the achievement of economic and monetary union, including a single currency administered by a single independent central bank. This is to be achieved in three stages. The third stage, which will start no later than January 1st 1999, but perhaps as early as January 1st 1997, commits those countries which fulfil four specific criteria – relating to inflation, budget deficits, exchange rates and interest rates – to proceed to the adoption of a common currency. A protocol provides that the UK would not be obliged to enter the third stage of EMU without a separate decision to do so by its government and parliament.

2 The development of common foreign and defence policies, with defence issues initially subcontracted to the Western European Union, whose membership would be opened to all EC member states.

3 The introduction of union citizenship, defining the rights and obligations of nationals of the member states. These include freedom of movement, right of residence, the right to vote and stand as a candidate at municipal and European elections, and shared diplomatic protection outside the union.

4 EC powers in areas such as education and vocational training, trans-European networks, industry, health, culture, development co-operation and consumer protection were confirmed or extended.

5 The establishment of a Cohesion Fund to transfer resources from the richer to the poorer member states.

6 The strengthening of judicial, immigration and police co-operation between member states, largely on an inter-governmental basis.

7 An agreement by 11 member states, excluding the UK, to use EC machinery to implement measures arising from the Social Charter of 1989 concerning the protection of workers' health and safety, working conditions, information and consultation of workers, equal opportunity and treatment, and the integration of persons excluded from the labour market.

8 Institutional changes, including an extension of the legislative powers of the European Parliament, the increase in the Commission's term of office from four to five years and the granting to the Court of Justice of the right to impose fines on member states for failing to implement its judgments.

9

ABBREVIATIONS AND ACRONYMS

Like other international organisations, the European Union has spawned a goodly number of abbreviations and acronyms, sometimes derisively referred to as "Eurojargon". The following list cannot claim to be comprehensive, but it does seek to include all those in common usage, including several derived from non-EU organisations with which the Union has dealings. In some cases the acronyms are based on the French language version, which may explain why the words do not match the initials.

ACE	Action by the Community on the Environment
Acnat	Action by the Community relating to nature conservation
ACP	African, Caribbean and Pacific countries party to the Lomé Convention
AGREP	Inventory of agricultural research projects
AIM	Advanced informatics in medicine
A1-Invest	Framework industrial co-operation and investment programme promotion for the countries of Latin America
Altener	Specific actions for greater penetration for renewable energy resources
ASEAN	Association of South-East Asian Nations
ASSET	Assessment of safety significant event team
Atlantis	Pilot measure to promote economic development and the environment in the Community's Atlantic regions
Avicenne	Science and technology co-operation with the Maghreb and other Mediterranean countries
BAP	Biotechnology action programme
BC-Net	Business Co-operation Network
BCC	Business Co-operation Centre
BCR	Community Bureau of References
BEMA	Biogenic emissions in the Mediterranean area
BEUC	The European Bureau of Consumers' Unions (Bureau Européen des Unions de Consommateurs)
BRIDGE	Biotechnology research for innovation, development and growth in Europe
BRITE/EURAM	Basic research in industrial technologies for Europe
Caddia	Co-operation in automation of data and documentation for imports/exports and agriculture
CAP	Common agricultural policy
CARE	Community database on road accidents
CCC	Consumers Consultative Council
CCITT	Consultative Committee on Innovation and Technology Transfer
CCT	Common Customs Tariff

CECAF	Fishery Committee for the Eastern Central Atlantic
Cedefop	European Centre for the Development of Vocational ⟨Training
CEN	The European Committee for Standardisation
CENELEC	The European Committee for Electrotechnical Standardisation
CERD	European Committee for Research and Development
CFSP	Common Foreign and Security Policy
CGC	Management and Co-ordination Advisory Committee (Comité consultatif en matière de gestion et de co-ordination)
CID	Centre for the Development of Industry (in ACP countries)
CIS	Commonwealth of Independent States
CIS	Customs Information System
CN	Combined Nomenclature
Coleacp	Europe-ACP Liaison Committee for the Promotion of Tropical Fruit, Out-of-Season Vegetables, Flowers, Pot Plants and Spices
COM	(or Comdoc) Commission documents
Comett	Community programme in education and training for technology
COPA	Committee for Agricultural Organisations in the European Community
Coreper	Committee of Permanent Representatives
Corinne	Co-ordination of information on the environment in Europe
COST	European co-operation on scientific and technical research
CRAFT	European co-operative research action for technology
Crest	Scientific and Technical Research Committee
Cronos	Database of macro-economic time series
CSCE	Conference on Security and Co-operation in Europe
CSF	Community support framework
CSO	Committee of Senior Officials (CSCE)
DAC	Development Assistance Committee (OECD)
DDR	Differentiated discount rate
Delta	Development of European learning through technological advance
Drive	Dedicated road infrastructure for vehicle safety in Europe
EAEC	European Atomic Energy Community (Euratom)
EAGGF	European Agricultural Guidance and Guarantee Fund
EBRD	European Bank for Reconstruction and Development
EC	European Community (or European Communities) – more often known, less correctly, as EEC
ECAS	Euro-citizens Action Service
ECE	European Commission for Europe (UN)
ECHO	European Community Humanitarian Office

ECIP	EC International Investment Partners
Eclair	European collaborative linkage of agriculture and industry through research
ECOS	European city co-operation system
ECSC	European Coal and Steel Community
ECOSOC	Economic and Social Committee (also known as ESC)
Ecu	European Currency Unit
EDA	Engineering design activities
EDF	European Development Fund
EDI	Electronic data interchange
Edicom	Commerce electronic data interchange
Edifact	Electronic data interchange for administration, commerce and transport
EDU	Europol Drugs Unit
EEA	European Economic Area
EEC	European Economic Community
EEIG	European economic interest grouping
EFICS	European forestry information and communication system
EFTA	European Free Trade Association
Ehlass	Community system of information on home and leisure accidents
EIB	European Investment Bank
EIC	Euro-Info Centre
EIF	European Investment Fund
Einecs	European inventory of existing commercial chemical substances
EMI	European Monetary Institute
EMS	European Monetary System
EMU	Economic and Monetary Union
Enrich	European network for research in global change
EP	European Parliament
EPHOS	European Procurement Handbook for Open Systems
EPO	European Patent Office
Erasmus	European Community action scheme for the mobility of university students
ERDF	European Regional Development Fund
ESA	European Space Agency
ESC	Economic and Social Committee (also known as Ecosoc)
ESCB	European System of Central Banks
ESF	European Social Fund
Esprit	European strategic programme for research and development in information technology
ESSI	European software and systems intiative

ETAN	European technology assessment network
ETSI	European Telecommunications Standards Institute
ETUC	European Trade Union Confederation
EUA	European Unit of Account (forerunner of the ecu)
Euragris	European agricultural research information system
Euratom	European Atomic Energy Community (also EAEC)
Eureka	European programme for high-technology research and development
EURET	European research for transport
Eurocontrol	European Organisation for the Safety of Air Navigation
Eurolib	European library project
Euronet-Diane	Direct information access network for Europe
Eurostat	The Community's statistical office
Eurotech Capital	European technology private capital
Eurotecnet	Community action programme in the field of vocational training and technological change
EVCA	European Venture Capital Association
FADN	EU farm accountancy data network
FAO	Food and Agriculture Organisation (UN)
FAST	Forecasting and assessment in the field of science and technology
FEOGA	French language acronym (very commonly used) for EAGGF
FIFG	Financial instrument for fisheries guidance
FLAIR	Food-linked agro-industrial research
FORCE	Action programme for the development of continuing voational training
GATT	General Agreement on Tariffs and Trade (UN)
GCC	Gulf Co-operation Council
GFCM	General Fisheries Council for the Mediterranean
GSP	General system of preferences
HCNM	High Commissioner on National Minorities
Helios	Community action programme for disabled people living independently in an open society
IAEA	International Atomic Energy Agency (UN)
IBC	Integrated broadband communications
IBRD	International Bank for Reconstruction and Development (World Bank) (UN)
IBSCF	International Baltic Sea Fishery Commission
ICCAT	International Convention for the Conservation of Atlantic Tunas
ICES	International Council for the Exploration of the Sea

IDA	Interchange of data between administrations
IDA	International Development Association (UN)
IDB	Inter-American Development Bank
IEA	International Energy Agency (OECD)
IEC	International Electrotechnical Commission
IEFR	International Emergency Food Reserve
IMF	International Monetary Fund (UN)
IMP	Integrated Mediterranean Programmes
Impact	Information market policy actions
INRO	International Natural Rubber Organisation
INSIS	Community inter-institutional integrated information system
INTAS	International Association for the Promotion of Co-operation with Scientists from the Independent States of the former Soviet Union
Interprise	Initiatives to encourage partnership between industries and services in Europe
Interreg	Community initiative concerning border areas
IRDAC	Industrial Research and Development Advisory Committee
ISDN	Integrated services digital network
ITC	International Trade Commission (USA)
ITER	International thermonuclear experimental reactor
ITTO	International Tropical Timber Organisation
IWC	International Whaling Commission
JESSI	Joint European submicron silicon initiative
JET	Joint European Torus
JICS	Joint Interpreting and Conference Service
JOPP	Joint venture Phare programme
JOULE	Joint opportunities for unconventional or long-term energy supply
JRC	Joint Research Centre
Konver	Programme to assist areas affected by the rundown of production for military purposes
LIFE	Financial instrument for the environment
Lingua	Action programme to promote foreign language competence in the Community
MAST	Marine science and technology (specific research and technological development programme)
Mattheus	Specific common programmes for the vocational training of customs officials
MCA	Monetary compensatory amount
MED-campus	Programme to support development co-operation schemes between the universities and higher educational

	establishments of Europe and the Mediterranean non-member countries
MED-Media	Programme to support co-operation between media institutions, organisations and companies in the EU and in the Mediterranean non-member countries
MED-Urbs	Programme to support co-operation between local authorities in the EU and those in Mediterranean non-member countries
Media	Measures to encourage the development of the audio-visual industry
MEP	Member of the European Parliament
MFA	Multi-Fibre Arrangement (arrangement regarding international trade in textiles)
Monitor	Community programme in the field of strategic analysis, forecasting and evaluation in research and technology
MOU	Memorandum of understanding
NAFO	Northwest Atlantic Fisheries Organisation
NAFTA	North American Free Trade Agreement
NASCO	Northwest Atlantic Salmon Conservation Organisation
NATO	North Atlantic Treaty Organisation
NCI	New Community Instrument (also known as NIC)
NET	Next European Torus
NGO	Non-governmental organisation
NIP	National indicative programme
NPT	Treaty on the non-proliferation of nuclear weapons
NOW	Community initiative for the promotion of equal opportunities for women
OCTs	Overseas countries and territories
ODIHR	Office for Democratic Institutions and Human Rights
OECD	Organisation for Economic Co-operation and Development
OICVP	Veterinary and Phytosanitary Inspections Office
OJ	*Official Journal* of the European Communities
ONP	Open network provision
OOPEC	Office for Official Publications of the European Communities
OPET	Organisation for the promotion of energy technologies
Ouverture	Co-operation network with East European regions
PEDIP	Financial assistance for Portugal for a specific industrial development programme
PETRA	Action programme for the vocational training of young people
Phare	Poland and Hungary – aid for economic restructuring
PISC	Project for inspection of steel components
Poseican	Programme of options specific to the remote and insular nature of the Canary Islands

Poseidom	Programme of options specific to the remote and insular nature of the overseas departments
Poseima	Programme of options specific to the remote and insular nature of Madeira and the Azores
PRO	Protracted Refugee operation (UN)
R&TD	Research and technological development
RACE	Research and development in advanced communication technologies for Europe
Rechar	Programme to assist the conversion of coal-mining areas
Recite	Regions and cities of Europe
REGIS	EU initiative concerning the most remote regions
Renaval	EU programme to assist the conversion of ship-building areas
RETEX	EU initiative for regions heavily dependent on textiles
SAVE	Specific actions for vigorous energy efficiency
SCENT	System for a customs enforcement network
SDC	Sustainable Development Commission (UN)
SDRs	Special drawing rights (IMF)
SEA	Single European Act
SIGL	Integrated licensing system
SPA	Special programme of assistance for sub-Saharan Africa
SPEAR	Support programme for a European assessment of research
Sprint	Strategic programme for innovation and technology transfer
Stabex	System for the stabilisation of ACP and OCT export earnings
STAR	Community programme for the development of certain less-favoured regions of the Community by improving access to advanced telecommunications services
STC	Scientific and Technical Committee
Sysmin	Special financing facility for ACP and OCT mining products
Systran	Computer translation system (system translation)
TAC	Total allowable catch
TACIS	Programme of technical assistance to the Commonwealth of Independent States
TAM	Trade assessment mechanism
TARIC	Integrated Community tariff
TEDIS	Communications network EU programme on trade electronic data interchange systems
Teleman	Research and training programme on remote handling in hazardous or disordered nuclear environments
Tempus	Trans-European mobility scheme for university studies
TENS	Trans-European networks
Thermie	Projects for the promotion of energy technology
TIDE	Technology for the socio-economic integration of disabled and

	elderly people
TNA	Telematics networks between administrations
TPA	Third-party access (to gas and electricity networks)
UDEAC	Central African Customs and Economic Union
UKREP	UK Permanent Representation to the EU
UMOA	West African Monetary Union
UN	United Nations
UNCED	United Nations Conference on Environment and Development
UNCTAD	United Nations Conference on Trade and Development
UNEP	United Nations Environment Programme
UNESCO	United Nations Educational, Scientific and Cultural Organisation
UNHCR	United Nations High Commissioner for Refugees
UNICE	Union of Industries of the European Community (employers' organisation)
UNIDCP	United Nations International Drug Control Programme
UNIDO	United Nations Industrial Development Organisation
UNRWA	United Nations Relief and Works Agency for Palestine Refugees in the Near East
Valoren	Community programme for the development of certain less-favoured regions of the Community by exploiting indigenous energy potential
VALUE	Specific programme for the dissemination and utilisation of research results (valorisation and utilisation for Europe)
VAT	Value-added tax
WEU	Western European Union
WFC	World Food Council (UN)
WFP	World Food Programme (UN)
WHO	World Health Organisation (UN)
WIPO	World Intellectual Property Organisation (UN)
WTO	World Trade Organisation (to replace GATT from 1995)
YES	Youth exchange scheme for Europe

10
CHRONOLOGY OF MAJOR EVENTS CONCERNING THE EUROPEAN UNION

1945 May — End of second world war in Europe.

1947 June — USA launches Marshall Plan to aid European reconstruction.

1948 April — Creation of the Organisation for Economic Co-operation (OEEC) to co-ordinate Marshall Plan assistance.

1949 April — North Atlantic Treaty signed, creating NATO.

1950 May — French foreign minister, Robert Schuman, proposes the pooling of French and West German coal and steel resources in a community open to other West European nations.

1951 April — Belgium, France, Italy, Luxembourg, the Netherlands and West Germany sign the Treaty of Paris, setting up the European Coal and Steel Community (ECSC).

1952 May — The same six countries sign a treaty to establish a European Defence Community (EDC), with a common European army.

August — The ECSC established, with its headquarters in Luxembourg.

1954 August — French parliament refuses to ratify the EDC treaty, which is immediately abandoned.

1955 June — Negotiations begin at Messina for the creation of a European Common Market.

1957 March — Two treaties signed in Rome, setting up the European Economic Community and Euratom, by the six member states of the ECSC.

1958 January — The EEC and Euratom treaties come into effect. The EEC Commission is established, with its headquarters "provisionally" in Brussels.

1960 January — The Stockholm Convention established the European Free Trade Association (EFTA), linking the UK with Austria, Denmark, Norway, Portugal, Sweden and Switzerland.

December — The OEEC is wound up and replaced by the Organisation for Economic Co-operation and Development (OECD), based in Paris.

1961 May — EFTA established, with its headquarters in Geneva.

July — The EEC signs an association agreement with Greece. Ireland applies for EEC membership.

August — Denmark and the UK also apply for membership.

November — Membership negotiations open in Brussels.

1962	April	Norway applies for EEC membership.
1963	January	President de Gaulle vetoes British membership; the other applicant states suspend their applications. Franco-German Treaty of Co-operation signed.
	July	Yaoundé Convention, providing for economic aid and trade concessions to 17 African states, formerly colonies of the EEC countries, is signed in the capital of Cameroon.
	September	The EEC signs an association agreement with Turkey.
1964	July	Common Agricultural Policy (CAP) comes into effect.
1965	June	Crisis in the EEC as France begins seven-month boycott of its meetings, refusing to be out-voted on issues which it considered of great importance.
1966	January	France resumes its active membership, after negotiation of the "Luxembourg compromise", under which important issues were, in effect, to be decided by unanimity, irrespective of the provisions of the Rome treaty.
1967	May	Denmark, Ireland, Norway and the UK make second application to join the EEC. In view of de Gaulle's continued hostility, the applications are left on the table.
	July	The EEC is merged with the ECSC and Euratom to form a single European Community (EC).
1968	July	All internal tariffs removed within the EC, which established a common external tariff (CET).
1969	December	France's President Pompidou agrees with other EC leaders at a "summit" meeting in The Hague to consider an enlargement of EC membership.
1970	June	Membership negotiations open in Brussels with the four applicant states.
1972	January	Treaties of Accession signed between the EC and Denmark, Ireland, Norway and the UK.
	July	Free trade agreements signed with the six EFTA states which did not apply to join the Community.
	September	Norway turns down EC membership in a referendum (46% for, 54% against).
1973	January	Denmark, Ireland and the UK become full members of the Community.
	May	Norway signs free trade agreement with the EC.
1974	April	At request of the new British Labour government, a "renegotiation" of the membership terms begins.
1975	February	First Lomé Convention, replacing the Yaoundé Convention of 1963, is signed, giving economic aid and

		trade concessions to 46 African, Caribbean and Pacific states (ACPs).
	June	Referendum in the UK shows a 2:1 majority in favour of staying in the EC.
		Greece applies for EC membership.
1977	**March**	Portugal applies for membership.
	July	Spain applies for membership.
1979	**March**	European Monetary System (EMS) established.
	June	First direct elections to the European Parliament.
	December	Row over British budget contribution to the EC at the Dublin summit, when Mrs Thatcher demands "our money back".
1980	**May**	Provisional solution to British budget problem, intended to last for three years.
1981	**January**	Greece becomes member of the EC.
1984	**June**	Second direct elections to European Parliament.
		At Fontainebleau summit agreement reached on reducing the British budget contribution and on increasing the financial resources of the EC.
1985	**January**	Jacques Delors becomes president of the EC Commission.
	June	At Milan summit agreement is reached on seven-year timetable to remove 300 barriers to the internal market, according to a programme devised by the UK EC commissioner, Lord Cockfield. An inter-governmental conference was also appointed to consider amendments to the Rome treaty.
	December	The inter-governmental conference produces the Single European Act, a series of treaty amendments designed to speed up decision-making, especially on internal market measures. It is signed by all member states.
1986	**January**	Spain and Portugal become members of the EC.
1987	**April**	Turkey applies to join the EC.
	July	The Single European Act comes into force.
1988	**February**	Delors I package, which set the guidelines for expanding EC budgets, but with tighter control over agricultural spending, over the five years 1988–92, agreed.
1989	**June**	Third direct elections to the European Parliament.
		Austria applies to join the EC.
	July	G7 summit asks the EC to co-ordinate western aid to Poland and Hungary. This aid is subsequently

extended to other East European countries, and negotiations follow to conclude trade and association agreements with the former Soviet "satellites".

November Breach of the Berlin Wall heralds the collapse of communism in Eastern Europe.

December Negotiations begin between the EC and the EFTA states to form a European Economic Area (EEA).

1990 July Capital movements liberalised throughout the EC.
Madrid summit conference approved in principle a plan to introduce economic and monetary union in three stages, with Mrs Thatcher reserving the British position.
Cyprus and Malta apply for EC membership.

October German unification: territory of former East Germany joins EC, as integral part of West Germany.

December Two inter-governmental conferences, on economic and monetary union and on political union respectively, begin work.
Rome EC summit approves programmes of food aid and technical assistance to the Soviet Union.

1991 July Sweden applies for EC membership.

September Following the failed Soviet coup, EC mission visits the former Soviet Union and the newly independent Baltic states to discuss an enhanced aid programme.
EC-sponsored peace conference opens on Yugoslavia.

November Agreement reached to set up European Economic Area on January 1st 1993.

December At Maastricht summit, agreement is reached on the Treaty on European Union. This included detailed arrangements for EMU, with a single currency, to be in force no later than 1999, with an opt-out provision for the UK, and for gradual progression towards a common foreign and security policy.

1992 February Delors II package proposes increasing EC budget by 30% over five years.

March Finland applies for EC membership.

May Switzerland applies for EC membership.

June Denmark narrowly rejects Maastricht Treaty in referendum; Jacques Delors is reappointed for two more years, from January 1993, at Lisbon summit; reform of CAP narrowly agreed by Council of Ministers.

November Blair House agreement aligns EC and US proposals on the agricultural sector of the Uruguay round of the

GATT negotiations.

December   Switzerland turns down EEA in a referendum; Edinburgh summit adopts reduced Delors II budget package, spreading it out over seven years instead of five, and approves establishment of European Investment Fund.

1993 February   Negotiations begin on accession of Austria, Finland and Sweden.

April   Negotiations begin on accession of Norway.

May   In second referendum the Danish people vote in favour of the Maastricht treaty.

July   Adoption of the TACIS programme to provide technical assistance to the independent states of the former Soviet Union.

August   After many delays, the UK finally ratifies the Maastricht treaty.

October   Germany, the last state to do so, deposits its ratification of the Maastricht treaty after a court challenge fails.

November 1   Maastricht treaty comes into force: the European Community becomes the European Union.

December   Brussels summit approves an action plan based on the European Commission's White Paper on growth, competitiveness and employment.

December   Uruguay round negotiations successfully concluded in Geneva.

1994 January   European Economic Area agreement comes into force, linking the EU and five member states of EFTA, but excluding Switzerland and, temporarily, Liechtenstein.

March   Accession negotiations successfully completed with Austria, Finland, Norway and Sweden. Subject to referenda, they become full members from January 1st 1995.

June   Fourth direct elections to the European Parliament. Austria approves EU membership in referendum. Partnership and Co-operation Agreement signed with Russia at Corfu summit.

SUGGESTIONS FOR
FURTHER READING

There is a vast literature on the EC, much of it of a very specialist nature. The best and most comprehensive guide to this literature is provided by David Overton, *Common Market Digest*, Library Association, London, 1983. It is very much to be hoped that this important bibliographical work will be regularly updated. The European Commission itself produces a stream of pamphlets and documentation of various kinds, much of which is available (often free of charge) from the information offices of the European Union in London, Edinburgh, Cardiff and Belfast. There are similar offices in all the major EU capital cities, as well as in other major centres including New York, Washington, New Delhi, Ottawa and Canberra.

The historical background to the creation of the Community is described in fascinating detail in Jean Monnet's memoirs, and placed in a wider context by two other well-known authors.

Calvocoressi, Peter, *Resilient Europe 1870–2000*, Longman, London, 1991.
Grosser, Alfred, *The Western Alliance: European-American relations since 1945*, Macmillan, London, 1980.
Monnet, Jean, *Memoirs*, Collins, London, 1978.

Among the very large number of books written about particular aspects of the Community's affairs, the following may be mentioned.

Brittan, Leon, *Europe: The Europe we need*, Hamish Hamilton, London, 1994.
Butler, Michael, *Europe: More than a Continent*, Heinemann, London, 1986.
Cecchini, Paolo *et al.*, *The European Challenge 1992: The Benefits of a Single Market*, Wildwood House, Aldershot, 1988.
Colchester, Nicholas and Buchan, David, *Europe Relaunched: Truth and Illusions on the Way to 1992*, Economist Books, London, 1990.
El Agraa, E.M., *The Economics of the European Community*, (2nd edition), Philip Allan, Deddington, 1991.
Emerson, Michael and Huhne, Christopher, *The ECU Report*, Pan Books, London, 1991.
Harris, Simon, Swinbank, Alan and Wilkinson, Guy, *The Food and Farm Policies of the European Community*, Wiley, Chichester, 1983.
Jacobs, Francis, Corbett, Richard and Shackleton, Michael, *The European Parliament*, Longman, London, 1990.
Kirchner, Emil Joseph, *Decision making in the European Community: The*

Council Presidency and European Integration, Manchester University Press, 1992.

Ludlow, Peter, *The Making of the European Monetary System*, Butterworth, London, 1982.

Mayes, David G. (ed.), *The European Challenge: Industry's response to the 1992 programme*, Harvester Wheatsheaf, London, 1991.

Owen, Richard and Dynes, Michael, *The Times Guide to 1992*, Times Books, London, 1989.

Palmer, John, *Trading Places: The Future of the European Community*, Radius, London, 1988.

Radice, Giles, *Offshore Europe: Britain and the European Idea*, I.B. Taurus, London, 1992.

Roney, Alex, *The European Community Fact Book* (3rd edition), Kogan Page, London, 1993.

Sbragia, Alberta M. (ed.), *Euro-Politics: Institutions and Policymaking in the "New" European Community*, Brookings Institution, Washington, 1992.

Tugendhat, Christopher, *Making Sense of Europe*, Viking, Harmondsworth, 1986.

Williams, Allen M., *The European Community: The Contradictions of Integration*, Blackwell, Oxford, 1991.

Finally, readers concerned to follow the work of the Union in some detail on a continuing basis may be interested in two quarterly publications: *European Trends*, produced by The Economist Intelligence Unit, and the more academic *Journal of Common Market Studies*.

INDEX

INDEX